Hardcover Edition
ISBN-13: 979-8-9890130-8-1
© 2024 Andreas Johansson

Published by Harker Press
http://HarkerPress.com
Book Design by Dustin McNeill

All rights reserved. No part of this publication may be reproduced, distributed, or transmitted in any form or by any means, including photocopying, recording, or other electronic or mechanical methods, without the prior written permission of the publisher, except in the case of brief quotations embodied in critical reviews and certain other noncommercial uses permitted by copyright law. Any unauthorized duplication, copying, distribution, exhibition or any other use of any kind may result in civil liability, and/or criminal prosecution.

This book is an independent work and not authorized by or affiliated with John Carpenter, Kurt Russell, or StudioCanal.

ESCAPE FROM NEW YORK INTERVIEWS

ANDREAS JOHANSSON

TABLE OF CONTENTS

8	John Carpenter [Director/Co-Writer/Co-Composer] *
14	Kurt Russell [Snake Plissken] *
22	Season Hubley [Girl in Chock full o'Nuts]
28	Adrienne Barbeau [Maggie]
32	Larry Franco [Producer/First Assistant Director]
36	Todd C. Ramsay [Editor]
42	Joe Alves [Production Designer]
52	Dean Cundey [Director of Photography]
60	Frank Doubleday [Romero]
62	John Strobel [Cronenberg]
66	John Cothran Jr. [Gypsy #1]
70	Garrett Bergfeld [Gypsy #2]
72	Joel Bennett [Gypsy #4]
78	Tobar Mayo [Third Indian]
82	Steven M. Gagnon [Secret Service #1]
86	Dale E. House [Helicopter Pilot #1]
90	Tony Papenfuss [Theater Assistant]
92	Alan Shearman [Dancer]
96	John Contini [Extra]
100	Jeff Sillifant [Extra]
104	Ken Tipton [Extra]
110	David Udell [Extra]
114	Dick Warlock [Stunt Coordinator/Stunts]
118	Jeffrey Chernov [Second Assistant Director]
124	Louise Jaffe [Script Supervisor]
130	Raymond Stella [Camera Operator]
136	Clyde E. Bryan [First Assistant Camera]
144	Christopher Horner [Assistant Art Director]
152	Cloudia Rebar [Set Decorator]
156	Arthur Gelb [Graphic Designer]
160	Steve Mathis [Flicker Box Technician]
164	Ken Chase [Makeup Artist Supervisor]

166	Kim Gottlieb-Walker [Stills]
170	Eddie Surkin [Special Effects]
174	Tom Thomas [Transportation Captain]
186	Geoffrey Ryan [Production Assistant]
190	Donald P. Borchers [Avco Nominee]
198	Mario Simon [Driver]
202	Sharon Tucci [TalentPlus: Extra Casting] [St. Louis]
204	R.J. Kizer [Project Supervisor: Special Visual Effects]
212	Brian Chin [Miniature Construction]
220	Tom Campbell [Engineer: Special Visual Effects]
224	Steve Caldwell [Camera Assistant: Special Visual Effects]
238	Eugene P. Rizzardi [Miniature Construction]
242	Bruce MacRae [Miniature Construction]
246	John C. Wash [Graphic Displays]
254	Mark Stetson [Miniature Construction]
260	John L. Hammontree [Special Thanks]
264	Gino LaMartina [Special Thanks]
268	Richard Hescox [Pre-Production Ad Artist]
272	Francis Delia [Pre-Production Portrait Photographer]
276	Barry E. Jackson [Poster Artist]
278	Stan Watts [Poster Artist]
282	Ben Bensen III [Poster Artist]
286	Renato Casaro [Italian Poster Artist]
288	Paul Chadwick [Poster Artist]
294	Kim Passey [Poster Artist]
302	Harold Johnson [Movie Tie-In Board Game Designer]
310	Bill Willingham [Movie Tie-In Board Game Artist]
316	Erol Otus [Movie Tie-In Board Game Artist]
318	E.T. Steadman [Movie Tie-In Novel Artist]
322	Mike McQuay [Movie Tie-In Novelist] *
328	Alan Howarth [Co-Composer/Special Synthesizer Sound] *

* This is a vintage interview/article.

INTRODUCTION

Who am I? Just a nut/loner from Sweden. I first saw the *Escape* movies back in 1997 and they immediately became a part of my DNA. Since 2002, I've become the biggest online authority on these films. (Should I seek help?)

Why do I like John Carpenter's *Escape* movies so much? The hero is much darker and cynical than usual, but is also a man of honor because he's incorruptible. Additionally, he's played by a guy named Kurt Russell, who made an unredeemable and disillusioned asshole named Snake Plissken an intriguing and sympathetic character. Furthermore, the director is a stylistic, prescient, and subversive guy named John Carpenter. He's dark and cynical as well, but doesn't take himself too seriously. I enjoy that he had fun with the sequel and basically remade his own movie, exaggerated it, and forced his hero to go through another similar mission that won't change things much. I find *Escape From L.A.* to be a very funny and rebellious movie with interesting themes about freedom.

Why did I do these books? When I did my first interview in 2011 for myself and fellow fans online, I never expected this to be the end result. Therefore, I want to sincerely thank all 113 interviewees for making these books possible. Hearing your stories, getting to know you a little bit, and preserving movie history is a BIG honor. John Carpenter rightfully puts his name above the title, but many people brought these cult classics to life and contributed to their legacy. I dedicate these books to you and your kindness.

Who else would I like to thank? Abe Perlstein, Alex Denney, Chris McQuay, David Weiner, Ken Hanis, Kim Gottlieb-Walker [Buy her book *On Set with John Carpenter* NOW!], Judi Raish, Mark Underwood, Philip D'angelo, Roger Romage, Steve Schapiro Photography, Wayne Gralian at Wayne's Books, Whitney Scott Bain, and everyone who helped me with contact information.

/Andreas

Author's Note: Some questions will be repetitive and scaled down for consistency and simplicity. Some interviews will also be a bit more personal than others.

Top: The Swedish poster logo for *Escape From New York*.
Bottom: The author.

ENJOY!

Escape From New York: An Interview with John Carpenter
By David Weiner

New York, 1997. Manhattan Island is a maximum federal penitentiary, and the president's plane has crashed in the middle of it. Snake Plissken [as played by Kurt Russell], a battle-hardened hero-turned-convict, is tasked by the government with extracting the president within 24 hours in exchange for a full pardon. Adding to the ticking clock is a mini-explosive in his bloodstream timed to detonate in 24 hours. Oh yeah, and the human race depends on Snake's success, because the U.S. is at war and the president was on his way to a summit meeting to avert a nuclear crisis with China and the Soviet Union. If Snake fails, we all fail.

That's the hook that made all of us want to go for a thrill ride with Kurt in John Carpenter's newest adventure in 1981, *Escape From New York*, a radically different film from his previous big-screen entries, 1978's game-changing indie film *Halloween* and his 1980 horror follow-up, *The Fog*.

Now, 35 years after its summer 1981 release, I got to chat with Carpenter about *Escape From New York* exclusively for *Famous Monsters* magazine, and it was a thrill to hear new tales and insights.

I'd love to have your CliffsNotes version of the making of *Escape From New York* from your perspective 35 years later. What sparked the idea for the film?

Well, there were a bunch of different things that propelled me to work on this movie and make this movie. One was a movie called *Death Wish*, which was out in the 70s. New York was having some big, giant problems at the time - I'm thinking bankruptcy and a crime problem. And this Charles Bronson movie, *Death Wish*, came along and he was a vigilante architect, of all things. And something about the movie struck a chord with me. It wasn't a great film, but it was a fun movie. And I read a lot of science fiction. I read a Harry Harrison story - there was this planet, the toughest, most evil place in the universe. So who're you going to choose to go in there and do something with some mission?

John Carpenter [Director/Co-Writer/Co-Composer]
(Photo by Steve Schapiro / © Steve Schapiro Photography)

The most evil guy in the universe. That idea stuck with me, and I thought of writing this kind of dystopian future story about New York as a prison and a guy has to go in to rescue the president. I thought about Charles Bronson playing the part, a tough guy at the time. ... [But] the project came along in '80 and I cast Kurt Russell. I'd just worked with him in *Elvis* and I really loved working with him. Here's this Disney kid and he's tough as nails, and he created a real memorable character [out of Snake Plissken].

Did you have carte blanche after *Halloween* in terms of your casting choices? Or was there any pressure from your distributor, Avco Embassy Pictures, to go with a more established star?

Well, we had discussions about it. They were uncertain about Kurt as a hero. They said, "Well, he's just this Disney kid." I said, "No, no, no. He can play this.

He can play anything. Believe me, he can play anything. He played Elvis, he can play Snake Plissken." So they relented. I mean, they wanted to talk about it and they wouldn't be doing their job if they didn't say, "We have concerns about this. I'm not sure that he can do the part." That's fine with me. I went ahead and defended him. I'm glad I did.

We're all glad you did! How collaborative was Kurt at that stage with developing his character? Or was he like, "This is what's on the page, let's just dive in?"

Well, Kurt as an actor, you have to understand he was Disney trained. So he doesn't come in with a lot of line changes at that time. As he became a big movie star later, he worked a little bit more behind the scenes. But then, it was just, "Say the lines that are there." His main contribution was as soon as he found out that Lee Van Cleef was in the movie, he said, "I know what I'm doing. Imitate Clint Eastwood!"

You've got a wonderful rogues' gallery of actors in this film. I know you love working with the same people over and over. What went into some of the casting choices for *Escape*? Was Jamie Lee Curtis ever considered?

There wasn't really a part for Jamie Lee in this. She was in a TV series as I remember. We had various parts written so we had to fill them up with actors who were good. Ernest Borgnine is just an amazing character actor. I mean, he's amazing! God bless him, you couldn't get better than Ernie. There's Harry Dean Stanton, who's still an awesome guy. I care for him very much. I mean, on and on. Everybody in the movie was great.

Were there any doubts this project might not get the green light because you didn't quite have the budget to build a rundown urban environment like you imagined in the script?

We knew it was going to go because it had a green light, so we were going to shoot the movie no matter what. The question was how big a spectacle could we afford to make. That was always the question. So we found St. Louis had had a fire in mid 70s and their downtown area was just ruined. And it was desolate. They were great. They let us come in there and shut everything down, shut the lights off - it was unbelievable cooperation. They had a lot of decrepit stuff around, so we found a location that worked that let us get the spectacle that we needed. So therefore, the movie didn't suffer a small look. It had a big look, which made me very happy.

Do you remember any specific surprises on the shoot or things you were unable to get due to budget or location constraints?

Every day we shot [at] night, because most of these [scenes] were at night - that was a new surprise. Sometimes good, sometimes very, very bad, and we had to punt. Every production is that way, unless you have all the money in the world. We didn't. Just to make the schedule is the big thing. Nothing big surprised me. Nothing big hurt the story. We didn't have to do anything to change the narrative, which is the thing you want to protect as a director - right to the very end is the narrative. If you start changing that, you're lost.

You're well-known for scoring your own films. Do you have a certain approach when you're doing a score? Do you take thematics into account, or is it more about tone and creating suspense?

I think it's everything that what you just mentioned. It's thematic, but it's also tone. Most of the music that I've done for movies is improvised at the moment with that footage. The main theme from *Escape From New York*, parts of that I had in my head before we recorded it. Just little snatches here and there. I stuck it together. These things come out of instinct - at least they do for me. I'm not a kind of a guy who can write music. So I don't write music, I improvise it, just play it to the image. And luckily, the music from *Escape* worked out.

How do you think *Escape From New York* holds up decades years later? Are you critical when you look back at your work? Or do you allow it to live in a time capsule from the era?

I can't watch it because I'm too critical of the things I've done. Once the movie's cut together and I've seen the print, that's it. I don't want to look at it again. Because it's over. Kurt's character, Snake Plissken, has lived in memory, and in the culture, and is extremely strong. And the cast and the acting in the movie is extremely strong. And the fun of it - the movie is just a silly adventure in the future, but it's fun. It's dark and fun. And that's lived on, so I'm really proud of the film. I'm really happy about it.

Was there ever any discussion of reuniting with Kurt as Snake Plissken after you did *Escape From L.A.***? Or was that the definitive end?**

That was sort of the end of talking about it. We had discussions about other kinds of projects, but no. And then now they're trying to do a remake of it, and they probably will go for a younger guy to play Snake Plissken. But that's the way it goes.

They've been talking about this remake for years and years.

They have. It has been years and years, you're absolutely right.

I remember after *300***, Gerard Butler was lined up to do it.**

That's right, then he dropped out, and then they moved on, and then [*Fast & Furious* producer] Neil Moritz took on the producing reins, and he couldn't get it set up. And now it's over at Fox and they're trying to get it done. I'm just sitting back relaxing, because I don't have to worry. I worried back in 1980 when we were shooting the film. I worried a lot back then. But now I don't worry at all!

I talked to Kurt about it a couple of years ago, and it was very important to him that whoever plays Snake is 100% American. What's your take on that?

[laughs] Well, you have to understand. Kurt is kind of a Tea Party guy. He's really right wing and nationalistic. So anything he plays, I think he would feel very proud of the fact that Snake Plissken is an American and has American values, and that's fine with me. As long as he's a tough-ass, I don't care.

Well it's a great, beloved film, and like Kurt said, regardless of where they remake it or not, the original is out there. If people want it, there it is.

That's right. It's not going anywhere!

[*This interview first appeared in* Famous Monsters of Filmland *(Issue 287, Sep-Oct, 2016) for the film's 35th anniversary. It appears here courtesy David Weiner.*]

John Carpenter [Director/Co-Writer/Co-Composer] after the film's release.
(Photo Courtesy Alamy)

Escape From New York:
An Interview with Kurt Russell
By Whitney Scott Bain

Back in the 80s, I had the good fortune to work on three John Carpenter films; two of them starred Kurt Russell. Not only was Kurt a pleasure to work with, he's a genuinely nice guy. In this rare interview, Kurt talks about working for Disney, his baseball years, and gives us the inside info on *Escape From New York*.

You started out working for Walt Disney as a child actor.

Mr. Disney was a wonderful man. I was in the *Adventures of Jamie McPherson* series. When I got the job, I was in Little League baseball and I was focused on wanting to become a professional ball player one day. We had a really good team. They were all really good. We went on to the championship. My father and I met with a man named, Mr. Anderson, who talked and acted like the same character from *The Matrix*. He said it would be impossible for me to play baseball and act because of the shooting conflict, so I decided that I'd rather play baseball than act. Little did I know that Mr. Disney had listened to the whole conversation in the other room on speaker and quickly had a talk with Mr. Anderson. When my father and I were walking down the hall ready to leave, Mr. Anderson came running up to us and made me a deal where I could have game days off during filming. Mr. Disney and I would sometimes have lunch and he'd ask me what I thought about certain rides and attractions he had planned for the amusement park. He'd listen to this nine-year-old kid to see what worked and what didn't, using me as a sounding board.

You did become a professional baseball player for awhile.

I worked my way up through the years and got to play professionally. I was a second baseman. Those days ended when I got hurt at 22. I fell back on acting because I figured that I needed another career to earn a living.

Kurt Russell [Snake Plissken]
(Photo by Steve Schapiro / © Steve Schapiro Photography)

Snake Plissken has become an iconic character throughout the years. He resonates and echoes with people.

Once in awhile you get the opportunity to play a really great character where you get to make it completely yours. Avco Embassy, the studio that produced *Escape,* originally wanted Charlie Bronson to pay the part because there were a lot of action heroes at the time like Clint Eastwood and Bronson that were making those types of films. John fought for me for that role.

When MGM acquired the rights to *Escape*, they were able to find the cut footage of your back story with Taylor [Joe Unger] and the master credit card robbery, except for the scene where you see the Indians roasting the headless cat on a spit in the World Trade Center. You tangle with them briefly and make your escape with them chasing after you. I know it's out there somewhere because I remember seeing it as a dirty dupe [black and white 35mm work footage.] on the Moviola at New World. Why do you think they cut those scenes?

The studio thought it was too long and cut them, but in a way it worked to our advantage. No one had ever done an opening sequence where this guy gets off a bus in handcuffs with this bad boy, f-you attitude. It set the mood for the film right away.

Not too many people know that Tom Atkins' character, Rehme, was named after the head of Avco Embassy, Bob Rehme who later on became a very successful producer. Warren Oates had originally been selected to play Brain, but had taken ill and recommended Harry Dean Stanton for the part. Adrienne Barbeau;, John's wife at the time, always liked to knit during set ups. The whole cast was a great ensemble of players and such a pleasure to work with.

Lee Van Cleef, Ernie Borgnine, Harry Dean, Tommy, Adrienne, Isaac Hayes, Donald Pleasence, Season Hubley; who I was married to at the time. I remember when my son was born and I had the duties of feeding him at night. Sometimes I'd get home from the set too tired to change, still in my wardrobe, and here I am feeding my son with a baby bottle. Kind of an incongruous look for Snake.

Isaac Hayes and I would get up early and work out together, I'd call him up in the morning and he already had a deep voice, but answer in the deepest baritone you'd ever hear. [imitates Isaac.] "Yeahhh... ohhhhkay..." then hang up. He was a really great guy.

We were at Roger Corman's New World Pictures hired by Avco to do the effects. I was a production assistant at the time, most notably known as a PA or piss ant as they'd call us because we did all the dirty jobs and got pissed on by everyone, even when we did a good job. Still, I got to work on the construction of Manhattan that consisted of cardboard shoeboxes and blocks of wood, Xeroxed pictures of buildings that we pasted on and shaded them in with pens, pencils, and white tape. All of that was destroyed after the production was over, but I did manage to save the top of the Woolworth building, which you see for a brief moment when Air Force One is about to crash. We shot the effects in 70mm, then brought it back down to 35mm, so it had this really great depth of field look to it. Most people think it was Jim Cameron who did the mattes. He did do one where it was a glass matte composite where the prisoners are flagging down the helicopters, but it was Jena Holman who was this incredible matte artist that drew the background landscape of Manhattan and the World Trade Center when we had the miniature Gulfire pushed off the top. Sadly, she passed away a few years ago. She was a very nice woman.

    There were a lot of talented people there that went on to do exceptional work in the film business that worked on *Escape*. It was like a big family. I remember when we were shooting inserts on the New World back lot for the Gulfire cockpit, which was a part of a plastic helicopter windshield that I pulled out of the junkyard, we called Keltonville because this one guy, Roger Kelton had organized the mess that was back there and it was a mess. We covered it with dubatine [black cloth.], I dug up a helicopter joystick and Dean Cundey lit it with a couple of lights with gels over them, Cundey had the .357 in a May Company department store paper bag that we were making jokes about that May Company got into the firearms business. Then there was the Station 19 block that was constructed for the close ups we used. Years later, we used that as a paint shed at Corman's. Afterwards, I remember you went home still in your wardrobe and John took Dean and I, buying us cheeseburgers at a place called the Oar House, which doesn't exist anymore. That was the best shoot I ever worked on. You kept the original wardrobe too.

Yes. John and I figured that we'd make a sequel one day and, seventeen years later, we did. I could still fit into Snake's wardrobe, but John decided that since *Escape From L.A.* was another story, Snake needed a new outfit. So, I ended up giving away the pants and shirt to my son's friends, but I kept the jacket.

Speaking of original wardrobe, how did that come about?

When John was trying to sell Avco on *Escape From New York* we talked about what Snake would wear. I got some green army fatigues, combat boots, and a black t-shirt and we took some promotional photos. It didn't look right. Something was missing. So, I went and got some black and white fatigues, and a pair of motorcycle boots with golf cleats I added. I thought Snake would look great with an eye patch, but the studio didn't want it. John fought for the idea and we won out. I remember when we were in St. Louis and it was in a bad part of town. They had a big fire there awhile back and it was deserted and desolate looking especially at night. No one was down there except the occasional drunk or group of gangs. It was a rough part of town. When we broke one night to set up another scene, I decided to take a walk. I went around the corner and saw these four rough looking guys staring at me. Here I am dressed as Snake, carrying a machine gun, a .357, and a knife looking back at them when they quietly walked away. I couldn't wait to get back to John and tell him; hey, this character's going to work!

John and Alan Howarth's score added to the film's quality.

It's one of my favorite scores ever.

You and John work seamlessly together the way John Wayne and John Ford or Howard Hawks did, which John is a big admirer of. Hawks' and John's films have this special rhythm and cadence to them.

John is like a big brother to me. He was always open to making a film better. When we did *Escape From L.A.*, there were a lot of questionable moments in that film that reflect on today's society. John wanted to point out how we were slowly losing our freedoms and that Snake's life is like a loop. Think about it. Try lighting up a cigarette in Santa Monica where you live.

That's true. They passed a law where you can't smoke at the beach or public property and, if you live in an apartment building, you can only smoke inside your home. Then you had to sign a paper whether-or-not you smoked. If you said you did, fine, but if you said you didn't and a friend came over and lit up, that would be grounds for eviction, driving up the cost of the rental unit for the next person.

That's right.

Totalitarianism at its best. I wonder when we're going to be goosestepping to Falco music next? On a lighter note, there's been the on again, off again rumor of remaking *Escape From New York*. I mean, why? The movie stands on its own merit and still holds up.

Remakes should only be made if the movie is extremely flawed or originally miscast. There seems to be no originality anymore. First of all, the actors they had in mind were from Scotland, Wales, England, and Australia. Snake needs to be played by a young man and an American. He's an American war hero. He gets into a ring to fight a guy twice his size with a baseball bat. How more American can you get?

Speaking of that; you did your own stunt work with Ox Baker in that scene.

Dick Warlock, who was my stand in and stunt coordinator on *Escape,* got a big baseball knot on his forehead from Ox during rehearsal, so it was impossible for him to do the scene. Ox was a professional wrestler and he accidentally killed his best friend in the ring, so you could say I was a little apprehensive to do this. Ox and I had rehearsed several times and he really got into it using his full weight on the swings and I was taking everything I got from him. I had to tap him a few times in the groin with my bat telling him that this is pretend. He got the message. Then it was my turn to get even in the scene where I drive the nail bat into the back of his skull. There was this wooden block placed on the back of his head with a nail sticking out of it and I had to hit it just right. I told him not to flinch or I could miss. During the first few takes, he did flinch.

So, I reassured him that I'd get it on the next take so we could get the scene over with. He calmed down, I brought the bat down on the nail perfectly and John got the shot.

What's the story on Snake's voice?

Ahh, the old wives tale… I was trying to find Snake's voice before we were filming and John said to me, "We just got Lee Van Cleef to play Bob Hauk." I thought, "Hey, since Clint Eastwood did all those films with him and made him a star, it could work for me." So, I worked on Snake's version of Eastwood. He's quieter than Eastwood, sometimes so quiet, you barely hear what he says.

You were originally in the lead role in *Ladyhawk*.

I thought it would be fun to shoot a film in Italy for a few weeks and then go home. Goldie, my wife, said that I'd be there for several months and I didn't believe her. When I got there, I see wardrobe and the character has to wear tights. I don't wear tights. That's not for me. On top of that, production got held up because of strikes and political problems. I went to Dick Donner; the director and told him that this was a mistake taking this role and I was sorry, so I recommended Rutger Hauer and said he'd be perfect for the part and I could get him. Dick said, "Really? You think?" I didn't know Rutger. I never even met him. So, while everything was being negotiated, Goldie flew over and we spent two weeks in the hotel room before we went home.

Who are your favorite actors?

Actors are amazing to me. I really don't have a favorite one. I'm amazed at what they do. I love all movies as an audience. I have a great time working in this business.

[*This interview was intended for* Starburst, *but never appeared in the magazine. It is previously unpublished and appears here courtesy Whitney Scott Bain.*]

L-R: Season Hubley [Girl in Chock full o'Nuts], Kurt Russell [Snake Plissken], with son Boston Russell in 1981.
(Photo Courtesy Alamy)

SEASON HUBLEY
Girl in Chock full o'Nuts

How did you end up being an actress?

I saw *Peter Pan* at the age of four or five or six. They called Mary Martin an actress and I wanted to be able to fly, too.

How did you get cast as Girl in Chock full o'Nuts [Maureen] in *Escape From New York*? You married Kurt Russell after co-starring in *Elvis* together, so you already knew John Carpenter from that.

John took me to lunch and asked me if I'd do it and of course I said, "Yes, it'd be a hoot!" He asked me how much money I'd want to do it and I just told him to get us a really nice alarm system and that was that.

Do you think Maureen is a crime groupie or a female gang leader?

Maureen is definitely a crime groupie all the way!

How do you think Maureen ended up in New York's Maximum Security Prison?

She had been the girlfriend of one of the hottest coke dealers and gang leaders in the Bronx. When he got busted and sent into Manhattan, she wanted to be with him. She sliced up some girl's face.

How was your experience filming your scenes such as the one with you being dragged through the floor by the Crazies?

It was quite nerve racking, actually. Boston [Russell] our son was in our motor home being baby sat by the producer Debra Hill while I was having an out of body experience on the set a few hundred feet away. I really have no recollection of number of takes, how long it took, etcetera. When I'm in character I'm not in 'my' [Season's] right mind. Aside from John's fantastic words, "You're a cop.", "I'm an asshole," it was pretty much all improvised. The only problem, if you

L-R/BG: Season Hubley [Girl in Chock full o'Nuts], John Carpenter [Director/Co-Writer/Co-Composer], Kurt Russell [Snake Plissken] /FG: Jeff Sillifant [Extra] (Photo by/Courtesy Kim Gottlieb-Walker)

want to call it that, was my invisible umbilical cord attachment to Boston. It was the first time I'd been in front of a camera since he had been born. We just kind of winged it. We discussed how it was supposed to go down - literally, ha ha. We walked through it and then just went for it because, obviously, the first time I could go through the floorboards had to be a take, but somehow they reset it and I did it again. He shot it from another angle for the second take. I think there were only two takes if I remember correctly.

If Maureen hadn't been attacked by the Crazies, do you think Snake Plissken would've allowed her to kiss him as written in the script and did you have any discussions about this?

Absolutely, the kiss and probably more would have happened. The real question was, is this going to be his ultimate downfall? John decided this, of course. That's the reason the Crazies carried me away.

How did Kurt Russell prepare for the role? Is it true that he bought a leather shirt from a guy he walked by in Paris before filming begun for instance? By the way, did you ever get to experience Kurt in his Snake Plissken clothes taking care of and feeding Boston Russell?

I have no memories of how Kurt and wardrobe came up with the Snake attire. I don't remember Kurt having been in France between our honeymoon and when he became Plissken, so that may have been a whimsical tale. But as you know, Plissken was pretty ripped, so there was a lot of time spent at the gym. Kurt tends to let himself go between flicks and loves to eat and packs it on a bit, so before a movie there's a mad dash to get beefed up. As far as the voice of Mr. Snake Plissken goes, it was Clint Eastwood all the way! And yes, Boston's male caretaker was Snake quite often.

How was your experience working with the cast and crew?

John and the crew were wonderful to work with. Of course, I only worked that one night, but I was on the set a lot and the cast became like family as it most always does on a film. Adrienne [Barbeau] [Maggie] and I became friends and we as two couples spent time together off the set as well. Kurt and I decided early on to try to work our schedules so that one of us was always home with Boston and the animals.

What's your favorite memory or memories of working on the movie?

Firstly, I love working with John Carpenter. He is an amazing man. He trusts the actors he hires and lets you fly. When asked a question, he replies with a question and puts the decision right back where it belongs on the actor. Whatever your decision is, he goes with it. It all just has an added layer of complexity, mystery, and intimacy. It was always a fun time working with Kurt and also it was amazing to have Boston aboard. To be working as a family, because Adrienne and John were our closest couple friends, was just really great!

Is it true that Kurt Russell couldn't get his family into the theater for free when watching it for the first time in a cinema in New York? Also, how did his family, you included, react to Snake Plissken and *Escape From New York*, which was a significant departure from his previous work?

We all loved it. As far as not being able to get his family into the theater in New York City for free. I've never heard that story.

What do you think of the movie personally?

I loved the movie. Kurt was amazing as Snake and so were each and every other actor in his or her character. Also, the miniatures were fantastic! To this day I get so many wonderful comments from people who remember the movie fondly and also remember the Girl in Chock full o'Nuts. I still get questions about how did we do the part where I was dragged through the floor and such. It's so funny how such a short time on film made such a big impression. That's John Carpenter for you!

What are you currently doing and what do you enjoy doing in your spare time?

I moved to Vermont in 2001 to get out of the business. I was getting to an age that they soon would have been demanding facelifts, boob lifts, everything lifts, and I didn't want all of that drama. I had always loved Vermont having grown up in Manhattan and then done L.A. for thirty years. Boston had moved away, so there was basically nothing holding me there. I really came here to move as far away and live a completely different lifestyle than I'd ever had the chance to live before. I guess you could call me kind of a vagabond, a searcher. I met quite a few people here that I really connected with spiritually.

Animal rescue and welfare is still huge to me. I do what I can do to bring awareness mainly. I was brought to consciousness in the 80s about the hideous situations many live their lives in when I joined an anti-vivisection group in L.A. called Last Chance for Animals after I had seen a film called *Hidden Crimes*. The head of Last Chance is a man named Chris DeRose. In 1988 [and I know before and since] there were multiple thefts of dogs and cats out of people's yards and there was a theory that many of them were being sold into medical research. Cedars Medical Center and UCLA were denying that they tested on any animals so just to make sure we got into Cedars and found two stolen dogs there. We then a few days later went to UCLA and as I was part of a decoy group of about five acting up to distract the campus police. Chris DeRose and another member broke into what they call the "vivarium" [ironic as that may be] and all they did was steal the truth. Hundreds of pictures of cats with electrodes attached to their heads, mismatched pupils, the whole nine yards. Hideous pictures! The law caught up with him so as he was being arrested he was able somehow to get the film over to us on the other side of the cops. We in turn were able to get it to the media and so within a few hours it was all over the news. CNN, NBC, CBS. Everywhere. That was a major break in where the animal welfare movement was at the time and raised the public awareness level monumentally!!! Possibly the proudest and most fulfilling day of my life second only to the day my son Boston was born!

I paint and I write and I try to help others who need help. That's pretty much my life today. It's a far cry from the life I led in the fast lane all those many years and I'm liking it very much! I support Hearts United for Animals. They are an amazing place! They take all the puppies and dogs that are rescued from Puppy Mills [are you aware of what puppy mills are? If not, please Google them. They are like Auschwitz for dogs and puppies. Hideous, hellish places!]. Anyway, when one of these puppy mills gets busted, Hearts United for Animals takes these poor abused animals to their rescue in Nebraska [HUA, PO Box 286 Auburn, NE 68305/Phone: [402] 274-3679] and treats them for physical neglect and abuse first, but all the while treats their traumatized minds, hearts, and souls. They socialize them to be with humans and then try to find them forever homes. Look them up: HUA.org

ADRIENNE BARBEAU
Maggie

How did you end up being an actress?

See biography on abarbeau.com

You had already married John Carpenter two years prior, but how did you get cast as Maggie in *Escape From New York*?

I loved the script, the character, and the director. What more could I ask for?

How did you prepare for the role and what kind of discussions did you have with John Carpenter about it?

Well, I roasted a turkey breast and then boiled it clean and used it as a hair clip. Somehow in my mind there must have been turkeys running wild inside that maximum security prison but no beauty supply stores.

How do you think Maggie ended up in New York's Maximum Security Prison?

I'm sure I did have a back story for Maggie. That's the way I usually work but whatever it was, it's long forgotten. Seems likely her landing in prison had something to do with her love and attachment to Brain [Harry Dean Stanton].

What's your favorite scene or scenes and which were the most challenging, problematic, memorable and fun to work on?

I love the scene on the bridge [69th Street Bridge] [Old Chain of Rocks Bridge] when Maggie takes a stand against the Duke [Isaac Hayes] and his badass Cadillac. All her morality is there. Her code of ethics and the depth of her feelings for Brain. And I love the scene in the taxi when Brain is giving Snake driving directions to avoid the land mines. Brain says something like, "I think there's one on the right." and Maggie says, "You think?" Makes me laugh.

L-R/FG: John Carpenter [Director/Co-Writer/Co-Composer], Harry Dean Stanton [Brain], Adrienne Barbeau [Maggie], Donald Pleasence [President] (Photo by/Courtesy Kim Gottlieb-Walker)

How was your experience working with the cast and crew?

I loved working with all the guys. Especially Donald [Pleasence] [President] who was one of the funniest men I've ever worked with and Ernie [Borgnine] [Cabbie] who was an absolute sweetheart. They all were. I scoured the antiques stores of St. Louis buying up handmade quilts and original Fiesta Ware and furniture I could ship back on the massive art department truck.

What's your favorite memory or memories of working on the movie?

I tell all my *Escape* stories in my memoir *There Are Worse Things I Could Do*.

What do you think of the movie personally?

I love it. It's one of my favorite John Carpenter films.

On November 4, 2011 you and Tom Atkins [Rehme] hosted a special screening of *Escape From New York* at the Andy Warhol Museum in Pittsburgh and did a Q&A afterwards. How was this experience?

Tommy is one of my dearest friends from way back in the mid-70s. I love him so much. I used him as himself in my second vampire novel *Love Bites* and I jump at any chance I get to visit him. Especially in Pittsburgh. We had a lot of fun at that Q&A. No one tells better stories than Tom Atkins.

What are you currently doing and what do you enjoy doing in your spare time?

First and foremost is spending time with my sons. These days that's usually on a soccer field. And I read non-stop. That's my true escape. I can't imagine getting through life without series detective novels. I love to write and I love to travel and I love my friends. Not necessarily in that order and I really do love to work as well. I'm almost always enjoying my life no matter what I'm doing.

L-R: Adrienne Barbeau [Maggie] and John Carpenter [Director/Co-Writer/Co-Composer] at the Century Plaza Hotel shortly after the film's release. (Photo Courtesy Alamy)

LARRY FRANCO
Producer / First Assistant Director

How did you end up being a second/first assistant director and producer and how did you and John Carpenter meet?

I worked as an extra from 1972 through 1974. During those years, I was applying to the Directors Guild of America Assistant Director Training Plan. I was finally accepted in 1974 and began my career in production. After a few years, I was working as a 1st AD [Assistant Director]. Kurt Russell [my ex-brother-in-law] called me and announced he had landed the role of Elvis for a TV movie and suggested I try to work on it with him. I called the production and asked for an interview with the director. I met John Carpenter the next day and he hired me as his AD.

How did you get the job of both producer and first assistant director for so many John Carpenter movies such as *Escape From New York* for instance and how did you manage being both?

After I had done *Elvis* and *The Fog*, John and Debra Hill [Producer], who had produced *Halloween* and *The Fog* with John, asked me to join the producing team. In those early days, the movies were less complicated and it was not unusual for someone to be the producer and either the AD or production manager at the same time. Nowadays it would be impossible.

How did you and Debra Hill [Producer] prepare for this project and how did you collaborate? Any issues prior to filming and such? You originally wanted to use BART [Bay Area Rapid Transit] in San Francisco for the opening bank robbery sequence [deleted]. Liberty Island [Liberty Island Security Control Exterior] also had bombings by Croatian freedom fighters three months earlier that made it hard to get permission for instance.

I was mainly in charge of the physical production and Debra was mainly in charge of the script, casting, and the interaction with the Avco Embassy. It was

L-R: Larry Franco [Producer/First Assistant Director], Debra Hill [Producer], John Carpenter [Director/Co-Writer/Co-Composer]
(Photo by/Courtesy Kim Gottlieb-Walker)

a great relationship. The studio wanted to cast Tommy Lee Jones as Plissken and John fought hard for Kurt. That was a big battle won and I remember John being upset when he couldn't get Warren Oates for the role of Brain [Harry Dean Stanton], but that turned out OK.

I don't recall any problems with any of the locations. The biggest challenge for the movie was where to shoot destroyed New York. We knew it had to be practical. We didn't have the money to build the streets. We put the search out for an urban environment that was abandoned. Fortunately, we found a three-block area in St. Louis that had been ravaged by a fire storm three years earlier. I don't recall ever discussing BART. We were always headed for Atlanta to shoot in the newly constructed but not yet opened MARTA system. As I recall, we shot in Atlanta for two nights.

What kind of challenges did this project provide and which scenes or locations were the most challenging, problematic, memorable and fun to work on? Did anything mess up the shooting schedule and such? The car chases took longer than expected due to intricate lighting setups for instance.

The most fun we had on the movie was the six weeks of all-nighters in St. Louis. We were on a roll and everybody was into it. The work on the bridge [Old Chain of Rocks Bridge] [69th Street Bridge] was challenging as were the car chases, but none of it was insurmountable. I remember it as being on schedule. If not on schedule, we were definitely on budget. There really wasn't an option then. I didn't realize until now that we were the first to shoot on Liberty Island at night, so it wasn't very special at the time!

How did John Carpenter and Kurt Russell collaborate and were there ever any disagreements between them?

Kurt and John had no disagreements as far as I can remember.

How was your experience working with the cast and crew?

We were all young and in the movie business on location. I can't think of any other experience that can top that. We were having a blast. All of us. Kurt and I even today are the best of friends, but we rarely talk about our movie experiences. We spend most of our time talking about our families.

What's your favorite memory or memories of working on the movie?

It has to be the St. Louis location work and the laughs we all shared together.

What do you think of the movie personally?

I love the movie. *Escape* and *Starman* are the top two favorites on my resume.

How come John Carpenter, Kurt Russell and Debra Hill reunited for *Escape From L.A.* and not you?

I wasn't involved because I was on another project when *Escape From L.A.* started production. I think the movie missed on several of levels. One of them being that audiences expected the visual effects to be better. It worked for *Escape From New York,* but *Escape From L.A.* was in a different climate.

What are you currently doing and what do you enjoy doing in your spare time?

I am currently working on *The Nutcracker* and *The Four Realms* for Disney. I enjoy traveling and playing golf when I'm not working.

TODD C. RAMSAY
Editor

How did you end up being an editor?

I am the classic story of the guy who started in the mail room. My father, Clark Ramsay, was executive vice president of advertising and publicity at MGM under the famous Howard Strickling. [My father later became famous in his own right]. In any case, he got me the mail room job. My father brought up the subject of nepotism at the time and he told me somewhat defensively, "No one cares if a baker wants his son to be a baker and this is no different." He also then told me that it didn't matter whose son I was. If I didn't do a great job, I could expect to be fired. Getting the job was a gift but keeping it was entirely up to me. Later, after walking away from college after my first year, he got me a job as an apprentice film editor in the splicing and coding room. At that time, the union required four years as an apprentice editor and then four more as an assistant before you could be qualified to cut. I put my years in here both as apprentice and then an assistant on a number of films and was taken under the wing of some great editors like Marge and Gene Fowler and John Howard.

    I became expert in optical effects as it was one of the few areas where, as an assistant, you could contribute something creatively to the film. I did all the design work for the first *That's Entertainment!* as well as *The Car* and *Sgt. Pepper's Lonely Hearts Club Band*. I was assistant editor on Robert Wise's *The Hindenburg* at Universal and also became the editorial liaison coordinating Albert Whitlock's [the famous matte painter] work with ours. In addition, I used a system of printing black and white negatives on color film I had developed at MGM for *That's Entertainment!* to do the black and white sections of *The Hindenburg*. Lastly, I found lost footage of the crash, which was used prominently in the film. This impressed Wise who, of course, had cut *Citizen Kane*. One day, he called me to come in and interview for editor on *Star Trek: The Motion Picture*. I had edited a few scenes but had never cut a picture or been an "Editor." I was stunned, forever grateful, and considered Robert Wise my mentor from that day forward. He was an extraordinary man who I will never forget.

How did you get the job of editor on *Escape From New York*?

I got an agent [again through Wise] and went in for an interview with John Carpenter. A few days later, as I was waiting to go in to interview for *On Golden Pond*, my agent called and said John had hired me. This was only my second film.

How did you get Alan Howarth [Co-Composer/Special Synthesizer Sound] involved with *Escape From New York*?

On *Star Trek*, I had hired a number of sound designers to make unusual sound effects for the film. The sound of the engines, for example. Alan Howarth was one of them. When John wanted to set up his own studio to do the film's soundtrack I recommended Alan as his technical [equipment] advisor, knowing that Alan was really interested in doing music. It worked out well for them both, I like to think.

How did you and John Carpenter prepare for this project and how did you collaborate? Any disagreements and such? Who chose the interesting fade in fade out transitions for instance?

I choose the fade in fade out transitions because I felt there was a certain elliptic style to the narrative that would benefit from it. It made for transitions and pauses in the pacing that achieved something that couldn't be had with straight cuts or dissolves or other means.

For the most part, John was very pleased with my first cut in terms of the scene edits themselves, but not the overall structure. I made less changes for John with regard as to how I edited individual scenes on the two films I did for him than any other director I have ever worked for. Our time together was primarily spent on structure. John and I had no disagreements between us, only shared concerns about whether certain things were working or not.

At one point, after the first cut, I said to John that having Snake Plissken captured in the film's beginning didn't align too well with the idea of him being a master thief. We could see him captured, but seeing him being captured undercut his credibility. Wise had taught me the value of test screenings in discovering a filmmaker's "blind side" in regards to how a film was working [or not working]. I suggested we organize a small screening ourselves. John was hesitant at first but agreed. A very young J.J. Abrams, still in school and not yet in films, was one of the invites. He remembers this screening so well he used it in his thank you address to the American Cinema Editors for their award to him last year. All I remember is that it was agreed afterwards to remove the scene of Snake being captured in the film's beginning and that was all I cared about.

He was very concerned at one point about the scene Kurt had with his then former wife Season Hubley [Girl in Chock full o'Nuts]. She was nursing her baby on the set and John felt that was very distracting to the acting process. I looked at the dailies and told him not worry. When he saw it cut he loved it. I loved it before I even cut it but, as always, all the glory goes to John and the actors. It was a fantastic cast and John was in top form.

However, there were a few things which I really learned from John about film editing. The first is the scene where Snake and cohorts are fleeing up an alley toward the taxi that [Ernest] Borgnine's [Cabbie] character is driving. I cut the scene realistically but John felt the suspense could be stretched out a bit longer. At the time I thought it might drag but, after doing it, I realized he was absolutely right.

In another place, the character played by Frank Doubleday [Romero] swings down suddenly from a rail car. I made nothing special out of the moment, thinking it stylish but not frightening. John thought it could be a surprise and make the audience jump. I changed it to accommodate John's idea and thought, Oh well. I doubt anyone will jump at that. When we previewed the film, the audience jumped.

The last and biggest change is in Snake's fight in the arena. Again, I cut this realistically. John who had cut his own films in the past asked if could take a pass at it himself. He had been so easy to work with that I wasn't bothered by this. He took a few hours and simply made about seven or eight trims [less than half a foot in length] on the heads or tails of shots to speed up the action. It was much better and I told him so. What he did was what we call "jam" cutting and it became part of my arsenal from then on.

Is it true that J.J. Abrams was responsible for John Carpenter's decision to film Maggie's [Adrienne Barbeau] death scene in his and then-wife Adrienne Barbeau's garage since the test screening didn't show what happened to her after the impact with the Duke's [Isaac Hayes] car?

I never knew or maybe I've just forgotten anything about this. Truthfully, I couldn't recall this shot when I read your question. It would certainly have to have been shot post-wrap as there would be no reason to shoot it beforehand [or have anything to match to].

What kind of challenges did this project provide and which scenes or sequences were the most challenging, problematic, memorable, and fun to work on?

At this point in my editing career, practically everything I did was new in some way to my limited experience as the actually editor. I enjoyed every day and everything I did. I didn't get to really spend any time with John before the shoot. He was on location for the majority of it and I didn't get to sit down with him until after my first cut was complete. All the scenes were very satisfying to cut because my method was always to keep cutting a scene until I was satisfied with it. I never believed in just "roughing out" a cut and then refining with the director. I wanted the director to be able to sit down and enjoy [as much as one can ever enjoy a first cut run] something as close to what I deemed their vision as possible. This allowed us to move right on to structure.

How come you chose Claude Debussy's "The Engulfed Cathedral" to be in the temp track for the glider flight and also in the final movie?

I had a complete temp score. I choose music that I felt supported the scenes and the film's dark tone.

How long did it take to edit the movie?

I don't recall how long it was until the film was finished editorially. It wasn't long as the film was relatively low budget.

Were there any significant changes or different cuts done and were there any scenes or material that you and John wanted to keep but had to drop at the very last second so to speak? You cut out a lot of scenes from this movie.

I don't recall how many different cuts there were, but it was not a lot. There is nothing I'd change or want to restore. I'm surprised you found 25 deleted scenes, but cutting the film down and pacing were our main goals. A lot of the dialogue scenes have a very meditative tone for an action film. Getting the right performances and taking the right beats was essential to keeping the film moving and not drag while making these scenes play.

Is it possible that the deleted scenes still exist?

All the dailies and lifts [deleted scenes] were put into storage. The company no longer exists and by now most likely has been discarded as the storage fees on such material are one of the first things companies cut as they devolve or dissolve.

Despite all the cut scenes, the movie still has a surprisingly slow pace that probably wouldn't work with today's audiences. Did it evolve naturally and did the studio have any issues with this? Also, would you edit the movie the same way today?

John's direction and the script determined the pace as it does with all directors. The approach as to how to deal with that pace editorially was mine and [style wise] remained unchanged as we simply cut things out to tighten the narrative. If the film were to be recut to more modern approaches, it would fail at what it so clearly succeeds at now. A mood. There was no studio interference on the style or execution of the film. I took the same approach in cutting John's *The Thing* and would do so today on any similar film which I might be presented with. The only other film which I have edited where I was permitted such complete authority besides John's two films is *Minus Man* directed by Hampton Francher of *Blade Runner* fame.

What's your favorite memory or memories of working on the movie?

It is all a favorite memory. One of my best experiences as an editor.

What do you think of the movie personally?

I think the movie is terrific and feel very fortunate to have worked on it.

What are you currently doing and what do you enjoy doing in your spare time?

I do more writing now than editing and have three scripts in various stages of development.

JOE ALVES
Production Designer

How did you end up being an art director and production designer?

I started at Disney when I was in art school for animation. I was nineteen. I did that for a couple of years, but I really wanted to get into live action. I also did some sets at the Hollywood Playhouse. It was a small theater, but it had some interesting people. Clifford Odets did a play there. He actually showed up and he liked what I did. He said, "I'm gonna use you on Broadway." Then from there, the producer or the director of the theater introduced me to art director Stan Galli. He told me how I should go about getting a job as a set designer. That's how you had to start. You didn't start as an art director or a production designer. You started either as a set designer or an illustrator doing either architectural drawings or illustrations. I finally got a job with Bob Kinoshita on *Man in Space*. He said, "I need somebody to draw the set drawings." Then I started as a set designer and worked at MGM, Fox, Universal, and Warner Brothers. I worked on some pretty good films.

    I eventually got settled at Universal where I was a staff set designer. Somebody came to the set department and said, "Does anybody know what a Lotus car is?" and I said, "What do you mean? There's a lot of Lotuses. Race cars, sports cars." He said, "You know cars." I said, "Yeah." "Well, we need somebody for the Indianapolis broadcast to do some displays and drawings." I did that and then went back to set design. The next year, the head of the department said, "They want you to do it again." I said, "Well, yeah, but I think you should make me an art director," so he made me an assistant art director. You worked until you got your own show. Then I started doing television shows. I did *Night Gallery* for [Steven] Spielberg and then eventually I did features. I worked on a lot of pictures. I worked with [Alfred] Hitchcock on *Torn Curtain* and I did *Sugarland Express*. Then on *Jaws*, for the first time, I got the production design credit. It's the same job, basically. Now, everybody gets a production design credit. It used to be that you had to do a movie that had special challenges where you design the whole production. Now, they all get production design credits and the art director works for the production designer.

L-R: Alan Levine [Production Manager], Debra Hill [Producer],
Joe Alves [Production Designer]
(Photo by/Courtesy Kim Gottlieb-Walker)

How did you get the job of production designer on *Escape From New York*?

It's an interesting story. I had an agent at the time, Phil Gersh. He had been around for years. He was Humphrey Bogart's agent, etcetera, very powerful, and I was fortunate to get him as my agent as a production designer. On *Jaws 2*, I had directed a hundred days of second unit. After that, I was interested in moving into directing. I had a project that was supposed to shoot in Europe about Formula One racing. I scouted all over - France, Italy, even Holland. When I came back, the studio had gone under so the project was dead. A couple of weeks later my father died.

My agent said, "You know, you should get back to work." He said, "I represent a young film director named John Carpenter and he's got this project called *Escape From New York*." I was older and had been nominated for the

Academy Award and won the British Academy Award. It seemed like a small film at the time, but Phil thought it would be good for me to get busy. I met John and Debra Hill [Producer] and they were very interesting. I thought the project had a lot of potential because of the futuristic setting and all that, so I got on board. Phil negotiated things. He put this together because of mutual agents. That how's it happened.

How did you and John Carpenter prepare for this project and how did you collaborate together?

Well, we would go through the script and he would express his thoughts about it. We just took it scene by scene. We needed an airplane crash, so I got him an airplane and set it up. Locations, we scouted all of that. It was interesting how the thing developed. I had to sort of motivate some of the people that he worked with [who weren't as aggressive] as I was having come off *Jaws* and *Close Encounters* [*of the Third Kind*], which were bigger pictures with bigger problems. Obviously, some of the big problems we had to look at involved New York and all of the very specific set locations such as a bridge that ends into a wall. That was the first thing to key off, finding a bridge that would end in a wall.

Did you have any sources of inspiration?

Not really. I think it just sort of grew as we got into it. I still have a lot of the original sketches. It grew from there, just doing sketches. John Carpenter, Larry Franco [Producer/First Assistant Director] and I went to New York City and we went to the top of the Trade Center because that was scripted. We just stood there and looked out at New York and said, "We don't have the budget to do New York. We'll have to do something different." I knew I would have to duplicate the top of the Trade Center somewhere else so that we could have the glider land there. The sad thing is that there is no Trade Center anymore.

What kind of challenges did this project provide and which scenes, locations, or sets were the most challenging, problematic, memorable, and fun to work on?

Here's how these things developed. We were looking all over for this bridge, which we found in St. Louis [Old Chain of Rocks Bridge] [69th Street Bridge]. It was a very controllable bridge that we could use, but it didn't have a wall. That was a fairly big build. It was about two hundred feet long and maybe fifty or sixty feet high. We did that all with scaffolding. We got a scaffolding company and covered their scaffold with plywood. Then I [brought in] my painter, Ward Welton [Paint Supervisor], who had worked with me on *Sugarland Express*, *Jaws,* and *Close Encounters.* I had some expert people on that. The bridge, of course, we dressed.

So, now we're in St. Louis. The thing about movies is that making them is very expensive. I said, "If we're in St. Louis, then let's see just how much of St. Louis we can use. Let's see if we can use downtown St. Louis as New York." There was a whole urban redevelopment area there, a big section they were going to redo, so we could pretty much do anything we wanted with it. We could trash it, though we'd have to clean it up. We also trashed a weird area where the helicopters could land. Then we found the old train station [St. Louis Union Station] [Grand Central Station] and that was pretty much deserted. That all made for a wonderful New York setting, a real rundown looking New York.

And the airplane, this is an interesting thing, the burning airplane where the President's [Donald Pleasence] pod comes out. I went to Arizona where they have a sort of graveyard for airplane parts. I went with my assistant and we were marking things that we wanted to buy or rent. As I was coming to the conclusion of my checking, somebody mentioned, "You know, they have an old DC-8 prop plane for sale for like $5,000." I said, "Really? That would make for great parts. Where is it?" He said, "In St. Louis." What are the chances of that? So, I cancelled all my parts, went to St. Louis, and found the DC-8. I thought, "Ok, I could take the engines out and the propellers." My painter, who became the coordinator, found a way of cutting it into pieces and we transported it to a lot in downtown St. Louis. We did this at night because we didn't have any permits. That worked extremely well.

We also found an old theater [Fox Theatre] [Theater Exterior] there, so St. Louis became the hub. We shot the exterior of the Trade Towers in Century City [Century Plaza Towers] in Los Angeles and then the interiors at CalArts [California Institute of the Arts]. I had to do a lot of graffiti, so I brought in rolls and rolls of butcher paper and put them on the walls there. Then we did the graffiti over that because we couldn't actually harm the walls. The Art Center [College of Design] [Liberty Island Security Control Interior] was a beautiful black and white building that also worked really well for us.

But we still had to shoot the Statue of Liberty, so here's what we decided to do for that. I had been designing this big set at a basin we have here called Sepulveda Dam [Liberty Island Security Control Exterior]. It has some nice big concrete structures, very sort of modern and geometrical looking. I had built a sentry post there where Tommy Atkins [Rehme] would come down and walk through. We put that set on a truck and drove it across the country [to New York.] We all flew there and put the set on the last ferry going to Liberty Island so that we didn't have to pay for a special boat. Then we set it up that night and got the shot.

John did that shot with a pan down from the Statue of Liberty. Tommy comes out, walks into the sentry post, and then you see him going through it. Dean Cundey [Director of Photography] was very clever with this. As he panned over from the statue, he came to a frame of total black and cut. Then we shipped everything back to Los Angeles. Dean measured and timed the exact same dolly shot and picked it up with Tommy in Los Angeles. That was very clever for the time. It was done very cheaply, but also in a way that worked because it flowed. It looked like one continuous shot that started with the top of the Statue of Liberty, panned down, and continued on into the building. Today, they'd do it with CGI or whatever was easy.

I think the thing that people remember a lot, and this is sort of funny, are the chandeliers on Isaac Hayes' [The Duke] car. What happened was, Debra said to me, "Can we do some kind of little chandeliers or something on the car that would reflect?" and I said, "Oh yeah, we could do that." I remember going to a decorative service in Yorba Linda, California and finding these chandeliers and I said, "Let's buy a bunch of those and put them on the hood of the car. Two on the fenders." Of course, we're doing stunts with this thing, so they're breaking like crazy and each time we have to replace them. Isaac is driving and it's going thump, thump, thump, thump, thump and then you see these crazy chandeliers. I get a lot of comments about that.

How did you come up with the designs for the Liberty Island Security Control, the Air Force One escape pod, the World Trade Center rooftop, Chock full o'Nuts, and the Grand Central Station gladiator ring and how were they all constructed?

With the Liberty Island Security Control, everything was pretty much extreme architecture there. I didn't want any soft curves or anything. I wanted everything straight, but also sort of angled, that kind of thing. Just angled, sharp, and black so that it would have that military look without using military colors. In other words, the United States Police Force wasn't the nicest. I was trying to express that the country had changed and become very militant.

The Air Force One escape pod was interesting. I did an egg-shaped pod because an egg is sort of a strong structure, and I thought it would hold together in a crash. Eggs don't really have weak sides to them. Of course, they can crack, but if it's made of metal then it would be pretty hard to break. I didn't want to make the pod into a box because that could collapse. I also made the pod orange so that, if it crashed, it would stick out and you would be able to find it. It was interesting because someone later used that idea on *Air Force One*, that they should have a pod like that to protect the president. We just made that up and John liked the idea. It worked out really good because you had this orange pod in all that rubble on the street and out pops the President.

For the World Trade Center rooftop where the glider lands, we just did that out in the desert [Indian Dunes] because we couldn't afford a soundstage. I just built it like it was supposed to be the top of the Trade Center. As for Chock full o'Nuts on Lexington Avenue, we did that out in the desert, too. We went to New York to get pictures of it and I just tried to match it as best I could. That's how it always works. We scout and take pictures of all these locations, like I scouted *Jaws* by myself up the whole east coast. Then I come back to the studio and put them on big illustration boards for the director, who looks at them and says, "Oh, I like this" or "I like that." Then we go back there and research. Today you can just Google it.

But with Chock full o'Nuts, we weren't gonna shoot that in New York because we were in Los Angeles. So, I built and matched half a block of New York out in the desert. Again, we were trying to save money. And I have to tell you something about John Carpenter. He was very, very similar in his shooting style to Alfred Hitchcock. When I worked with Hitchcock, we would build half sets because Hitch would only wanna build what he was gonna shoot. So, in *Escape From New York*, Kurt Russell is walking down toward Chock full o'Nuts and then he goes inside. If John had panned slightly to the left, you would've seen cactus because we were out in the desert. John just shot the minimum. He didn't do any reverse shots. We just built the front of it and then inside where the girl pops up [Season Hubley]. John was very disciplined in that way. Some directors are like, "Build me everything, then I'll figure out how to shoot it." John pretty well knew what he was gonna do before we got there.

And let me tell you about the Grand Central Station gladiator ring, which was interesting. We built the ring and I was trying to make it look harsher, so I put a chain link fence around it. Interestingly, years later they started doing that in wrestling with chain link fences. But I just wanted to make it look real brutal. Normally, boxing rings would just have the ropes, but yeah - I added the chain link to make it look a bit more sinister.

There's an interesting storyboard print on your website showing the taxi driving through Times Square past walls of stacked cars. The revised shooting script dated July 20, 1980 doesn't have a scene in Times Square. Can you shed some light on this?

I think that was somewhere in one of the scripts, although I might have just taken it for granted that we were gonna go to Times Square. I do remember talking to Roy Arbogast [Special Effects Supervisor] about how he was going to build the walls of cars. But I've been asked about that before when I was doing the *Jaws* Blu-ray for the Universal 100th anniversary thing. They asked me to come to the studio there in front of the *Jaws* display and talk to these various reporters. I talked to around twenty-five of them. One said, "You know, the new Batman movie [*The Dark Knight Rises*] copied a lot of your stuff from *Escape From New York*." I said, "What are you talking about?" He said, "Well, you know, they blocked in Gotham City with these walls made of cars." I said, "You know, yeah." I still have all these pencil drawings I did in 1980 of walls made of cars. And that's exactly like what the recent Batman movie did.

Was there any talk about actually doing this scene?

There was talk about driving through New York, the taxi thing with Ernie Borgnine [Cabbie]. Such a nice man. We had plans to do lots of things, but I guess we were limited by having to shoot in St. Louis. When I did the conceptional sketches, obviously I thought we'd be shooting in New York. Those are just hangovers from very early thinking.

Were there more ideas from you, John Carpenter, or someone else that didn't make it into the movie? Were there any other scenes you would do if the movie had been shot in New York for instance?

Storyboard [Times Square] [Omitted]
© Joe Alves

There are always ideas that don't get into a final film, but I can't remember anything in particular that really bothered me that didn't get in. It's hard to say what we would have shot if we had used New York. Other than Liberty Island, we really didn't scout anything in New York. We probably would have used the entrance to the Trade Towers.

How was your experience working with the cast and crew?

It was one of the most fun movies. It's one of two movies that I really had a lot of fun shooting just because the crew were all good people. One was *Sugarland Express*, the first thing I did with Steven Spielberg, and we were just all over Texas and that was fun. I think *Escape From New York* was just good people. I had a good time with Larry Franco, who was the first assistant director, and John and I had a good relationship. I became very good friends with Debra Hill and eventually she dated one of my best friends for many years. She was going out with Dick Smothers. The Smothers Brothers were very big on television around the time of the Vietnam war. They were very progressive and anti-war. Richard Nixon got them taken off the air because they were sort of protesting, but they were very, very big. Anyway, Dick is a good friend of mine. I met him racing cars. I used to race formula cars and so he met Debra. It's very sad that she passed away so young. Dean Cundey is an incredible cinematographer and I think we had a great relationship. We could talk about this and that. He shot a lot of night scenes, but you could still see everything. A lot of these shows that have night scenes, it's just all black and you can't even see the actors, but Dean managed to do it.

What's your favorite memory or memories of working on the movie?

I think it was, yeah, just the relationships with the people was the most rewarding.

Did you learn anything particular to your profession from making this movie that was useful in your later work?

Having done bigger movies like *Jaws* and *Close Encounters*, it made me feel very rewarded to do this smaller picture and still get so much notoriety for the innovative look of it. Vincent Canby, a critic for the *New York Times*, mentioned *Escape From New York* three times that summer, talking about the look of the movie. I think that's what I learned from it. It's not about the budget. It's about the ideas and working with a director as creative as John and a nice team.

What do you think of the movie personally?

At first, I didn't quite know was John was going for, but I think it had a good balance of humor and also an innovative quality about it. I thought Kurt Russell was quite commanding in it. Yeah, it was a very interesting movie because it didn't take itself too seriously. It was sort of lighthearted and you could just go with it.

What are you currently doing and what do you enjoy doing in your spare time?

Oh, what do I do now? I've been retired. Beside these lectures I have probably in the last ten years done thirty sculptures. Big sculptures. Full-size people. I got into a thing of doing mermaids. I don't know why. Someone interviewed me from Sweden. This is for a Swedish talk show of all things, you being from Sweden. This was some kind of reality show, and this woman went up to interview the guy who scared everybody. So, I come in and a film crew comes in and a very tall blonde lady comes in. Very nice and she looks at all my mermaids. I have a fishpond in the house with big coy and mermaids and she said, "Oh my gosh, the softer side of *Jaws*." It was sort of fun but I have so many sculptures. I do them in wood or clay or in carbon foam. Plus, I'm looking outside through the windows. I've got. Oh my gosh. I got a half a dozen there. I had originally sculpted the shark in *Jaws* and I sculpted some aliens for *Close Encounters* so that was something I always wanted to do so that's what I'm doing.

DEAN CUNDEY
Director of Photography

How did you end up being a director of photography?

It's something I always wanted to do. Even as a kid, like twelve years old, I was fascinated by movies. Fascinated by the creative process and the people who made them. In high school, I'd decided I wanted to go into film, so I went to UCLA film school. When I got out, I was fortunate enough to start working in small low budget movies. I took any job I could get, so I didn't start out as a cinematographer. I actually did some makeup. I did editing, special effects, anything I could, always wanting to be in the camera department. I then got an opportunity to shoot a movie when the cinematographer couldn't do it. I was going to be the gaffer, but the director said, "Well, maybe you can do it?" and gave me the opportunity. I had that credit and I did a total of five films with him because the relationship worked out and then just continued on. It was something I always wanted to do and I've been fortunate enough to be able to do it all my career.

How did you get the job of director of photography on *Escape From New York*?

I had been working with John Carpenter starting on *Halloween* and *The Fog*, so it just sort of came naturally when he was doing *Escape From New York*. So, I continued working with him on that film and it was a great experience.

How did you and John Carpenter prepare for this project and how did you collaborate?

It was interesting because it was the biggest film that we had worked on with the most production value and the biggest locations. Originally, the thought was to shoot it in New York, but it was quickly obvious to us that we wouldn't be able to do that. The streets were so crowded. You couldn't shut off the areas that we wanted to. As a result, they looked around for another city and found that St. Louis was rehabilitating some older areas with old brick buildings and factories. These buildings were all closed off. The streets there were rarely used, so we were

L-R/FG: John Carpenter [Director/Co-Writer/Co-Composer], Dean Cundey [Director of Photography], Ray Stella [Camera Operator]
(Photo by/Courtesy Kim Gottlieb-Walker)

given the freedom to block them off. It was this old part of town they were gonna tear down and modernize. So, we had a big location.

It was very fortunate because, if we hadn't found that, we would have had a lot of difficulty in trying to make it look big and desolate and rundown. The prep was pretty sophisticated. I had to go and scout the locations with John. We talked about what direction we would shoot in, how big the shots would be, and how we would dress it to make it look like a derelict New York. Then we started making storyboards, but also working with the crew to come up with a lighting package and a camera package, all that. It was the biggest prep that I had been involved with up until then. It was actually very lucky that we found that part of town. We had complete freedom to shoot however and wherever we wanted.

Were there any disagreements and such?

No. John and I got a long extraordinarily well. We respected each other's talents and creative skills. He would say, "I would like a shot that did this or that." and he would pretty much let me set it up and light it the way I thought it should be and he would look at it and say, "Okay. That looks good." We had a very good creative relationship on the film.

How did you and Joy Brown invent and build the computerized light modulator? And how were the new ultra speed Panatar lenses from Panavision utilized? And the HMI [Hydrargyrum Medium-Arc Iodide]?

Let's see. With the computerized light modulator, I knew that we were going to be creating the illusion that most of the light for the prisoners of New York came from fires. We created this idea that they took big metal forty-five gallon drums, built fires in them, and then set them around town so that they would have some light because we went with the idea that they had no electricity. So, the computerized light modulator was something I had wanted to make. The idea was to be able to flicker a movie light in such a way that it looked like it was fire, flickering brighter and then dimmer. I went to a friend of mine who lived about three houses away from where I was living. He was an electronic engineer and worked on heart simulators for hospitals and doctors and stuff, so he was used to making an electronic signal that fluctuated. I explained the problem and the challenge to him, and he was very interested. So, he and I developed this thing.

He would develop the circuit and then he would say, "How about if we have it do this?" and I said, "Great. And it should also do this." I showed him how I wanted the controls and so forth. He developed this thing, and I built two or maybe three of them in my workshop in my house. I was amazed that they worked so well because they really became an important part of the lighting scheme.

We also had other new technologies we were using like these very fast lenses from Panavision that allowed us to shoot with less light. That was good because I knew we were going to be lighting large areas of nighttime exteriors. Then there was this new device, the HMI light, which also helped us do that. It produced a much brighter light with less electricity. The HMI light also had a very specific color, a kind of interesting blue color. That sort of became the signature look of the streets in New York, along with the flickering light modulator and the very fast lenses.

Which scenes did you use the computer light modulator in?

That scene with the crashed airplane was one. I had two units and we put four or five lights in each one to create the flickering fire. I think that's probably the largest shot, but it was used quite a bit for all kinds of smaller scenes, interiors and so forth. Now with contemporary cameras and digital technology, you can actually shoot with real fires as a source and you can even shoot with candlelight. It's very often done nowadays, but in those days we were shooting on film, which was slower than digital. It needed a lot more light. A LOT more. So, the light modulator worked inside a lot of interiors where we wanted to create the illusion of a small fire or candles or whatever.

What kind of challenges did this project provide and which scenes or locations were the most challenging, problematic, memorable, and fun to work on? Any technical issues and such?

I think the biggest challenges were the night exteriors, especially the one where Kurt Russell is walking through the large square. I guess it was a parking lot where the airplane had supposedly crashed. It was challenging because we had to see the buildings in the background, but we also had to light the foreground with the flickering fires. That was probably the largest night exterior setup we had. We also had the sequences by the train in the train station. That train station was old and no longer in use, essentially deserted. It had been a very important part of St. Louis' history of trains coming and going, but it was quite large and old. We had to light a big area there. Other areas that were difficult or tricky were... actually, there were quite a number of them. The streets at night and the inside of the theater [Wiltern Theatre] when they're putting on the musical concert, a lot of things like that. So, the larger exteriors and the bigger scenes were always the most difficult to light and get enough light on, but also to hide [the light sources] on and make it look natural. The smaller scenes inside the little buildings and rooms were easier and more conventional.

Is it true that the chase scenes as well as the 69th Street Bridge [Old Chain of Rocks Bridge] scenes took longer to light than expected and were among the most challenging ones?

Oh yes, yes. Yeah, that was interesting because we were lucky enough to have a bridge that was old and abandoned. They had built a new bridge just across the river, so the old bridge was okay for us to use because we needed something old and rusty looking. It was tricky to light due to its length. Then we had to have it lit for when the car drives through it and there's the crash and people on it and everything. I would say that was one of the trickier sequences.

How was your experience lighting places such as Hartsfield-Jackson Atlanta International Airport [Colorado Terminal Corridor] [Deleted Scene], Atlanta Subway [Colorado Subway Platform] [San Francisco Subway Platform/Upper Lobby] [Deleted Scenes], Sepulveda Dam [Liberty Island Security Control Exterior], and Liberty Island [Liberty Island Security Control Exterior]?

With [the airport and the subway], those were supposed to be - I guess you could call it the modern world. They were outside the prison, so we used a lot of the available light in lighting those locations. They were still challenging, but in many ways a little easier because we didn't have to bring as much light to it. The Sepulveda Dam worked out very nicely because it was a very stark and large area. Of course, we had to light it at night.

Liberty Island was very interesting because we went there at night to do just a few shots, but it was interesting for us to be essentially alone on the island. There were some police men that guard the island, but we were the only other people there. It was a very inspiring thing to be able to light the Statue of Liberty and be up close in areas that the public doesn't get to go. That's one of the advantages of what we do in film is that very often we get to visit places that the regular public can't visit. We get to see things and experience things that the public can't, and Liberty Island was one of them. We just went there for the night. We arrived during the day, of course, to load equipment and so forth. We worked almost all night out there.

Is it true that the Liberty Island scenes were the last scenes to be filmed for the movie and, if so, did you celebrate after the last shot in any way?

Yes, I think they were, if I remember it right. When you're tired and you turn to each other and say, "Well, that's the last shot," you're very pleased. You say, "Thank you very much." but you don't really get to celebrate until later on. That's why they have wrap parties. Maybe a few days or a week later, the crew and cast get together somewhere in a restaurant or facility and have a little thank you, goodbye party.

How was your experience working with the cast and crew?

When a film is logistically interesting, it doesn't matter how challenging or difficult the work is. We worked almost the entire time in St. Louis at night. We would work all night, sleep during the day, and then come back the next night. Those are the things that can be difficult for a crew. I think everybody knew that we were doing something creative. Something special. Something intriguing. As a result, everybody was very dedicated and enjoyed the creative challenge that we had, so the crew worked very well together. It was my first movie with a union crew, so we had key people who were all members of the film union. They were extremely experienced. They had been working for years and years on films, so they were a tremendous help in accomplishing what we needed to do.

Did any of the actors/characters have to be lit a certain way?

I think we always knew that Kurt was going to look rugged. There were no real women with the exception of the girl that Kurt runs into in the deserted coffee shop [Girl in Chock full o'Nuts] [Season Hubley], so most of the cast were men who were supposedly the prisoners on the island. It gave us the ability to just light them in more contrasting and dramatic ways. We didn't have to worry about making the women look beautiful. We just made the men look ruggedly handsome or like derelicts.

What's your favorite memory or memories of working on the movie?

The film was so full of many memorable experiences. I think it would be hard to pick out any one that was better than the others. I look back and say, "What a great experience it was," and the fact that it has become such a popular cult favorite makes it all worthwhile.

How come you were chosen to be in the theater scene as a sax player in the band consisting of Nick Castle [Co-Writer] on piano, John Carpenter on guitar and kazoo, Barry Bernardi [Associate Producer/Location Manager] on violin, and Clyde Bryan [First Assistant Camera] as a trumpet player, and how was your experience filming this scene and collaborating with Low Moan Spectacular [Dancer] for instance?

That was an amusing thing. When they decided they wanted to have a musical sequence with a band playing, they said, "Why should we go and hire musicians or extras to play musicians when John plays the guitar, Dean plays the saxophone, and we have a drummer?" So, we just put together a little band of background players out of the cast and crew. As a result, we all appeared very briefly as a cameo in the movie and that was fun. Every time I watch the film, I see all of us playing in the little band and it's kind of fun.

What do you think of the movie personally?

When I look at the film, I'm actually quite proud of it. Especially knowing of course what we had to do to accomplish it with our night exteriors and lighting and the rugged conditions we were working under on streets at night that we deliberately filled with junk and trash. There's a lot of the film I look at and say, "Well, we accomplished quite a lot and have created a film that's very popular, so I'm especially proud of it." It's one of my favorite films that I've worked on.

Which shots, scenes or sequences are you most proud of?

There's so many shots where we had to accomplish something or overcome difficulties that I don't know. I think I enjoyed the Steadicam [Panaglide] move of following Kurt through the area with the crashed airplane. It was a very large location inside a large scene. Anytime you're moving the camera like we did with Kurt walking, it makes it more difficult. You have to hide your lights in an area that needs a lot of light. Then you want to stay on Kurt and keep things out of frame that you don't want seen. I think that's one of the trickier shots that I appreciate. Although there are others that stick out in my mind. Kurt coming across the street or the alley and coming across the escape capsule that the President [Donald Pleasence] used. That's a fairly dramatic moment where we deliberately composed the shot looking down the street. There's a lot of shots like that I remember and am proud of.

What are you currently doing and what do you enjoy doing in your spare time?

I've always been interested in a lot of different things. As a kid growing up, I loved music. I played the saxophone all through high school and college and played in two or three musical groups in college. The marching band, the regular band, the jazz band. It was a lot of fun and it has affected me in that I understand music. I appreciate what it takes to play in an orchestra or a band. I don't play anymore for my amusement, but I certainly appreciate music. In my spare time, I've always enjoyed little things like woodworking and making useful little things. I've never built anything giant like a cabinet or bookcase. Well, actually, I guess I have, but I've always enjoyed working with my hands. I enjoy trying to keep up with technology from the standpoint of what's developing. I'm not a computer wizard, but I enjoy reading about them and trying to understand the modern world, technology and things that we deal with. I don't have any big, you know, hobbies like playing golf or whatever. Although I have played it some. I guess you can say I just enjoy puttering.

FRANK DOUBLEDAY
Romero

How did you end up being an actor?

I started acting in college. I did not want to be an actor until I saw a production of *Waiting for Godot*. Once I saw that production, I knew I had to do this.

How did you get cast as Romero in *Escape From New York*?

I had worked for John Carpenter on *Assault on Precinct 13,* so he knew me. He looked for me for *Escape From New York* and gave me the role.

How did you prepare for the role and how was your experience filming? How much of Romero's bizarre behavior was improvised for instance?

I totally created the role myself. John gave me total creative freedom. The voice and the look were my ideas. I like that kind of work. I did a lot of character work and worked on Romero through voice, costume, and movement. All my behavior was improvised. Once a character is created and is in one's skin, the behavior just comes naturally. All the behavior, the hissing, etcetera, was not planned. That kind of thing is the actor playing and, again, if the character has been internalized, it all just happens. That was a rich, fun character to create.

How do you think Romero ended up in New York's Maximum Security Prison and why do you think the Duke [Isaac Hayes] chose him to be his right-hand man?

Not sure why he ended up in the prison, but was probably chosen to be the Duke's right-hand man because of his propensity for evil and his comfort with danger. Romero was referred to in *Newsweek* as Carpenter's most menacing villain to date.

What's your favorite memory or memories of working on the movie?

I don't really have a favorite memory.

How was your experience working with the cast and crew?

Cast and crew were great. No ego problems.

What do you think of the movie personally?

I think the movie is excellent for the style of movie it is. Also, John Carpenter is a great and underrated director.

What are you currently doing and what do you enjoy doing in your spare time?

I continued to work in the theater and in television. I directed a lot of theater and taught for several years. My interests are literature, science, history, and physics. I read a great deal and love the internet for listening to lectures. I also like listening to the BBC recorded radio plays.

JOHN STROBEL
Cronenberg

How did you get cast as Cronenberg in *Escape From New York*?

I was friends with his casting director. I already had worked for Carpenter on *The Fog*. Originally, I was a dead body that fell on top of Jamie Lee [Curtis]. Not a bad job. I also played the grocery clerk in the opening credits. When we were shooting the scene at the Canyon Country Store up Laurel Canyon, the police came by, and shooting had to wrap up quickly as no permits were pulled for this. Always surprised that I got credit in the film as this was off record to some degree. Debra Hill [Producer] and John knew they were sneaking this bit of shooting which made it more fun really. They told the police that it was a student film as I recall.

How did you prepare for the role and how was your experience filming your scenes such as the one with Snake Plissken choking Hauk [Lee Van Cleef] for instance?

We did run through/rehearse the scene with Kurt and Lee. We actually did one run through with all of us doing a fey act. While very much not politically correct, it was pretty funny at the time. Especially considering it was Lee and Kurt. I also ran lines with Lee for another scene we did. He was very gracious and giving in doing so. Small anecdote: The injection device in the scene actually broke before we shot. The wires became unconnected. I had to hold the injection bit and the wire in such a way that the wires looked attached. Just an odd moment but, on relatively low budget movies, waiting for a repair would have eaten up time.

How was your experience working with the cast and crew?

The interesting thing about *Escape From New York* is where it sits in the careers of the actors - not me, the stars. For Kurt, this was really his first go at an action hero type character. He was extremely focused and took the entire process very seriously and I think it shows in the quality of his performance. I loved working with Lee. I was a huge fan of his work in westerns, especially of the spaghetti

L-R: Lee Van Cleef [Hauk], John Strobel [Cronenberg], Kurt Russell [Snake Plissken]
(Photo by/Courtesy Kim Gottlieb-Walker)

variety. On screen, his look was terrifying! In life, he was the kindest and gentlest guy you could imagine.

Carpenter did not do a lot of takes in general was my impression. He used his storyboards extensively and shot what he needed. I do know that he sometimes had to shoot inserts after primary shooting was completed, stuff like the face of a clock or a hand. Little snips that he needed in editing. Also, Carpenter used matte shots a couple of times if I remember correctly, which are fascinating. Even then, pretty much a dead art. He also loved fade to black and extended pans - see *Halloween* - to extend his shots and shift locations, which was cool. I got to see a couple of those set up and executed. His ability to shoot on a bridge outside of St. Louis [Old Chain of Rocks Bridge] [69th Street Bridge] and then shift to the Sepulveda Damn [Liberty Island Security Control Exterior] in L.A. was pretty neat.

What's your favorite memory or memories of working on the movie?

Really meeting and working with Lee Van Cleef. Also meeting some of the other actors involved. Ernest Borgnine [Cabbie] was amazing. His portrayal of Marty was off the charts, great as was most everything he ever did, but the high point for me was meeting Isaac Hayes [The Duke]. This was the man who wrote the theme music to *Shaft*. Amazing talent and a very large presence.

Is it true that you were responsible for the *Escape From New York* t-shirts sent to the cast and crew after the movie was made? If so, how come you chose to make them and how were they made?

Jeez, how in hell did you find that out? I had some made up that had a number like on the watch Kurt wore in the picture. It was something like "00:00:15 To Escape From New York". I think I used the count down time that was on Kurt's watch when it stopped after Cronenberg deactivates the explosive charges in his neck. Not sure about this. I did it just a gesture of thanks is all. Just designed it and had them printed at some t-shirt joint in Hollywood, as I recall.

What do you think of the movie personally?

The older the movie gets, the better and more fun it is. It was good when it was released, but viewing it now, the rudimentary special effects seem somehow quaint and you can accept them for what they are - antiquated. They seem better now than they did then for some odd reason, kind of like watching an old Roger Corman film now versus then. It was cheesy then but now viewing a guy in a rubber suit playing the monster, I love that stuff. While CGI is amazing, the art of actually filming live action models was cool and is more fun to watch.

The interesting thing, and this is news to no one, was some of the locations, especially the Statue of Liberty shots. I would think security concerns would make shots like that impossible and so they would be CGI. In *Escape From New York*, it was all shot on location. One thing to remember is, when this film was shot, the idea that New York could be abandoned and turned into a big pit to throw bad guys into was not a gigantic stretch. I lived in New York in the mid-70s and it was nearly as trashed out and dirty as depicted in the movie. I have read that they have tried a couple of times to remake

Escape From New York. The problem is that no one would accept New York being abandoned now. Back then, as I said, it did not take a lot of imagination to accept the premise.

How come you stopped working as an actor after *Escape From New York*?

I decided I liked eating more than not eating, I guess. I co-owned some restaurants in L.A. for a while which took care of the eating part. Later, I owned a logistics business and now I am an angel investor and CEO of an equity investment firm focused on commercial real estate.

What are you currently doing and what do you enjoy doing in your spare time?

Playing music, guitar, and the normal stuff. Hiking, biking, travel, dining, cooking, reading.

JOHN COTHRAN JR.
Gypsy #1

How did you end up being an actor?

I started acting when I was in high school, and I majored in theatre in college. Around twenty-one or twenty-two, I finally made a commitment that I had to make a living at it, so I started acting professionally. I had a lot of jobs before that, but acting was always my first love.

How did you get cast as Gypsy #1 in *Escape From New York*?

I was in Kansas City, Missouri working at a repertoire theatre when my agent called me and told me that they were shooting a feature film in St. Louis. Kansas City, which is where I was, was about a four hour drive from St. Louis. I lived in St. Louis, but I was working in Kansas City. I agreed to drive to St. Louis and I auditioned not realizing that it was gonna cause me even more problems. I auditioned for John Carpenter. He wanted me to do Gypsy One and have a couple of lines, but I wasn't a member of the Screen Actors Guild. That meant I had to make a trip to Chicago to join SAG, which cost me more money than I got paid to do the film, but it was unusual that a feature film would be shooting in St. Louis. That's how I got cast. They were shooting in St. Louis, which is my hometown, and I was already an actor. *Escape From New York* was my first film. I had never been in a feature film before. All of my work had been in the theatre up until then.

How did you prepare for the role and how was your experience filming?

Well, again, it was such an unusual experience because it was my first film and *Escape From New York* was an incredibly complicated action film. They used the old union train station, which had fallen into complete disrepair and wasn't used anymore. It was quite a showplace in the 40s and 50s. I was a gypsy and the whole Union Station was transformed into Grand Central Station. Isaac Hayes [The Duke] was in control of the city and that room where the big fight took place was the main hall of the train station. I had a lot of friends who were in the film too. A lot of people I knew in St. Louis were used as extras, so it was just an incredible first-time experience. I worked on the film for I think two days and hung around probably for another five or six days just talking to people - Lee Van Cleef [Hauk], Ernest Borgnine [Cabbie], Donald Pleasence [President]. I was smitten by Adrienne Barbeau [Maggie], that's for sure. We all knew her from television as she had been on *Maude*.

It was just a fun experience and I remember my big line. I had to make Snake get off the table and I had a crossbow. I had buddies in St. Louis for years who would always tease me about my line, "Get up, Snake!, Get up, Snake!" If I remember right. That big scene. Get off the table and then leading him into the arena. We did that maybe two or three times. The time-consuming part of that was once we got him into the arena, he had to be put into the ring for the fight and that took forever. That fight with the big hairy guy [Ox Baker] [Slag] with the club with nails in it that was quite something. That was a world that was completely new to me. Like I said, I had never been on a film, let alone an action film, so seeing how that was done was incredibly interesting. His death and all of that was new and exciting stuff for me and Isaac Hayes back then was iconic. He was only known in the music world, so this was a big deal for him to be acting and for him to be there acting and giving his big speech to the hall. We were all excited by it. The costume designer decided what we were gonna wear. I mean, they made real choices because the people who populated the city had to look a certain way. You know, the underlings. If I remember right, there were like two different kinds of people that populated the city. Obviously, the convicts and then the regular people had been reduced to almost a homeless kind of look.

How was your experience working with the cast and crew?

Again, I was new to all that and, because I didn't have a major role, my involvement with the cast and crew was very minimal. I wasn't one of the people that got the chance to really talk to them or deal with them. My memory was, they were all pleasant and nice to everybody. I did have one friend who lived in St. Louis who injured himself. He had to jump off a train or something and he really hurt his legs very badly. That caused him problems for years. The production company's insurance took care of him and all of that because of it. I just remember that my interaction with the crew and all that was minimal, but the interaction I did have was pleasant. I didn't have any problems at all, and they really took care of us.

What's your favorite memory or memories of working on the movie?

My favorite memories of working on the movie have to do with the filmmaking. For example, it was the first time I had ever seen a hand-held camera like a Steadicam [Panaglide]. That was a new thing back then. They were just beginning to use the Steadicam and that whole scene of us walking down the hall leading Snake to the auditorium, that was shot with a Steadicam. So just watching how things were done was one of my most favorite memories. Just being a fly on the wall and watching how film worked.

My next favorite memory certainly was meeting people like Ernest Borgnine. I remember having a really pleasant conversation with him in front of the train station. He was a big deal.

What do you think of the movie personally?

I think it's a really fun movie and it was really ahead of its time. I mean, think how many movies we've had since then that deal with that kind of subject matter - the disintegration of a city. In fact, right now I play the president of the United States on a show called *The Last Ship*. This last season I became the president of the United States in the last eight episodes. It's a show that deals with an apocalyptic kind of thing that's going on in the world. I think *Escape From New York* was one of the first films that dealt with that kind of thing going on. That's basically what's happened to New York. It's been walled off and it has returned to the most basic and primitive of man's instinct, so it was ahead of its time even in terms of the technology that was used in the film. The digital time on the watch and all that was stuff we hadn't seen before. It turned out to be such an iconic film, but when it was being done, none of us knew really what we were in and what it really was. I'm not even sure I was given an entire script because I know when I finally saw the film, I was wide-eyed at what was going on. I didn't really know what was really happening. At that time if you didn't have a major role, you only got sides of the pages you're involved in.

What are you currently doing and what do you enjoy doing in your spare time?

I'm just a regular working stiff actor. I live in Sherman Oaks, California. I do a lot of television and occasionally I do theatre still. If you go to IMDb, you can see I've been staying pretty busy over the years. I feel incredibly blessed about being able to practice the craft that I love so much. I have a family. Just a regular guy.

GARRETT BERGFELD
Gypsy #2

How did you end up being an actor?

I was very shy as a teenager and got into high school plays as a way to express myself and also to escape into the persona of someone else. Over the many years since then I've done nearly one hundred plays including turns as Hamlet and Macbeth. I've only done a few films, but *Escape From New York* is certainly the most well-known of those.

How did you get cast as Gypsy #2 in *Escape From New York*?

My initial audition was taped by a local talent agency and then sent to John Carpenter. Now, you have to remember that this was 1980 and there was a TV commercial airing selling televisions sets and using the tag line, "My shirt is blue, my jacket is yellow and my tie is bright red. If these colors don't look right to you, then you're not watching on a Motorola TV." So, in an attempt to get noticed, I introduced myself on the tape and described the opposite of what I was actually wearing. I then said, "If these colors look right to you, then you're doing the same drugs I am." It worked and when John interviewed me in person we had a good laugh about it.

How did you prepare for the role and how was your experience filming?

I'm in two scenes. The first is a very brief close-up as my character spies Brain [Harry Dean Stanton] and Maggie [Adrienne Barbeau] absconding with the President [Donald Pleasence] during the wrestling match. Then a few minutes later, as the fight ends, I'm seen running up to the Duke [Isaac Hayes] in the balcony to tell him about it. The Duke leaves and I jump on the railing of the balcony with the line, "The President's gone! Brain took him!" John Carpenter told me before the shoot that he'd given me, "The worst line I've ever written, but I have to clear the room of about three hundred people. Do whatever you can with it." When it actually came time to shoot the scene, John was downstairs by the wrestling ring and I was up on the balcony. I realized that the crowd of extras down below was still loudly cheering Snake's victory and would never hear the line. So, I took it upon myself to adlib and very loudly shouted, "Listen! LISTEN! LISTEN!" Once the crowd quieted down, I delivered that immortal line of John's.

How was your experience working with the cast and crew?

I was impressed by the efficiency and professionalism of the cast and crew. I was blown away by how the set designer had transformed St. Louis' Union Station into that wrestling arena. The atmosphere was exactly what the scene required. The first actor I met was Harry Dean Stanton. When I asked him where I could find one of the PAs [Production Assistant], he responded by describing the guy down to the color of his socks, explaining that he was playing a memory game he had learned from his acting classes. I briefly spoke with Donald Pleasence who I found was quite aptly named. Ernest Borgnine [Cabbie] had already wrapped, but I got to use his trailer for my dressing room. I did not get a chance to talk to Kurt Russell. He seemed to want his privacy. At the wrap party, I spoke with Adrienne Barbeau for a few minutes, and she was very kind and friendly.

What's your favorite memory or memories of working on the movie?

My favorite memory comes from the wrap party after the shoot. John Carpenter told me that I should come out to L.A. to work as an actor. I told him I'd do that if he would promise to cast me in his next movie. John smiled and just said, "Okay." His next film was *The Thing* and I've always wondered if he was serious and, if so, what role I might have been given.

What do you think of the movie personally?

I can't honestly say it's one of my favorite movies, but I think it was a good film that achieved exactly what the director wanted it to. I believe it was one of Carpenter's best.

What are you currently doing and what do you enjoy doing in your spare time?

Even though I've worked in theater semi-professionally for decades, acting was always just an avocation for me, albeit an important one. My actual vocation is as a college professor of physiology, which I love. I recently came out of a self-imposed retirement to do an original play called *Black and Blue* about the Michael Brown shooting in Ferguson, Missouri.

JOEL BENNETT
Gypsy #4

How did you end up being an actor?

I lived from birth until ten in Appalachia near the western foothills of the great Smokey Mountains. My "Gomer Pyle" accent was as thick as cold molasses. Moving to the Midwest was a shock. I had to fix my pronunciation to the horrid and flat sounds heard in the wonderful Coen Brother's movie, *Fargo*. I had to adapt as soon as possible or face the taunts and physical abuse of neighborhood bullies. This was a tough blue-collar area of North St. Louis County about a mile and a half from the notorious Ferguson. I guess that was a forced lesson, but it got me interested in pretending to be someone I was not. My fascination with accents, but mostly my desire to fit in, led me to being a comical extrovert and that led to high school acting. I did school and college plays and got hired professionally by the seminal Theatre Project Company at twenty-three. I did non-union roles and local TV and radio and at twenty-four got cast in *Escape From New York*. The first college I attended had a vicious instructor who reviewed my attempt at a scene from *The Lion in Winter* by telling me in front of the class that her kindest advice was to quit acting. She was fired that year and I attended another school with classmates like John Goodman, Kathleen Turner, and other future successes.

How did you get cast as Gypsy #4 in *Escape From New York*?

I had an agent as I was working a lot in professional theater and in St. Louis. I rehearsed both Gypsy parts in the scene. When I got called in to read, it was just a small room with a long haired and very calm yet powerfully intense John Carpenter. He looked at me the way a few other creative geniuses have looked at me. He completely took what I brought into the little room in a calm focused and positive manner. Most actors don't account for this, but casting people really, really want you to succeed. Then they can go home for the day. To calm myself, I remembered what local acting legend Bobby Miller had told me. Picture them in their underwear. It is much less intimidating. I read the scene, taking extra time for the death shot, and slumped down in submission to Snake

Plissken's prowess. Mr. Carpenter was happy and shook my hand. I got a call from my agent a week later and the earth moved. I got that call the afternoon of my twenty-fifth birthday to be on the set the next several days as John Carpenter wisely used me as a double, an extra, and a few small roles without lines. I missed my birthday party but WHO CARED?

How did you prepare for the role and how was your experience filming?

I arrived at the set, the [Old] Chain of Rocks Bridge [69th Street Bridge] where my high school graduation party had ended eight years before. I learned that August 20 was also Isaac Hayes' [The Duke] birthday and he generously gave me a slice of his birthday cake. That night I was one of the cops on top of the wall that were trying to help Snake back to safety at the end. It was my first experience with razor wire and I got a nice little cut on my finger. They used stunt doubles for Donald [Pleasence] [President] and Kurt for the scary parts of it. Jesse Wayne was Donald's stunt double and Dick Warlock was Kurt's stunt double. Dick gave me excellent advice for a scene in a play I was rehearsing where I lay dead on the floor center stage for five minutes. He told me to die with an arm under me. The shallow breaths I needed to take could be under my body instead of rising and falling from the top which is far more visible. On the bus to a location, Jesse Wayne fooled me into believing he was related to John Wayne.

    The following two nights, I doubled for the extraordinary Frank Doubleday [Romero]. No pun intended. Night one was simple exterior shot of the Duke's pimpmobile pulling up to Brain's [Harry Dean Stanton] library lair. That car was memorable to ride in. I merely wore a similar wig and was, at most, a silhouette as we were shot from a distance. That night I got a treat as Carpenter wisely gave me as much experience as I could get before my "big" scene. I stood directly behind the camera operator as Mr. Carpenter explained the shot where Cabbie [Ernest Borgnine] and Snake make their separate arrival to the lair. He explained where he wanted Mr. Borgnine to park the cab, where he was to say his first line, and that he was to finish his last line just as he passed the camera. Mr. Russell and Mr. Borgnine got into the cab as the crew sprayed the street with water and drove around the block just out of sight waiting to hear "Action!" via a radio. I watched in the awe of youth as Mr. Borgnine parked perfectly, said his first line perfectly, and finished his last line EXACTLY as he passed the camera. As he passed the camera, "Cut! Print!" was announced and he noticed me wide-eyed a few steps behind the camera and gave me a big wink as if to say, "THAT's how ya do it, kid!"

The following night, I was actually a stand-in for Mr. Doubleday. It was a scene at Union Station where the Theatre Project Company was located. This was another coincidence as much of the movie took place there as the almost abandoned building "doubled" for an abandoned Grand Central Station in an awful future time. Stand-ins literally assume the position of the actual actors or "First Team" as they are sometimes called while the tedious process of getting the lighting just right is performed. I was astonished when they had me leaning against a statue with its hand on my face. One of the many bold, bizarre, and wonderful choices Mr. Doubleday made. When the lights were right, the stand-ins left and the first team came back from their "break" to shoot the scene.

I was in several crowd scenes and saw Ox Baker [Slag] accidentally bash Kurt Russell with his bat. The bats were rubber, but he caught him pretty hard and there was a brief time out as Snake got his composure back. Kurt Russell had been a professional actor since childhood, and I am sure he was pissed at the pro wrestler's disregard for combat acting.

One other thing. I always felt kinda sorry for the stupendously sexy Adrienne Barbeau [Maggie]. She was almost ALWAYS the ONLY woman on set and her outfit brought about continued and helpless stares. She was a pro as well and could kill anyone's too lustful ideas with a single ice-cold glance.

I got all the "extra" work because John Carpenter knew it was a big scene and that, although I had maybe ten professional theater gigs and a few local TV commercials, I had a lot to learn and needed to get used to the process of making a major motion picture. By the way, only on the day of my big scene did I receive SAG scale, which was $330 for "under fives" in those days. All of the other days I got the same forty bucks cash that the other extras got. Hell, I would have done it for free. That day I got permission for my best friend to visit the set. His name was Lance Cleveland and he died of liver cancer three and a half years ago. Permission was granted by relatively new producers Debra Hill and Larry Franco. They were both as gracious as could be. Ms. Hill doled out all the extra pay every dawn and Mr. Franco made a point of speaking to Lance and making him feel welcome. Lance got to meet Donald Pleasence and Kurt Russell who were professional and courteous. So much happened in that one night it is hard to remember it all.

The first shot was easy as I worked the hacksaw blade and delivered my first line. The second shot was from behind Mr. Pleasence's back as Snake snuck in to break my fellow Gypsy's [Robert John Metcalf] [Gypsy #3] neck. I was told not to say my second line, "What are you lookin' at?" until Carpenter cued me from behind the camera which was maybe eight feet behind Mr. Pleasence. I heard the direction clearly but when Mr. Pleasence's eyes grew wide [invisible on this shot], I reacted and said my line. "Cut!" was called and I was gently reminded that, even though I was watching the President as I used my hacksaw on his mysterious undoubtedly valuable briefcase, I was to wait for Mr. Carpenter's cue. "Action!" was called. I did it again. "Cut!!!" was shouted and I was not so gently reminded again. Carpenter hated to do three takes and God forbid you needed any more. Third time was a charm. I rose and turned, dropped the hacksaw, and got off a hurried left headed shot with my crossbow.

You would have laughed to see the actual crossbow shot. It went about all of six feet. Not to worry. It was planned that way as they edited just as soon as the trigger was pulled and the bolt began to "fly". There followed a setup where a thin fishing line was run from the Snake's leg [actually a thin piece of Styrofoam inside his pants leg] all the way past my hip to an effects guy behind me. He had a half-arrow hollowed out to slide along the line pulled back with a damn slingshot. The camera was placed just behind my knee so when "Action!" was called the angle looked real as the slingshot whipped the hollow half-arrow into the Styrofoam in Snake's pants leg and STUCK. Then, stud that he was and still is, the wounded Plissken hurled a ninja star into my forehead kinda.

When we first met earlier that night, Kurt carefully explained that he was trained and had practiced diligently and would miss me by a good three feet. He was as good as his word and the actual star hit a big plywood target just about where he said it would. Since the shot was from behind my knee you only saw him let fly at an angle that suggested it would strike me up high. Then there was a break where I marched over to makeup and they glued a silver painted piece of balsa wood that had been cut in half into the middle of my forehead. Putty and a few other tricks were also applied. Now I walk back to the set with the ninja star stuck in my head feeling very strange. Back in the railroad car, the effects guy ran a small hose under the back of my shirt and hid that end in my bushy dirty hair about two inches above my forehead. The other end of the hose ran to something like a large enema bag completely filled with stage blood. On "Action!" I flipped my head back as if receiving the blow and started to "die". "Cut! Where's the blood?" asked Carpenter. The effects guy said my hair was thicker than he thought so we went for take two. Same problem again. Third time was a charm and as soon as I flipped my head back the blood began to flow and I "died," taking my time as Carpenter advised and since it was my only close-up it worked out well for me. I used to joke with fellow actors that if you REALLY watch me, I go through all five stages of death. Ha ha. One regret is, the close-up was deemed gory enough to be cut whenever it was shown on non-premium cable. Oh well.

How was your experience working with the cast and crew?

Kurt Russell was a great guy. He had dumbbells just out of sight so he could pump his Plissken guns when he felt the need. He was "tryin' to quit," but he owes me about half a pack of Marlboro reds. If you run into him, tell him they were my treat.

What's your favorite memory or memories of working on the movie?

My favorite moment was that magical, knowing "wink" from the enormously talented Ernest Borgnine. Shooting the big scene is a close second.

What do you think of the movie personally?

I liked the movie. The story was great and the casting was phenomenal. I think I got around fourteenth credit as Gypsy #4, but Jesus, the first eight or so names were Oscar and Emmy winners or nominees. I am glad that it is still popular and still occasionally remind folks that I am the only character who seriously hurt Snake Plissken. How the Duke missed him with his Uzi, I will never know.

What are you currently doing and what do you enjoy doing in your spare time?

I found myself unemployed last month after five great years with a poorly run company. I performed well but downsizing from fifteen to two locations was too much. I outlasted almost everyone. I am seriously seeing this is as an opportunity to pursue acting professionally again. The crazy highs and lows are both unhealthy unless you have "The soul of a rose and the hide of a rhinoceros." I got talked into doing a union waiver show a few years ago and I wound up co-starring in a scandalously hilarious political operetta called *The Beastly Bombing*. We won *LA Weekly*'s "Musical of the Year" and got to perform it two weeks off-Broadway in Manhattan. For the past several years I have satisfied my creative itch by sitting in with local bands who know me. I usually sit in with bands around my age and do old school country. Hank Sr. [Williams], [Johnny] Cash, Buck [Owens] and classic rock. The crowds know me and demand "White Lightning" by George Jones and "Crocodile Rock" from Elton John.

Last summer I finally decided I wanted to do my own thing. The part owner/musical genius Cody Bryant runs the shows at Viva Fresh Cantina in Burbank. It was voted "Best Place to Hear Live Music" by *LA Weekly*. Being old and wise enough not to argue with a guy like Cody, I heeded his advice and found my sound and style AND repertoire with only a solo acoustic guitar. It was quite the learning curve as I insist on the finest local players and they get late calls for tours and huge paying gigs. As Cody explained, "Finding good sidemen at the last minute is a valuable skill." After a few months, I got promoted to a later slot and finally got paid enough to hire a top guitarist and bass and break even. Last gig I raked in over one hundred in tips, so I am seeing bigger and better gigs. Paying my own band. I get to do fantastic and unheard new "Americana" songs by geniuses like Ryan [not Bryan] Adams, Jason Isbell, Guy Clark and the late great Townes Van Zandt. We also KILL with our duet of harmonies in "The Sound of Silence." My next gig is in two weeks, and I have a decent amount of hardcore fans. I sing soul music that tells deep stories and I do my best to go there. The rest is easy. I have a successful wife and two fine sons and a very cute home in Encino.

TOBAR MAYO
Third Indian

How did you end up being an actor?

I sang and danced in elementary school and got into barbershop quartets and school plays. When I got to high school, in my time, you couldn't be a senior player until you were in the last year of school. I was singing with acapella choirs and doing stuff with the Parent-Teacher Association and little community theaters. I ended up doing a play called *Harvey*. I don't know if you've heard of it, but it's about a young man who imagines an invisible rabbit. Then I started doing some extra work. I didn't do much because I didn't know what I wanted to do. I did some stand-in work and I ended up doing that for like Jim Brown and Fred Williamson. Then one time I got lucky. My first union TV show was called *Mannix*. The way I got the part was that someone else was supposed to do it and he got sick. So my agent called me and said, "Get down to Paramount Studios right away to look at that part for this show," but I wasn't in the union. What happened was, I went into the office there. The secretary gave me some pages out of a script and just when I sat down to read it the director walked out and said, "Is that the man?" and she said, "Yes." He said, "Alright. Send him over to the wardrobe," and all that. "You got to be kidding me. I just walked in here!"

So anyway, I got the part. The shoot was in San Francisco, so I got there and the assistant director said, "Tobar, you're not in the union." I said, "I know I'm not in the union. Nobody asked me." There were no other men, so I had the job. I don't know how familiar you are with substantiative provisions and such, but it's called Taft-Hartley. You can work on a film once on a union production, but on the next job you have to join, so that's what I did. It was pretty exciting for me. In San Francisco, we started out at Fisherman's Wharf and I had to chase Mannix. Have you heard of it? It's an old series. In fact, when they show reruns, I expect to get a little 10 cent check out of that I guess. So anyway, I had to chase him from Fisherman's Wharf to the cable car because San Francisco is famous for their cable cars. I chase him up from Fisherman's Wharf and we have to turn a corner and I thought I was still chasing him but it ended up being his double. By the time we got up to the cable car, people were stopping me wanting my autograph. I said, "What do you mean autograph? This is my first job." They wanted an autograph from the bad guy. Then the show got cancelled. The next season got cancelled. They asked me if I was interested in coming back. I said, "Are you kidding? Heck yeah!" but it got cancelled the next season. It's kind of a quick jump from being a stand-in to actually having a part in a hot show.

How did you get cast as Third Indian in *Escape From New York*?

I originally read for the part that Isaac Hayes [The Duke] got. Of course, he had a bigger name than I did. The director called me back because he liked my audition for the Isaac Hayes part. I guess that's how I got the Indian part.

How did you prepare for the role and how was your experience filming? You had the misfortune to be involved in two scenes that were cut out of the movie. The first one saw the Indians roasting a cat in the lobby of the World Trade Center and Snake Plissken almost getting garroted by a fourth Indian from behind. The second was the Indians running out from The World Trade Center and looking for Snake.

I don't remember roasting a cat. I remember we had a fire and that was done at a university [California Institute of the Arts]. It wasn't in the city area. It was in the county of L.A. I do remember the three of us Indians sitting around a fire. I don't remember doing the cat but we were doing something there with that fire. I'm just guessing. I was pretty good. I don't remember taking two takes of anything that ever I worked in. Maybe one project. My resume is not as long as everybody else's. There's another scene we were suppose to do. We were suppose to get rid of the glider but they used other people for that.

Did Kurt Russell use a flare gun in the first scene and did he run behind a concrete wall in the second scene as written in the shooting script?

Yeah, I remember Kurt Russell doing that and I think he ran straight ahead. I think I looked right at the camera as he was spying around. I think that's why it was cut. I also think that shoot was day to night.

Were you disappointed that the aforementioned scenes were cut out of the movie?

Yeah, I was disappointed but, like I said, the camera was on me. I'm supposed to just keep turning my head looking to the right, I think it was. I'm almost sure that I stopped where I wasn't supposed to stop. I was very disappointed because that was a good part. I was playing an Indian you know.

How was your experience working with the cast and crew?

One good surprise was getting to my dressing room once we were on set and meeting Ernest Borgnine [Cabbie]. Very nice guy. I got all excited getting to meet him. I mean, I was like a young kid, man. Frank Doubleday [Romero], who was also in the film, played the nasty looking guy. He and I had done a show at the university, so there were some people in that movie that I knew but I didn't get to shoot with. I didn't even know they were in it because my part was so small.

    I was excited meeting John Carpenter because I knew who he was, but I wasn't excited about being cut. He was cool too. My plan was to work for John Carpenter again. I was hoping to do that. I think I looked into the camera, but he was happy with what I was doing from the start because I heard him talking to someone. I think it was the AD [Assistant Director]. He said, "The guy is an actor." That was before the scene where I screwed up. What happened was, the other two Indians, they were screwing up and it kind of threw me off. Not that they were bad actors. I don't know what they were doing. They were doing something they had no business doing. They were kind of laughing and having a good time. I remember John talking to the AD, "This guy is an actor. He's the only one acting in here." Then I turned around and screwed up. I'm blaming myself for that.

What's your favorite memory or memories of working on the movie?

My favorite memory of the movie was meeting Ernest Borgnine. It was a joy to meet him. My other favorite memory came in TV. I did a couple of TV shows with some people who had hot shows at the time. I played a gay guy in one of them and I did a good job on that. The next time I had the most fun would've been a show called *The Jeffersons*. I loved working on that show because I got to play a part being in jail and I have been arrested before. I've never been to jail or prison but just being a black male in America when I was coming up as a kid was enough to go to jail, so I was excited to be in jail and getting paid! It was also the first time they had used a large cast of speaking parts, and I had the first line. The episode was called "The Blackout". That was one of my favorite parts. I got a good, nice fat check and I was in jail, so I was happy about that.

What do you think of the movie personally?

I liked the movie. I liked the script. Carpenter always came up with something, man. He did some stuff that I enjoyed seeing, but I've only seen a couple of his movies.

How come you stopped working as an actor after *Escape From New York*?

I didn't stop. You see, my family was living in a bad neighborhood. It was low income and all that stuff. I'm the oldest out of nine. I always had to stop and help my family. I was a desperate young man. I wanted to be a part of it, of anything. My idea was that I wanted to make big money and get them out of that neighborhood but they're still there except my mother. She died a month ago and my father has been gone for a while. From there I just kept hustling, going to auditions, and getting beat out sometimes. Sometimes I got a part and the show was cancelled. One time a lead actress went on a strike the day before I was shooting, so I lost that part. I was in New York auditioning for a cop show and then I got calls to do a shoot in L.A. for another cop show and I didn't get the job because I couldn't get back in time. I just kept on pounding. I had to get a job. Then I'd go back and try to do it again.

What are you currently doing and what do you enjoy doing in your spare time?

Since I've been healing for the last five years, I haven't had much fun. I haven't worked because the last five years I've lost eighteen people, man. Family and friends. I've also had knee surgery and back surgery. I'm also a veteran, so I'm waiting to get some patriot housing. I did end up working at UCLA my last ten years so I would have some health benefits. I would prefer to be doing something with my theater Open Gate Theatre. I like to travel.

STEVEN M. GAGNON
Secret Service #1

How did you end up being an actor?

I was an actor all through high school. What I really wanted to do was to make the baseball team. Any time I got cut from baseball, I went back to the stage, which I always found to be easy and enjoyed. It was a lot of fun. I realized that, by doing stage in high school, I could hang out with jocks and people that come watch me perform on stage. Unfortunately, I couldn't get the coaches to come, so they kept cutting me. That was really my first love, to play baseball, and it didn't work out, but acting was where it was at, and I fell back into acting. So when I left high school, I kicked around doing a few different jobs. I worked at a supermarket for several years and was a gardener for my dad, things like that. Various jobs.

Then I had friends that became teamsters, drivers for the studios, and they said, "Hey, we want to get you a job as one of the drivers." So they got me into being a driver for the studios and it was a wonderful job, a great union job. You know, teamsters for the studios. They drove everything and it got me into the field from behind the walls, which is so important for people that had a craft whether you wanted to be a costumer or a stuntman or a cameraman. My friends started as teamsters and they went on to become cinematographer Denny Hall and stuntman Michael Vendrell and people like that. Becoming a teamster got you inside the walls, so it broke all the ice and people started to know you and trust you. I was driving for Aaron Spelling. I was driving Cheryl Ladd's motorhome on *Charlie's Angels,* believe it or not, and they threw me a couple of bones here and there. Different shows like *Family* and a TV movie called *Love's Savage Fury,* so they threw me a couple of lines. It started my acting career again and I kind of fell back into it. Then I kept studying in L.A. with a really good acting teacher named Al Ruscio and one thing led to another. Someone in the editorial department had a good friend who was a casting director and she recommended me to an agent and that agent signed me the day I walked in. I did hundreds of commercials, so that was how it all got going. That agent led to my manager, which led to me becoming an actor with a bigger agent. It was with ICM [International Creative Management Partners] where I got buried reading for different roles.

How did you get cast as Secret Service #1 in *Escape From New York*?

I was sent in by Phyllis Carlyle, who was my manager at the time. John [Carpenter] was a really nice guy. It was funny because I didn't do any reading. He just wanted to talk with me and he said, "Well, you've done some theatre in town," which I had and he said, "How do you feel about theatre compared to film?" I said, "Well, it's a whole different medium. It's a whole different ballgame." Doing real theatre back in the 80s was a big deal. Now in L.A., I don't think it's what it was back then. It doesn't have the glow to it. It's more of an - I don't know - I wouldn't say a nonentity, but I've seen some little theater in town and to me it's not half as good or even close to what we used to do back in the 80s. There were a lot of really, really good actors doing little theatre in Los Angeles back in the day. So John and I just talked and the next thing I knew I was cast for Secret Service Agent #1 and that was it. I had a few lines in the existing script and that was what happened.

How did you prepare for the role and how was your experience filming?

It was only a one-day shoot for myself and, as you know, Steven Ford [son of former U.S. President Gerald Ford] was Secret Service Agent #2. He's had a great career. It was a simple, nice set over at the old Selznick Studios. I don't think John did very many takes. I remember him telling me, "Listen, I'm gonna give these lines in the script to Steven. I'm gonna write you a better part." and I said, "Okay, that's great." Of course, this only made me more nervous because, although I'd done another feature film called *Cheaper to Keep Her*, this was a much bigger show. I think it was my sixth part I had worked on, so I was kind of green in the industry. I was still pretty young, so this was a big deal. I mean, today it's got quite a following and, as far as my part, I'm nothing. I mean, I'm a blur. I really am a blur. So John wrote this speech for me, and I tried to learn it on a lunch break and we came back. It was my speech to Donald Pleasence playing the President as I put him into the escape pod because the plane is going down. It's been hijacked by a terrorist and it's going to crash. As I'm giving him the speech, I'm putting him in the escape pod and, I gotta tell you, I was so nervous. I don't know why. Some days as an actor you can't say two words in a row without tripping over your own tongue. The funny thing is that it didn't go well. I got him into the escape pod and Donald was very quiet from what I remember. He wasn't very conversational. Long story short. I don't think John was happy with what I did and I really felt bad about that. I felt that I had let John down. I really, really did. After having our conversation I really thought that he felt I was better than that and as an actor when they put their trust into you and you fail or you trip, I think it hurts them and I felt terrible about it.

I went to see a viewing of it when it first came out in Hollywood and I'm a blur. I'm in the background. You see me standing by the door. "Let's get him into the escape pod," says Steven. I get him in and here's my dialogue and it's been looped. It's not even my voice. They didn't even bring me back into the looping session and use me, my voice. I was so hurt when I left that theater. Plus, they spelled my name wrong in the credits, so I guess the only good thing about it is that people think it's great that I was in the movie. I still get residuals, which is nice, but I was very disappointed. I never got to work with John Carpenter again and he used to use a lot of the same people, which is great. I certainly don't blame John. I blame myself for being green and for being a rookie. I've learned so much from that. I've gone so much farther now after forty-three years of doing this. I'm basically a blue-collar journey man actor and you can plug me in to feed the stars. That's how I look at it and I've had a decent career, so that was it in a nutshell. It's funny because you see people down the line and a lot of people back then are not even in the business any longer, so I've got some good stories.

It's funny. A couple of years ago I did a small movie called *Brampton's Own*, which is a small independent baseball movie. I played the hitting coach. At the wrap party, the 1st AD [Assistant Director] comes up to me in a really great mood, maybe he's had a couple of drinks, and says, "This guy right here. This guy. This guy was in *Escape From New York*!" and I thought, *wow*. So, I guess this movie has got quite a following. I wish I could have done more or taken any credit for anything because I really, really can't. I'm happy I did it. I learned a lot from it, but I wished I had learned more. That's right. I learned in the future to really be on top of your game because it's really on you the actor. It really, really is.

How was your experience working with the cast and crew?

Wonderful. They were great. Everybody was so nice, very professional. I don't think I ever heard anybody raise their voice and I think he probably uses a lot of the same crew people. I think they had a pretty good working relationship. For me, that part was fine. Totally, totally fine. I wished I had the chance to work in some other movies down the line. That would've been wonderful. It would've been great to work in like *The Thing*. Something like that. It would've been great. Again, I was disappointed with myself, but they could not have been nicer to me. That's for sure.

Did you know that Steven Ford was former president Gerald Ford's son?

Yeah, I think we were all aware of the fact that he was the son of Gerald Ford. I don't remember if he had some actual secret service people around. He probably did.

What's your favorite memory or memories of working on the movie?

I gotta tell you, probably my favorite part of that movie was when I had the interview with John. It was such a nice one-on-one conversation, purely talking about acting and some theatre. He was just a really nice man.

What do you think of the movie personally?

I like it. It's a fun cult film. I had done another movie after that called *Savage Dawn* and it was sort of a cult biker film, but it doesn't even compare. It's a good movie. To this day, I think *Escape From New York* still holds up. People still love the movie and still talk about that movie. As you know, it got a great, great following. Kurt's great. They're all great. It's a great cast. Wonderful, wonderful cast. A very dark film way ahead of its time. It's a good movie.

What are you currently doing and what do you enjoy doing in your spare time?

Currently, as we all are with the pandemic, the business is pretty much shut down, so I'm at home in Sherman Oaks with my wife. I have twin daughters. They're twenty-three years old and have careers and live together in Northern California, so they're fine. I just work out at home and help my wife around the house. My wife has a business called Emerald Forest in Studio City, a very successful fine gifts and jewelry store. That's pretty much it for me. I go on auditions. There was something sort of hanging for me when this all came down, an acting part in a movie. If it will still be there or not when I come back, I don't know. I'm still going along and getting what I can as an actor and doing what I can as far as commercials. I've just been lucky that people still know who I am in the business and still give me chances here and there, so I haven't retired. I haven't bought that farm in Montana yet. Someday but not now. I got a good life. I can't complain. I really can't.

DALE E. HOUSE
Helicopter Pilot #1

How did you end up being a helicopter pilot?

I became a pilot in the U.S. Army in 1968 and flew in the Vietnam War.

How did you get cast as Helicopter Pilot #1 in *Escape From New York*?

I was working for National Helicopter Service and Engineering Company. They were one of the premiere helicopter companies in the Los Angeles area. We did quite a bit of motion picture and television production work. We advertised heavily. I personally advertised in a couple industry publications. I cold called from *Variety* and a few other publications as well. Between them I captured work. So it came to pass that the production company needed helicopters and we could get them and I did. I ended up getting helicopters from the U.S. Army Reserve unit [National Guard] and the 336th Assault Helicopter Company, which I flew in for the Huey [Bell UH-1 Iroquois] scenes.

How did you prepare for the role and how was your experience filming? John Carpenter himself played an uncredited Helicopter Pilot in the Central Park scene for instance.

I was already an accomplished helicopter pilot and had done quite a bit of film work, so preparing for the role was routine. All that was needed was a storyboard and some direction. John Carpenter did that for us personally and through production assistants. It was all first unit production. All the scenes that I flew in or coordinated were shot in California. The National Guard was also used and filmed in another state. I arranged for four Huey's from the National Guard out of Los Alamitos one night for multiple night shots to the delight of John Carpenter. I also flew a Jet Ranger as a security helicopter. The location was the Sepulveda Flood Basin [Liberty Island Security Control Exterior]. We were on location for most of the night. It may have been two nights. I can't remember. I didn't know that John Carpenter was in one of the helicopters.

How was your experience working with the cast and crew? I know this was the first time John Carpenter got exposed to helicopters and, the following year, he started taking lessons himself and became a pilot for many years.

I didn't know that was John's first time with helicopters. You wouldn't have known it. He knew exactly what he wanted and conveyed that perfectly so that he got what he wanted. I didn't know that John had learned to fly helicopters either. I know James Cameron [Director of Photography/Matte Artwork: Special Visual Effects] did following *Titanic*. I know because I was his instructor for a brief time until our insurance wouldn't insure him because of the liability. I admire Kurt Russell and Goldie Hawn for their enduring relationship and their acting abilities.

What's your favorite memory or memories of working on the movie?

I enjoyed working on movie sets. I'm not an actor per say. The helicopter is an extension of my arms, legs, and thought processes, so I act with the helicopter. It's all very rewarding as it allows me to use the helicopter in an artistic way.

What do you think of the movie personally?

I thought the movie was very entertaining. It became a "cult classic," as you know. I have a VHS and a CD copy of it. I also have a movie poster, which I have yet to frame. I went to the premiere for cast and crew and it felt like I was at the Academy Awards. I'm not star struck by any stretch of the imagination, but I did enjoy the ambience. I do my job the best that I can and go home.

How do the Huey helicopters differ from other helicopters?

The Huey helicopter is iconic. It's been around since the early 60s. It is a work horse. It is easy to fly and forgiving in so many ways. It proved itself in battle so many times. It continued to function despite extensive damage, flying in the most inhospitable environment imaginable [Vietnam] and still brought us home. Although we all thought we were invincible in it, nearly five thousand aircrew men paid the ultimate sacrifice. That represented a nearly 10 percent casualty rate in a war that became known as "The Helicopter War." The Huey helicopter will forever be remembered by its distinctive wop-wop sound of the rotor blades slapping the air into submission.

Did the *Twilight Zone: The Movie* accident affect you in any way?

Twilight Zone affected the whole industry in a lot of ways. Some good, some bad. The *Twilight Zone* accident was a tragedy, to be sure. The pilot became the fall guy in the end. It came about as a result of many failures on the set that night. It was not just the pilot's fault. In fact, he was following direction from the ground. The industry was scared. A lot of people were in line for manslaughter and other charges. For a short time, the industry was understandably shying away from helicopter use in filming. It took over a year for things to settle down. The members of the helicopter community banded together to come up with safety guidelines. This resulted in industry safety standards for motion picture and television production. Also, at the same time the Federal Aviation Administration required everyone who was involved in aerial filming to comply with their written safety standards. This became the motion picture and television production manual, which became a requirement for anyone who was conducting filming activity within the U.S. This is still in use today.

Here is how it affected me personally. Totally unrelated to *Twilight Zone*, but still connected in an adverse way. I was doing some aerial filming of a train in the City of Industry, California. I was orbiting a train depot waiting for a train to leave. Although I was between 300 to 500 feet above the ground, the helicopter I was flying created enough noise that it became a nuisance to people on the ground, which produced a public complaint to the FAA. The complaint finally made its way to the same FAA attorney that was prosecuting the pilot on the *Twilight Zone* accident. He had stacks of folders on the floor in his office at regional headquarters. The case on *Twilight Zone* was basically an indictment against that pilot. He did not like helicopter pilots much and was very vindictive toward them. He wanted to revoke my pilot certificate. I hired an attorney and eventually made a settlement with the FAA on the condition that I was not admitting to any wrongdoing and paid a fine.

What are you currently doing and what do you enjoy doing in your spare time?

I've been flying for nearly fifty years. Next year will be that milestone. I'm still flying. I flew just last night. I was flying a gyro-stabilized infrared camera mapping the heat signature of four high rise buildings in downtown Denver. Last week I escaped from New York after ferrying a helicopter there from Denver. Not as exciting as working on a movie and doesn't pay as well either, but I love doing it. I'm involved in a lot of veteran activities, most notably the Vietnam Helicopter War Museum. I'm the curator and also chapter president of the organization. You can find more about our chapter and museum on our website at rmcvhpa.com.

TONY PAPENFUSS
Theater Assistant

How did you end up being an actor?

I got involved in acting in high school. I was enamored by it and never looked back. Got to L.A. through a teacher from college who was working for the Mark Taper Forum and hired me there.

How did you get cast as Theater Assistant in *Escape From New York*?

John Carpenter was holding interviews just to see people and said I had a good look and that my long hair was an asset. I don't think I cut it for at least three years after that. Apparently, that was good enough to get me the part. My very first in any film.

How did you prepare for the role and how was your experience filming? You had the misfortune to be in a scene that was cut out of the movie where you and Borah Silver [Theater Manager] have an altercation with Snake Plissken in the Theater.

Memories are hazy. The most I recall is that the scene was shot in its entirety, probably three or four takes. Can't remember the location. Borah looked ragged, dusty, hairy, big, and menacing. I looked ragged, dusty, and weaselly. I had no idea what the movie was about and there were no lines [Author's Note: This is false. Tony forgot that he did have lines.], so my prep was basically keeping a grip and not becoming a babbling fool and not getting in the way. I'm not sure since it was my first experience, but I recall it being a quick and efficient shoot. Especially compared to a lot of my experiences after that, which involved endless waiting. No improv that I recall. I believe most of Carpenter's direction to me was to keep my acting to as much of a minimum as possible. In other words, I was too much. Maybe I was trying to make a walk-on part into *Hamlet*. Classic rookie.

Were you disappointed that your scene was cut out of the movie?

Of course, I was crushed and heartbroken when I saw that my bravura debut performance was distilled down to Snake walking past my left shoulder. But that only lasted about two days. Then oddly, I was kind of amused about being part of the Hollywood cliché: "My best work winding up on the cutting room floor." Classic start of a career in the movies.

How was your experience working with the cast and crew?

Backstage was friendly and comfortable and professional. Borah and I had a friend in common, so that helped conversation and passing the time. Nice man.

What's your favorite memory or memories of working on the movie?

My clearest and fondest memory is having makeup with Kurt Russell in the next chair. He said, "Hi," and "Welcome to the set," and we were just a couple of guys on the job. That made it real. I was really there and I was really gonna be in a real movie. Kinda dazzled.

What do you think of the movie personally?

At first, I was entertained by the film but very skeptical about its relative worth. Then I saw it twice and knew it was damn good. Now I realize its place as a true classic of its type. That's another cliché right there, but in this case right on the money.

What are you currently doing and what do you enjoy doing in your spare time?

I'm still at it here in Minnesota doing stage and film surprisingly often. More going on than one might expect. That, golf, and reading fill the time. I guess that's it.

ALAN SHEARMAN
Dancer

How did you end up being an actor, playwright, screenwriter, and director?

Since childhood, I wanted to be an actor but common sense prevailed, and I went with my other passion - travel. I then spent six years working for a travel agency arranging other people's travel plans with my own travel limited to commuting on the London Underground every day and spending all my time translating foreign rail schedules. I learned how to say, "This train does not run on Sundays," in fourteen languages. Figuring there was more to life, I quit and joined up with Ron House [Dancer] as a co-founder of the comedy theater group Low Moan Spectacular to create *El Grande de Coca-Cola*, *Bullshot Crummond*, *Footlight Frenzy*, *The Scandalous Adventures of Sir Toby Trollope* etcetera and never looked back. All four shows continue to be performed across the country and around the world. *Bullshot Crummond* became George Harrison's HandMade Films movie *Bullshot* in which I played the title role. As a result, I also satisfied the travel bug by working around the globe writing and acting in movies shot in Africa, Asia, North America, and Europe. About twenty years ago, I quit stage acting to instead direct stage comedies, musicals, musical comedies, and comedies with music collecting five Best Director awards along the way. I still work both on and off-screen as an actor, writer and director with voiceover credits on several hundred movies, TV shows and video games. Do not be surprised to see me at weekends, however, waiting for a train that will never come as I wistfully recite the only phrase I learned in fourteen foreign languages.

In other words. I have been professionally acting, writing, directing, and producing since 1971 but, until moving to Los Angeles in 1978, all this experience was related to theater. Specifically, I was a co-founder with Ron House of the comedy theater group called Low Moan Spectacular. Originally based in London we created our own shows as writers and actors, directing each other and producing whenever needed wherever we went. Our first show *El Grande de Coca-Cola* was a big hit in London in 1971 and subsequently at the Edinburgh Fringe Festival of 1972 where it was picked up for New York to open in early 1973. The show ran off-Broadway for two and a half years and our replacement

L-R: Ron Vernan [Dancer], Alan Shearman [Dancer], Ron House [Dancer], Nick Castle [Co-Writer], John Carpenter [Director/Co-Writer/Co-Composer] (Photo by/Courtesy Kim Gottlieb-Walker)

cast spawned such stars as the late Ron Silver and Jeff Goldblum [who took over my role]. Ron House and I have stayed in the U.S. ever since [although he was originally from Chicago]. During our time in the U.K., we also created a second show *Bullshot Crummond* which followed a similar path as *El Grande de Coca-Cola* but ended up being hugely successful in San Francisco [a five-year run from 1975-1979] and Los Angeles for over a year at the Westwood Playhouse [now the Geffen and the Coronet Theatre [now the Largo] on La Cienega [1979-1980].

How did Low Moan Spectacular get cast as dancers in *Escape From New York*?

It was while we were enjoying the success of *Bullshot Crummond* at the Westwood Playhouse and the Coronet that John Carpenter came to see the show and offered us roles in *Escape From New York*. That's why Low Moan Spectacular is credited on IMDb. Sadly, both Joseph Perrotti and Ron Vernan have passed away. Ron

House and I are still going strong as is Rodger Bumpass, who has made quite a name for himself as the voice of Squidward on *Sponge Bob Square Pants*. We are all still in touch with each other. It's hard to remember exactly when we did this. I know the movie was released in 1981, but I suspect we shot it in 1980. I have a feeling that our *Bullshot Crummond* production had closed by then because, aside from Ron House and me, nobody else in the picture had ever been in that show. Joseph Perrotti was in Low Moan Spectacular, but as our line producer/company manager. Purely administration. He died in 1990. Ron House, myself, Rodger Bumpass, and Ron Vernan [who passed away earlier this year, 2015] were all working on our third Low Moan Spectacular comedy called *Footlight Frenzy*. We were getting ready to produce and take the show to San Francisco. It was a big success there at the Marines Memorial Theatre and then transferred to the Alcazar Theatre on Geary Street.

I'm also hazy about the year because this was a terrible time for the movie industry. There was a massive three-month actors strike in 1980 followed by a massive three-month writers strike in 1981. It closed down the whole industry. I remember walking around the lot at Universal with my footsteps literally echoing off the walls. The place felt like a ghost town. It was terribly depressing to have arrived in L.A., having made a huge splash with *Bullshot Crummond* that won us screenplay and TV deals with 20th Century Fox, Paramount, ABC, HBO, Showtime, and Disney and then have the whole thing collapse. I couldn't believe it. We'd achieved the impossible dream of coming to Hollywood only to have the whole town close down a year or two later. We were desperate and broke and never really recovered until we made the *Bullshot* movie with George Harrison's HandMade Films in 1983.

How did you prepare for the role and how was your experience filming?

As I recall, we only had one day's work on *Escape From New York*. Possibly an additional rehearsal day, I forget, and then the pick-up day. Costumes were provided by the costume designer. The roles were such that character input was unnecessary.

How was it to be choreographed by Nick Castle [Co-Writer] whose parents were famous dancers?

I remember that we had choreography rehearsals with Nick at the location where we shot the scene. A temple or some such on Wilshire Boulevard [Wiltern Theatre].

How was your experience working with the cast and crew?

All very straightforward and un-stressful, mainly thanks to John Carpenter. It was certainly a fun experience. I do remember chatting with Ernest Borgnine [Cabbie] at the lunch break.

Were you disappointed that the original song by Steven Sondheim that you used during filming, "Everything's Coming Up Roses" had to be replaced by "Everyone's Coming To New York" written by Nick Castle?

I can't say I was disappointed [additional work is always good] but I certainly sympathized with the music clearance issues. We in Low Moan Spectacular had been through something similar when we were doing our *El Grande de Coca-Cola* show in New York. I seem to remember there being some concern on our part that the lip synch wouldn't work but they told us not to worry. That's probably why we're mainly kept in long shot.

What's your favorite memory or memories of working on the movie?

I remember it being a lot of fun. We really didn't understand much about the plot or premise of the film, so everything seemed very strange and bizarre.

What do you think of the movie personally?

Hugely entertaining and, in many ways, way ahead of its time.

What are you currently doing and what do you enjoy doing in your spare time?

As mentioned earlier, for what now amounts to forty plus years, the comedies of Low Moan Spectacular continue to be presented across the country and around the globe. A recent revival of our *El Grande de Coca-Cola* show at the Ruskin Theatre in Santa Monica ran to sellout houses for six months and wall-to-wall rave reviews. This extraordinary success prompted us to create a sequel called *El Grande CIRCUS de Coca-Cola*. Also, Ron House and I have collaborated on a sequel to the *Bullshot Crummond* show that John Carpenter enjoyed so much. Ron is credited as author and I shall be directing the world premiere production in Portland, Oregon early next year.

JOHN CONTINI
Extra

How did you end up being an actor?

I grew up loving film and TV and my parents supported my love. I went to St. Louis University and majored in theater and education. I worked as a drama teacher yet always kept my acting career going. About twenty years ago, I went full time as a professional actor.

How did you get cast as an extra in *Escape From New York*?

I was called in by my agent for an audition and then called back in by director John Carpenter. I was interviewed by him and read with him. He cast me as a prisoner in the film.

How did you prepare for the role and how was your experience filming?

I shot about ten days overnight until four or six in the morning. Each evening would begin with a trip to wardrobe and makeup, then to the weapons trailer, and then to the location sites. There was not much time for rehearsal as most of the shooting time was used in setting camera and lights. We spent a great deal of time sitting and waiting. I was involved in probably a half dozen scenes, and some wound up on the editing floor. There was one incredible scene involving at least two hundred extras that took a whole night to shoot and never ended up in the final cut. It takes place right after they discover Brain [Harry Dean Stanton] took the President [Donald Pleasence]. All the extras in the wrestling arena charge out of the front doors of Grand Central Station. There were three cameras set up across the street from the doors and I was the lucky one to push them open and lead some of the charging prisoners out. I believe it could have been a very impressive looking and epic scene, but for some reason it fell on the cutting room floor.

    Originally, I was to have lines, but they wound up being cut also [I suppose for time]. I was in the street scene after Snake first arrives and walks past the downed aircraft. I was warming myself by a street fire. I was also in the scene where Frank Doubleday [Romero] hands the severed finger of the President to Lee Van Cleef [Hauk]. I am standing behind. I am also in the train station arena when Donald Pleasence is handcuffed to the wall and Isaac Hayes [The Duke] was shooting at him. I am sitting on the floor by the bench Isaac Hayes was sitting on. My biggest scene is when I am standing above Kurt Russell with a crossbow pointed at him. Interesting story. The crossbow was real and the arrow was real. There was only a small nail jamming the trigger. I was impressed that Kurt would let me, this nobody extra, point this lethal weapon at him with such little security on the bow.

How was your experience working with the cast and crew?

Carpenter's direction was very prepared. He would calmly set the scene and tell the actors what he was looking for. Then he let them create. He would allow overlapping dialogue, which is very similar to one of his idols Howard Hawks.

Most of the stars were very friendly. Kurt Russell was very polite and pleasant. Ernest Borgnine [Cabbie] and Lee Van Cleef were always nice enough to spend time and talk with us. Donald Pleasence kept us entertained with impromptu and hilarious presidential speeches as his character. One evening was especially memorable as I sat at the catered dinner table with John Carpenter. He was very down to earth and easy to talk to. We shared our likes and dislikes of horror films and I was glad to say we had similar taste. He told me at that time about his next project, a screenplay by William Lancaster based on the 1951 version of *The Thing*. We both agreed this was a classic.

What's your favorite memory or memories of working on the movie?

My favorite costume piece was the weaponed glove I got to wear. It was like something out of a *Mad Max* movie. Another great moment was spending time talking with Lee Van Cleef about his appearance in *Beast From 20,000 Fathoms*. He was surprised that I knew and remembered he was in that. It was one of his first screen appearances and I enjoyed it. We also talked about his western movie appearances and he was a very classy gentleman. I will always remember being a passenger in one of the stunt cars with Jesse Wayne [Stunts] as we did 360-degree doughnuts in the middle of an intersection. Scary but exciting.

What do you think of the movie personally?

Besides it being a cult favorite, I thought it was well done and an original science fiction film. It had a unique and clever premise. I was also impressed that John Carpenter created the music in the film.

What are you currently doing and what do you enjoy doing in your spare time?

I am still working professionally in theater and film. I have received many awards for my work and I just recently finished another film called *Four Color Eulogy*, which should be out soon. I directed and acted in over two hundred theatrical productions around the mid-west. I am an avid comic book collector and, in fact, was going into comic book art before I fell into acting.

JEFF SILLIFANT
Extra

How did you get cast as an extra in *Escape From New York*?

I owe that to Ann Robinson, star of 1953's *War of the Worlds*. She hooked me and some of our mutual friends up with a lady she knew who cast non-union extras from her agency.

How did you prepare for the role and how was your experience filming?

I was part of the group shouting at the helicopter making a food drop [Central Park] in the only daytime sequence filmed. We shot that at Sepulveda Dam [Liberty Island Security Control Exterior] in the San Fernando Valley heat and did around three takes running through high weeds and stickers. The scene was cut to the bone, of course. It began with the guys running toward the incoming chopper until we got under it and the boxes were pushed out. We then gathered them up as the chopper zipped off. Everything was filmed, but only the brief bit landed on screen. Another element of the sequence was a skyline matte painting lined up with the foreground trash. Bob Skotak [Matte Artist: Special Visual Effects] [Supervisor: Special Visual Effects] [Uncredited] had a little bit of trouble getting it all matched perfectly, I think. Bob and his brother [Dennis Skotak] [Director of Photographer: Special Visual Effects] were there. We talked between takes. They're both old friends. I believe the dam shoot took two days.

The Chock full o'Nuts [Indian Dunes] shoot was quite an experience for me as a newbie to film acting. I'm whistling past Kurt Russell as he sidles along the outside restaurant wall before we moved inside. While John Carpenter put Kurt and Season Hubley [Girl in Chock full o'Nuts] through setups, stunt man Dick Warlock [Stunt Coordinator/Stunts] and I were getting prepared for the take-down scene in a cubbyhole under the floor. As Kurt is machine-gunning Crazies bursting through the front door, Season tries to run away but yours truly grabs her legs and pulls her under. This was pretty tricky. Dick elevated me with his shoulder and arms in the cramped chamber and blew smoke from a canister

Jeff Sillifant [Extra]
(Photo by Mark Groseclose, courtesy Jeff Sillifant)

after the hole was boarded up with balsa wood. We had to hold our breath as the scene above unfolded and the "fog" came close to turning me blue by the time Season and I got up close and personal. Two takes on that. Don't think I would have survived a third. I was filmed crashing up out of the floor and crawling directly toward the camera all mean and gnarly, but my close-up ended up on the ole cutting room floor.

Between filming, a couple of fun things happened. The Smothers Brothers, friends of Carpenter, showed up and we had some laughs. The next night a giant screen remote was rolled onto the outdoor set in order to watch a Mohammed Ali boxing match, which he lost. The restaurant shoot lasted four nights and took us into the early morning hours. A lot of hurry up and wait as I'm sure you know. Then came the stage show sequence in which Ernest Borgnine's Cabbie spies Snake walking past him. The theater audience pan shot captures my zombie-like presence before focusing on Cabbie happily rocking in his seat. Men in drag pranced around and sang as Carpenter played the guitar and kazoo with his band at the stage pit. A funny bit but somehow I managed to keep a straight face. Got my close-up after all!

The entire sequence that began with Snake entering the building was shot at the Wiltern Theatre [Theater Interior] in West Los Angeles before it was remodeled. During a break, two of us wandered down the block to a grocery store to glares and stares. The look on the cashier's face when two scummy-looking tramps produced twenty dollar bills to pay for snacks was priceless. Only then did we spill about our movie roles. It was too hard to resist. The only input any of us had dealt with choosing our wardrobes. I had three changes that included dirt, makeup, and black spray paint to make the costumes look even more grungy. Other than that, we just followed the 2nd AD's [Assistant Director] directions. My scene with Ernie only took two takes each for the head-on and the side view when Snake passes by.

How was your experience working with the cast and crew?

The entire experience stood out since the only other part I played was victim in a much smaller science fiction yarn called *The Aftermath*, my only screen credit. A small business I started in 1977 regrettably prevented me from continuing with extra work. Just being involved in a John Carpenter film, one that ultimately earned cult classic status, rewarded me with a life highlight.

What's your favorite memory or memories of working on the movie?

You know, my favorite memories involved the goof-off time with my two best friends Mark Groseclose and Eric Caidin acting out our characters with a juvenile lack of aplomb. I miss them terribly. Mark was part of the theatre and restaurant [Chock full o'Nuts] gang, but didn't get used for the drop. He died in 1988 at only forty-two. My best friend for many years, he was the most talented soul I've ever known. He excelled as a surfer, band drummer, and artist. One of his greatest paintings hangs on my living room wall. He did backgrounds on the animated TV series *BraveStarr* from 1987 until his passing. Eric Caidin, owner of Hollywood Book and Poster Co. and my dearest friend. We lost him May 18, 2015 at age sixty-two while attending a Palm Springs film convention.

What do you think of the movie personally?

It ranks second on my John Carpenter film list. I have to go with *Assault on Precinct 13* as my first.

What are you currently doing and what do you enjoy doing in your spare time?

After a four-year stint in the Air Force followed by a career as a newsman and police reporter in Los Angeles, I began the aforementioned memorabilia business called Still Things. I sell movie and TV photos, posters, autographs, and other goodies through mail order and eBay after a lifetime of collecting. Up through the 1990s, I also sold at science-fiction and other types of conventions. From 1995 to 1998 I co-hosted Starcon and Hollywood Memories shows at the Pasadena Convention Center sometimes bringing more than one hundred celebrity guests together. I quit that entire scene by moving to Las Vegas with my wife in 2000. I wanted to get closer to my money. Since moving to the gambling capital, I've written eleven thoroughbred horse racing handicapping booklets, all of which have been top ten ranked by a racing newsletter considered the bible of the biz. My wife, meanwhile, cares for all variety of dogs in our Northwest valley home. Area friends and neighbors appreciate having a place other than a kennel to leave their pets when taking a vacation. That's the pinnacle of our adventure at the moment but plans for our fiftieth wedding anniversary next April are in the works, speaking of adventures.

KEN TIPTON
Extra

How did you end up being an actor and entrepreneur and can you tell us a little bit about your movie *Heart of the Beholder*, which is based on a personal true story that you also directed, wrote, produced, and acted in?

In grade school, I was chosen for a fourth-grade class play. I played Stephen Foster and I kind of liked it, so I continued on acting. In high school, I was in musical plays and dramas and stuff like that. Any movie that was shot in St. Louis, I tried to get on. My first movie was *Corvette Summer* and then *Escape From New York*. *Corvette Summer* had Mark Hamill in it. In fact, this was after Mark had been in *Star Wars* and he actually crashed one of the Corvettes in that movie, which is how he got his scars. At that time, I was working for IBM as a computer engineer. After the Air Force, I had electronic experience, so I got to work in IBM in St. Louis, but I was still a movie geek. I opened the very first movie cassette rental place in St. Louis in 1981. It was called Video Library and that is what my movie is about.

How did you get cast as an extra in *Escape From New York*?

Anytime they shot a movie in St. Louis, they usually advertised the auditions for smaller roles, extras and such. The first audition I saw after I got out of the Air Force was for *Escape From New York*. I auditioned to be one of the gypsies, the bad guys, and I didn't get anywhere from the audition. They just didn't take me, even when I applied to be an extra. However, I later found out where they were shooting and I just showed up. When you watch the movie, there's a lot of people in the crowd scenes and stuff like that. They weren't paying attention to who was doing what. After a couple of nights of me just showing up, they just kind of accepted that I was part of it. I didn't sign in, so I didn't get paid or anything like that, but I got fed and got treated like a background extra. That was my very first real experience. It was fun to watch them making a real movie because I grew up being a movie geek. I mean, every weekend I watched two, three movies. What intelligence I had came from watching movies. It didn't come from home or school, I know that.

How did you prepare for the role and how was your experience filming?

We had an extras wrangler, I think it was the second assistant director, who basically put us in an area where there were chairs and snacks and things like that. We just sat there until background actors were needed. They would say, "I'll take you, I'll take you, I'll take you," or they take everybody. It depended on how many background actors they needed and how many times you've been seen before. If you've been established in one scene and they go to another scene, there's no way you have gotten across town in two seconds. They would keep track of that. A lot of us blended in. We all just kind of looked like scrubby homeless people, but still they were careful to what they call continuity. They didn't put people in the same places. We just sat there a lot and talked, read books, whatever, until they said, "Ok, background extras. Let's go." What was nice about it was that this was all in like a ten-block area, so we would just move from block to block. There is a scene in the movie where there's nobody there. Snake Plissken and maybe another person. He would walk around a corner and there would be two hundred people sitting there. You just don't know it because you don't see it.

It was a total of twelve to sixteen nights. We did get rained out a few nights. Everything was shot at nighttime. We had about ten o'clock to eight in the morning or something like that. It was chilly most of the time because it was nighttime. It was fun just to watch all the stuff that went on. When we sat in the theater, we had no clue what it actually took to make that. It's hard work. Shooting the same scenes over and over in different angles. It can be fun, but it's really, really hard work. When you see all the people that it takes to shoot one simple little scene, it freaks me out still. It amazes me.

Working on the movie was interesting because of that time. St. Louis had parts of it that used to be really great looking, but had become run down and had started to look like shit. That's why they shot this movie there because it was supposed to be New York City in its decline with beat up buildings and stuff. This was really how St. Louis looked. There was a section of St. Louis down by the Arch called Laclade's Landing [69th Street Bridge Ramp] and it was just old warehouses and stuff like that. It looked like crap. They shot also at Union Station [Grand Central Station], which was once one of the biggest railroad hubs in the nation. By 1980, it was all closed down and abandoned and just looked like crap.

The one that was hurt the most was the Fox Theatre [Theater Exterior]. It was called the Fabulous Fox. This was one of those old timey, absolutely beautiful theaters. In fact, the very first movie I saw was at the Fox Theatre in 1959. When my grandmother took me there, it was like a church. It was big and beautiful. The organ came up from a hole in the stage and it was like, *Oh my God*. I remember asking her, "Is this a church?" and she says, "Well, it can be." Movies became my religion in a way. So here we are shooting *Escape From New York* and the Fox Theatre is just plain terrible. After the movie came out, it made St. Louis look so bad because of all these derelict places that they got some bonds and put some money together to clean up St. Louis. The Fabulous Fox is now back to its glory. Lacklade's Landing is beautiful. The Union Station is now hotels and shops. That movie did more for St. Louis than anything. It basically embarrassed the hell out of them. About five miles north of where the Arch is there was a bridge called the [Old] Chain of Rocks Bridge [69th Street Bridge] across Mississippi and it really was falling apart, so they shut it down. People couldn't use it anymore. That's where they built the scene at the end where the bridge goes into a wall. That wall was basically just a plywood wall that they just threw up. That wall stayed up there for a long, long time and people came up there to play on it. They'd get on top of it and say, "A number one." and whatever Donald Pleasence [President] is yelling at the end of the movie. It was weird how they were able to take piece of crap locations and make them look cool.

My kids and I, we got the DVD, put it on a big screen, and we have played it frame by frame. I can show you the scene I was in, the match at the St. Louis Union Station. I'm there, but you can't see me. In some of the other scenes, it's either too far away or I'm in the dark, so it makes me nuts, but I know I was there and that's all I care about. In fact, later on when I actually had a feature role in a movie, I took all my family and friends to see it. It was called *Naked Gun 3 1/3: The Final Insult,* and I took all my friends there and found out I was cut from the movie, which is embarrassing. I kind of learned not to tell anybody anything until I've seen it and I can see myself.

How was your experience working with the cast and crew?

The absolute best part of making that movie, besides actually sitting there and getting to see Kurt Russell who I was a fan of and Adrienne Barbeau [Maggie] who I had a big crush on, was Isaac Hayes [The Duke]. I remember in college how his number one hit was the *Shaft* theme. It was cool. The person I got to sit to and talk to was Harry Dean Stanton [Brain]. He only lives like three blocks from where I live now. He was cool because I was sitting in line with the other extras to get food and he got in line with us, which was kind of strange. All of the principle performers, they had their trailers and their food was brought to them. They didn't get near the extras. That's the way it was. Not Harry. He was just a guy. He had already had some exposure with *Alien* and stuff and we just treated him like a normal guy. I remember sitting down at a table and he came and sat next to me. Then we're just talking. I was in the Air Force and he told me all about his time in the Navy and he was just telling me all kinds of stuff and great stories and it just made me feel good. Here I am working on a major motion picture. Director of *Halloween*, John Carpenter. James Cameron [Director of Photography/Matte Artwork: Special Visual Effects] is doing the second unit visual stuff and special effects. Even if I'm not suppose to be here, I'm having the time of my life just being a part of it. Me and Harry Dean Stanton are just talking like guys. It was funny. I actually called him years later because I wanted him to be in my movie and I was able to get his phone number and he remembered me. It was very cool twenty or thirty years later, this well-known actor remembers this extra from St. Louis.

What's your favorite memory of working on the movie?
Obviously, looking at Adrienne Barbeau. She was hot. There was one actor, the skinny kid, blond hair with lots of makeup [Frank Doubleday] [Romero]. He's the one that approaches the military and he kind of walks in an almost John Wayne walk side by side by side and hisses. I never know who that was, but damn that guy was a good actor. I don't know if he went on to do other things, but it was great watching him do the rehearsals and prepare for the scene and everything else. He'd go from just talking like a normal human being to all of a sudden, "Ok, action!" Boom! He was creepier than anything. I'm just looking at him, "Wow. How the hell is he doing that?" It was fun to watch everybody work their craft from the actors to the grips to the catering to the lighting to the makeup. All of these people getting together with all these different skills. At the beginning of the night, nothing existed. But by the end of the night, they all created something that was entertaining, educational, whatever. I just thought that was fascinating. That's what movies are all about. Entertainment. Education. Just enjoyment. I just love movies.

What do you think of the movie personally?

I thought it was great. I watched it just the other night. It's what I call a popcorn movie. When you go to movies, you go in there to forget your problems, to sit in the dark, to be entertained and eat some popcorn and that's what it was. When you come out of that movie, you should not feel any worse than when you went in. You feel good. It was a good story. Snake Plissken wins. It had an interesting plot. I mean, you've never seen that topic before, Manhattan being turned into a Maximum Security Prison. That's a cool idea. The President's plane gets blown up and his pod lands in the security prison. That's kind of cool. I thought the whole thing was cool. I didn't really know about John Carpenter before that. I'm not really a horror movie fan. I scare too easy. I didn't watch *Halloween* and stuff like that, but to sit there and watch John Carpenter direct was fascinating. On a scale of one to ten I give it about eight point five because I enjoyed it. Then we get around to *Escape From L.A.* When I heard they were gonna make that, boy I was gonna do everything I could to make sure I got on that movie in a speaking role or a non-speaking role. I don't care. I'll even show up just like I did on the other movie. It was a little bit different now. I couldn't find out where they were shooting, but I really wanted to be in that movie because again, what goes around, comes around. I started in that movie and here's a sequel.

What are you currently doing and what do you enjoy doing in your spare time?

I have passion projects that have to do with sequels and stuff like that, but right now I'm acting as a producer for my wife. She's retired. We believe in karma. We absolutely are believers in karma as a concept of what goes around, comes around. A non-religious concept of what comes around, goes around. I'm actually working on a website now that will be released in a month or two that is hers, but I'm helping her produce it. I am doing everything on the website. The design, the art, the music. It's like I'm producing a movie. I'm writing, directing, and producing a movie but it's an internet thing and she's the star of it. This is what we wanna do because we're at the fourth quarter of our lives. We're both sixty-three and we've lived good lives and had ups and downs and paid our dues and stuff, but now we want to kind of give it back. We want to do things that help others for the greater good of people of the planet. I know it sounds very Californian, very fufu, but there's nothing wrong with it.

DAVID UDELL
Extra

How did you get cast as an extra in *Escape From New York*?

There were no films being made in St. Louis at the time. The want ads said there would be open auditions at TalentPlus [a modeling agency]. A friend and I thought it might be fun to try out. We showed up at the last minute and got right in. They said there had been a line around the block all day, but it was all winding down. I'm not sure who did the casting, but my friend and I stood in front of a small panel. Someone pointed at me and that was it. I was around twenty with long hair and a beard. I think my friend may have cleaned up a bit and that's why he wasn't chosen. Years later I tried to get a part in *White Palace*. All of Soulard had an agent and they got in as a group. I didn't make it, but I did get to know Glenn Savan before he died.

How did you prepare for the role and how was your experience filming?

I was in the Ox Baker [Slag] fight scene. We were the screaming mob around the ring. St. Louis Union Station was abandoned at the time, and they used it to emulate Grand Central [Station]. The scene took two days to shoot. I was at the side of the ring one day and up in the rafters another. There was a lot of waiting around. The camera people were in the ring with Steadicams [Panaglide]. I think these were new. I had never heard of them, and I was a bit of an amateur filmmaker myself. The cameras had gyroscopes that allowed them to remain still even though they were hand-held. Friends of mine have been renting the movie for years insisting they could make me out in the scene.

To be honest, I was just able to make out the poncho I was wearing freezing the frame on a friend's giant screen TV. After the fight scene, we had to run from the building. They shot it three times. They had stunt drivers drive right into us going fifty miles per hour. Twice a car came to a stop right up on my leg. I had a genuine look of horror on my face. Both times I was right next to Kurt Russell. I thought I'd be right up there in the movie, but they cut the whole scene.

How was your experience working with the cast and crew?

Between takes I was getting pretty chummy with Ox Baker, Isaac Hayes [The Duke], Isaac Hayes' stunt double [Bob Minor] and a local actor named Duane. Duane was a friend of my parents, and he was walking around like he owned the place. When the film came out, he had a tiny bit part in an alley at the beginning. John Carpenter was strictly business. Adrienne Barbeau [Maggie] was kind of cold and stand-offish. Her sister was a blast, really fun to talk to. I think she was having a good time. Isaac Hayes and his stunt double hung out with us and were really open and fun to talk to. I think Donald Pleasence [President] was there, but I didn't talk to him. The only people on the set that weren't incredibly friendly were Kurt Russell and Adrienne Barbeau.

My favorite was Ox Baker. What a giant and what a sweetie. With all the down time, we carried on like old friends. It was a little grueling for all of us. In contrast to my thuggish look, Reed Nesbit was there. He was very fashion conscious. I'm sure they chose him for his futuristic appearance. Nesbit was a local post punk guitarist. I picked up as guitarist for Delay Tactics second LP after he left. We were on recordings together, but I never knew him. Rick Buscher, singer for Ray Milland, was an extra. You only see his hands opening a manhole cover at the beginning.

What's your favorite memory or memories of working on the movie?

There are several. We were waiting for the catering trailer to show up, but it was so late they sent for KFC boxes. The first day of shooting, I picked up my wardrobe from a truck. They were rags from the siege of the Atlanta scene in *Gone with the Wind* where the wounded lay at the train station. I was very impressed. We made $75 a day. Before the film's release, they had two showings for the extras. The first was at the Des Peres 14 Cinema. Four screens were a multiplex in those days. I don't remember any stars at that one, but the second was at the I-44 Drive-In theater and that was a party. I took my brother who was totally star struck with Isaac Hayes. In his personal life, Hayes was famous for having ridiculously lavish limousines. I think one had a bathtub in the back. They probably contributed to his bankruptcy. He drove the Duke's Cadillac into the drive-in. It was a hoot.

What do you think of the movie personally?

Kurt Russell was a Disney child star and it seemed like they were looking for an inexpensive actor. Union Station was nowhere near as cavernous as Grand Central Station. I mentioned that at the time and someone told me their lenses would make up for it. It didn't. The soundtrack was pretty simplistic and unimaginative. Everything about the film struck me as low budget. I kind of feel that way about all of Carpenter's films. For some reason, that's what makes them so enjoyable for me. He gets 'em out there.

What are you currently doing and what do you enjoy doing in your spare time?

I was and still am a recording musician. There were a lot of St. Louis' post punk musicians who were extras in the movie. We had a really vibrant scene in the late 70s/early 80s.

DICK WARLOCK
Stunt Coordinator / Stunts

How did you end up being a stunt man/coordinator and Kurt Russell's stunt double for many years?

Go to dickwarlock.com. All of the answers to this one are there. Back in 1965, his dad suggested that he put me in his contract so that when they called him, they would have to call me to double him. He didn't know how to do that at eighteen, so his dad Bing [Russell] did it for him. It was a pretty good marriage for twenty-five years.

How did you and Kurt Russell prepare for this project and how did you collaborate?

We never discussed this film regarding what, when, where, or how, except for the battle with Ox Baker [Slag]. He did one hundred percent of that fight routine. He did tell Ox after Ox started playing it like he would have in the ring with another pro wrestler that he would bury the bat in his balls if he even came close to hurting him during the routine. There was not one stunt that I ever did for him that he couldn't have done better than me. Kurt is one heck of an athlete, but the insurance companies wouldn't let him do something that could jeopardize the movie or the company, so he would ask me if he should do it or have me do it.

What kind of challenges did this project provide and which stunts, scenes, or locations were the most challenging, problematic, memorable, and fun to work on?

The crash of the baddie car into the parked car during the chase [deleted scene]. The crash car was to hit the catch car at such an angle that it would cause the inertia to carry the rear of the crash car around the catch car, causing the crash car to roll. Hopefully several times. To this day I have no idea what happened. Did I lift too soon, drive into the catch car too deep or at slightly off angle? I wish I knew.

L-R: Dick Warlock [Stunt Coordinator/Stunts], Kurt Russell [Snake Plissken] (Photo by/Courtesy Kim Gottlieb-Walker)

How was the station wagon going through the pile of cars scene done?

I just went out there with a crane driver and had him stack the cars in a particular order much like dominos. When I ran the car through the hole, the remaining cars filled the gap.

Is it true that Ox Baker [Slag] gave you a lump on the head and another guy a broken nose while coordinating the gladiator ring fight?

That is absolutely BOGUS. No lump and no broken nose. Ox was an easy-going guy and wouldn't want to hurt anyone intentionally. He was used to wrestling with professionals and Kurt was no match for him, besides being the star of the film. Ox got a little anxious a time or two and that is when Kurt laid down the law.

Is it true that Adrienne Barbeau [Maggie] and you practiced gun control on her bed and she never remembered you doing it?

John [Carpenter] came to me and asked if I'd go to Adrienne's home and work with her regarding gun control. When I got there, I suggested that we practice over something soft. She suggested her bed so if she dropped the weapon, it wouldn't be damaged. I agreed and that is the end of the story. I met her again at a convention a few years ago and reminded her of that, but she couldn't remember that happening. Oh well. I made one heck of an impression, didn't I?

Were there any accidents during the making of the movie?

None that I know of.

How was your experience working with the cast and crew?

Outstanding cast and crew.

What's your favorite memory or memories of working on the movie?

Just being a part of the film with such an outstanding cast and crew. It was pure cake and something I will always treasure in my memory box.

What do you think of the movie personally?

I like it very much.

Do you have any favorite memory or memories of working with Kurt Russell during your years together?

Not really. He treated me very well during our tenure together. Since *Tango & Cash,* I have not spoken to him.

What are you currently doing and what do you enjoy doing in your spare time?

We enjoy traveling. We used to do more when we had the motorcycle but not so much in the Miata. We are together almost 24/7 without fussing and you can't say that about too many couples.

JEFFREY CHERNOV
Second Assistant Director

How did you end up being a second/first assistant director, unit production manager and producer?

My first job in the film business was as a production assistant on Dino De Laurentiis' remake of *King Kong* back in 1975. After that, I got involved in working on commercials which is where I learned a lot. Then I was given the opportunity to become a location manager on a very small movie, which taught me a lot. Through those two or three years, I was able to get into the Directors Guild as a second AD [Assistant Director] and the guild opened up the doors to allow more membership.

Once I got in as a 2nd AD, I was invited to go to work for a whole week on a very small movie, which is where I met Larry Franco [Producer/First Assistant Director]. After that one week of working with him, he took a liking to me and hired me on a movie called *Cutter & Bone,* which eventually became known as *Cutter's Way.* The movie was actually released once and then re-released. After that, Larry established a relationship with John Carpenter and asked me to come work on *Escape From New York.* Then Debra Hill [Producer], who produced many movies for John Carpenter, asked me what I wanted to do next. I told her I wanted to be a production manager, so she granted me that wish, and we started working on the *Halloween* movies. I went on to work on many movies with Debra. I was eventually able to get enough experience to start working as a line producer. That's kind of my climb to what I do now.

How did you, Larry Franco [Producer/First Assistant Director] and Geoff Ryan [Production Assistant] prepare for this project and how did you collaborate?

Larry, as the 1st AD, had a very specific way of working, which he learned from another 1st AD named Jerry Ziesmer. Jerry was an amazing assistant director of some of the largest movies back then. Larry basically laid out how he worked, and I took that and just started applying myself to what I thought would be the best way to support him. One of my big questions to Larry when we were

L-R: Unknown [Extra], Kurt Russell [Snake Plissken],
Jeffrey Chernov [Second Assistant Director]
(Photo by/Courtesy Kim Gottlieb-Walker)

doing it was, "Who's in charge of the background?" and Larry said, "You are." and I said, "Great. I love setting background. It's one of my favorite things." On *Escape From New York,* I set all the background, which I'm very proud of. I think the background of that movie had as much to do with its overall success [as anything else.] I feel that the background, in a way, was a character in the piece.

I brought Geoffrey Ryan on. Unfortunately, Geoffrey is no longer with us. He's passed on. It was very unfortunate getting that news. He was a friend and a fellow worker. We used to dress up as the background so that we could intermingle with the background while we were shooting because otherwise, we stood out so much. We used to go to wardrobe and put something on and dirty our faces and arms and everything. Then we would go out every night and set background. I learned through the process that, if you're not amongst the background, sometimes you don't see what's going on. Back then, having video playback so we could go and look at it wasn't something that was common. I used to find myself ducking and hiding behind cars or whatever and then I wouldn't know what we were doing because I couldn't get back behind the camera quick enough once I set the background. I decided that I would become one of the backgrounds so I could actually be a part of it all and see what was going on. That was kind of how I found my craft of setting backgrounds and, to this day, that was one of my favorite things. I loved doing background.

What kind of challenges did this project provide and which scenes or locations were the most challenging, problematic, memorable, and fun to work on?

I have to say the movie was pretty problem free. We spent a month shooting in St. Louis. It was almost all night, something I don't think I can even fathom today. It's a young man's business when you're working nights all the time. This is a testament of John Carpenter and Larry Franco. The movie was so well prepped and things went so smoothly that you really didn't run into many problems. No problems at all really. When we went to St. Louis, they were so excited to have us that they would shut down streets and reroute traffic. They would ask us, "What do you want us to do next?" Back then in the late 70s, it was a lot easier to make movies. It wasn't as difficult and there weren't as many restrictions, so I have to admit that everything went very smoothly and there were never really any problems. I never look back on it and say, "This was a horrible day, this happened." It wasn't one of those movies at all. I have plenty of other stories to tell from other movies, but it didn't happen on *Escape From New York*. It really didn't.

How was your experience working with the cast and crew?

In terms of the cast, I mean, you couldn't have asked for a nicer assemble. You know what they say, if you have a good time making a movie, usually the movie isn't good. If you draw blood, then usually the movie is good, but that was one of the few movies that was a lot of fun and was successful. The cast was wonderful. There was no drama. Everybody got along back then. Actually, it was a lot more fun than sometimes now where they can be much more problematic. For me, it was my first movie with Kurt Russell and I went on to do *The Thing* with Kurt. He's the greatest guy you can possibly imagine. Down to earth. Generous. Friendly. Funny. Just a regular guy. Ernest Borgnine [Cabbie], you couldn't ask for a sweeter man. Adrienne Barbeau [Maggie], lovely. Harry Dean Stanton [Brain], just one of the great guys, great actors of our time. Isaac Hayes [The Duke], that was a trip. Isaac Hayes was like the coolest you could ever be around. All of them were. You couldn't have asked for a better group of actors.

How did you collaborate with the extras and how were they chosen for the different scenes?

We had a big casting call that I did with the extras casting, and thousands of people showed up. We met everybody and divided them up into separate groups such as the sewer rats as I call them. They're the people who lived underground and would come up from the sewers. I'm sure you remember how they moved, like they dragged their leg when they went across the pavement. That was something that I introduced to John. I didn't know if he'd like it. We did it on take one and I went up to John and said, "Do you like that or should I change it?" and he said, "No, I like it. Have them drag more. Have them more like they've lived in the dark and are scared to come out." You know, they're very ghoulish and very kind of like low to the ground, so that became the signature for the sewer people. Then there were just kind of like the mad hatters, the ones that were like the stronger of a group who tried to dominate the streets. Then there were the gangs and the various groups within the gangs and the ones that were afraid of gangs and didn't come out. We were very careful to make sure we cast everybody to the proper areas of gangs and people that were less violent. You know, children. We took a lot of time. At least I did to make sure that I gave John a little bit of everything when he needed it. Then we would grab different groups of people and make sure that we had created a kind of class within the prison on this island.

How was it working on the Broadway and Grand Central Station scenes with so many extras?

That was the coolest. Do you remember the shot where they all come running out [of Grand Central Station] charging down the stairs and out [deleted scene]? I really wasn't sure how to get people to go at different times and I really didn't know what to expect when I told them to run out of there. I basically told everybody I was gonna call out the months of the year and if you were born in that month then you had to run. I was inside so I didn't get to see the shot, but after we had done take one, I went outside and said, "So what do you think guys? How does it look?" and they were like, "What did you tell them?" and I said, "I just told them to run." and they said, "They came out like they were crazy." I have to say that, maybe it was good casting or we got lucky, but really it was just go, run, get out there and that's what they did. I can't remember how many takes we did but I do remember the energy in that first take was extraordinary.

What's your favorite memory or memories of working on the movie?

I'll tell you the whole thing. I've never had more fun. I was never more excited to go to work. I saw that we were doing something that had never been done before and it was just so exciting to be a part of it. It was a great crew. This is a crew that's been together for many, many movies. Everybody just loved going to work every day. We just tried to better ourselves every day to bring John's vision to the screen. We knew it was unique. We knew it was different and we knew that maybe we could do something that could change the course of film a little bit, so I hope we succeeded at that.

What do you think of the movie personally?

It's one of my favorites. When people see it on my resume, it's usually one of the movies they first get drawn to that they want to talk about.

What are you currently doing and what do you enjoy doing in your spare time?

I decided that my hobby is making movies, so I don't really do much of my spare time except recover from a hard day's worth of work. I'm currently working on a movie for Warner Brothers. We tried to do a movie called *Flashpoint,* which is a superhero movie based on Justice League. We are doing the standalone movie for The Flash and prior to that I did *Shazam!*, which comes out in April and prior to that I did *Black Panther,* so I've been having a great time in the superhero world.

LOUISE JAFFE
Script Supervisor

How did you end up being a script supervisor?

I was about to go to graduate school for a degree in geology when I had an epiphany that I really wasn't that great at the sciences. I also didn't want to go back to school and I knew that you could work in film without having a higher degree. [This is somewhat ironic because in my non-script supervising life I have been a public schools advocate and a trustee for Santa Monica Community College all about the important of education!]. My uncle Herbert Ross was a film director and had invited me to be a production assistant on *The Seven-Per-Cent Solution*. I was impressed by the work the script supervisor [in England then called continuity girl] did. My uncle thought if I wanted to work in film, I should become an editor because that was a more creative and well-paid position. Also, something where women were already accepted, but it was something like a seven-year apprenticeship to become an editor! I didn't like the idea of sitting in a windowless room all the time. Working on a set, especially on location and freelancing so that you didn't work all the time but also could travel or whatever, was much more appealing to me as a twenty-one year old [actually still].

I left my job at an oceanography lab [Skidaway] and came out to California where I was able to apprentice under the wonderful and experienced script supervisor Cynnie Troup on my uncle's film *The Goodbye Girl*. Cynnie was my first new friend in L.A. and remained a good friend for the rest of her life. which sadly ended this year [2023]. Anyhow, the short answer is: One, I didn't want to go back to school. Two, I didn't want a nine to five year-round job. Three, my uncle introduced me to the film world and gave me the opportunity to learn the craft.

How did you get the job of script supervisor on *Escape From New York*?

I was the script supervisor on *Halloween* and I got that job from being very good friends with Nancy Kyes, whom I had met working on another film. Nancy's then husband Tommy Wallace was very good friends with John Carpenter and we all worked on *Halloween*. Debra Hill [Producer] was the co-writer and

L-R/FG: Ray Stella [Camera Operator], Ernest Borgnine [Cabbie], Terry Marshall [Electrician], Dean Cundey [Director of Photography], Louise Jaffe [Script Supervisor], Clyde Bryan [First Assistant Camera]
(Photo by/Courtesy Kim Gottlieb-Walker)

producer for *Halloween* and she hired me again for *Escape*. [Debra had been a script supervisor herself before becoming a producer]. This was a huge break for me because she managed to get me into the union, which opened many more opportunities for work. I will always be grateful to Debra and *Escape From New York* for that! I can't possibly overstate what a big deal it was for me for Debra to hold out to get me into the union. It was something my uncle had definitely not been able to do. I wasn't a friend of Debra's, but she knew my work and really went to bat for me. I'm forever grateful.

How did you prepare for this project and how did you collaborate with cast and crew?

I prepared for this and every project I worked/work on by really meticulously breaking down the script so I know everything I might need to know about it before we are on the set so I don't have to do any last-minute thinking about things. Like, what time is it [in the unwelcome event that there is a clock on the set!] or is this directly continuous from the scene before [so that I know to match not only clothes but hand props, relative positions, etcetera]. What props is the actor going to need in this or subsequent scenes [so that they have them when they need them].

What kind of continuity problems during or after the production were discovered and how were they solved?

Yikes. I really don't remember any continuity problems. You would have to ask the editor if there were problems that had to be fixed. I hope not!

When you discovered a continuity problem or an error on location, how did you deal with it?

In terms of continuity, I would always check the main actors and sets for wardrobe and props or any prominent set design feature before the shot begins, so hopefully anything that may have been forgotten or misplaced gets righted before we begin filming. If it involved wardrobe or props, I just talk to those people or just sort it out with the actor. Like if a shoulder bag gets switched from the right shoulder to the left or something simple like that. Lots of little details to double check and keep straight so the shots and action flow seamlessly.

If something goes askew during the shoot, like forgotten or adlibbed lines or mismatches between shots, I let the director know so if he wants to reshoot it he can. In John's case, he didn't do much coverage [close-ups] so that wouldn't have been a problem.

What kind of challenges did *Escape From New York* provide and which scenes or locations were the most challenging, problematic, memorable, and fun to work on?

The most memorable part of filming to me was filming nights in St. Louis during the summer. I think we were there in August. There were huge street scenes with trash strewn everywhere and big/long lighting setups so lots of waiting [which I always find challenging!]. It was hot and we were out all night on these desolate streets. It was otherworldly. I also remember filming at the

Sepulveda dam [Liberty Island Security Control Exterior] in Los Angeles. This is some place I often drive by so it was fun to have it be transformed. Again, mostly night filming. And lastly [since I don't have a very good memory and it was a long time ago] I remember filming at the Wiltern Theatre [Theater Interior] in L.A. This is also a landmark and a really elegant building on the outside which was totally trashed on the inside even before the set designers got to work when we filmed there. Happy to report it has been restored and is again in use and not as a dump.

How was your experience working with the cast and crew?

Collaborating/working with the crew was pretty seamless because I already knew most of them. At least the camera, lighting and sound crew from *Halloween*. I wouldn't use the word "collaborate" for the relationship with the cast but no one [that I recall] was at all difficult to work with. We all did our respective jobs and it was fun to work with and see such legendary actors work. I didn't really develop any kind of close relationship with any of the cast. I think they may have stayed in character mostly while on the set. Not unfriendly, just professional. I think we all felt like strangers united in a strange land working hot summer nights outside in the *Escape From New York*/St. Louis dystopia.

What's your favorite memory or memories of working on the movie?

One day off, a group of us, camera crew mostly, rented a van [I think] and drove to Hannibal, Missouri to see where Samuel Langhorne Clemens [Mark Twain] lived. The gaffer Mark Walthour was a big Mark Twain fan and he organized it. That was a really interesting, fun, and good break. Good to spend a day as tourists.

What do you think of the movie personally?

I just rewatched it to refresh my memory. It was fun to watch. Suspenseful without being terrifying, which I appreciate. Fun to see all those great actors at work and all the locations. It all works great! Funny that it is supposed to be 1997. We escaped that dystopian reality. At least for a while.

What are you currently doing and what do you enjoy doing in your spare time?

I've been working as the script supervisor for *The Simpsons* for the past three plus decades! We are on season 35 now with over 750 episodes. I was also the script supervisor on *King of the Hill* for its 13 seasons. Working on the animated shows for me is much less consuming than working on a feature film like *Escape*. Especially on location. I loved working on location, but it definitely is not conducive to having a family. I was lucky enough to be able to make the switch from features to *The Simpsons* when my daughter was born. Because my work on *The Simpsons* and *King of the Hill* were both just part time I was able to become very involved in education as an advocate and PTA [Parent Teacher Association] leader. Eventually leading to my election as a trustee at Santa Monica College where I served for four terms, 16 years. This is my first year off the board. I'm still working on *The Simpsons* [except there is a WGA strike now] and still doing some education advocacy. Especially for early childhood. And I now have three grandchildren and a dog! I have been very fortunate in every aspect of my life. *Halloween*, *Escape From New York* and Debra's willingness to fight for me all set me up for everything I've been able to do in my personal and professional life. Who knew?!

RAYMOND STELLA
Camera Operator

How did you end up being a camera operator and director of photography?

I guess you can say my career started while I was in the Army stationed in Frankfurt, Germany. I bought a 35mm still camera because the base I was stationed at had a darkroom. I started taking pictures and taught myself how to develop and print. When I got out of the Army, I went to Los Angeles City College and took a photography class. I met a couple of guys that were making their own film and they asked me to work on it as still photographer. About two years later I answered an advertisement from the *Hollywood Reporter* to work on a short film. Dean Cundey [Director of Photography] had also seen the ad. We met each other, did the film, and stayed together for many years to come. At that point in time, I was a camera assistant and stayed a camera assistant for the next six years on little films that we did together. Dean would always allow me to operate an extra camera so I could get experience as a camera operator which was the position I had always wanted.

In 1977 we met up with John Carpenter to do *Halloween*. We ended up doing the first three *Halloween*'s and then *The Fog*. All non-union. When John was going to direct *Escape From New York* which was the first union movie for any of us he asked Dean to shoot it. We were on a program called the [Industry] Experience Roster through Contract Services, which enabled us to work on union movies if we could possibly get hired on one. Dean hired me as camera operator. By then I had operated twelve non-union movies, so the confidence and experience were there. That's how we became unionized. Needless to say, *Escape From New York* was very instrumental in our careers. Having gotten into the union on that movie was huge. I worked the next thirteen years as camera operator splitting off many times to shoot the second unit. I then moved up to director of photography on a movie called *Honey We Shrunk Ourselves,* which Dean directed. The next fifteen years I continued as director of photography shooting mostly bigger second units. Having shot fifty-nine episodes of *Buffy the Vampire Slayer* and moving on to shoot five non-union movies and various other assignments before retiring in 2013.

L-R/FG: John Carpenter [Director/Co-Writer/Co-Composer], Steve Tate [Second Assistant Camera], Clyde Bryan [First Assistant Camera] [Unseen], Ray Stella [Camera Operator]
(Photo by/Courtesy Kim Gottlieb-Walker)

How did you, John Carpenter, and Dean Cundey [Director of Photography] prepare for this project and how did you collaborate?

As a camera operator, a lot of preparation is not required. Most of it is done by the director of photography by scouting locations, looking at sets, figuring out the lights he would need, and having plenty of meetings concerning all aspects of the film. How I would prepare was to help the assistant pick out the best lenses, find the Panaglide I most wanted to work with, and make sure that I knew the script from top to bottom. Once that was taken care of, I was ready to go. John was the best director we had worked with to date. I never really saw much improvisation or altering of shots. He storyboarded a lot of the scenes but not all, from what I remember. He always knew where to put the cameras, never hemmed and hawed about the next shot or any of the shots he needed. He never had to shoot very many takes, shot very little film, and was very confident in what he was doing. A fine director. He and his actors and the crew were very prepared. John liked to move fast and, when he felt he had the shot, he moved on. The combination of John and Dean on the set was a beautiful thing to watch as they talked over the best way to shoot a scene. I even got to throw my two cents in the pot now and again. I was very fortunate and happy to be a part of it.

How come you chose to use the Panaglide extensively and is there any difference filming in anamorphic widescreen which John Carpenter prefers as opposed to other formats?

John loved the Panaglide. We used it extensively in *Halloween* and all of his movies for that matter. The Panaglide was a quick way to shoot. You could get plenty of movement in the shot. Long walks and talks, for instance. Not having to lay dolly track which was a big time saver. We could get into small places where the dolly couldn't. The anamorphic format was essentially a 65mm format squeezed onto a 35mm frame of film and then de-squeezed through the lens of the projector for a 2.35:1 widescreen look. With the 1.85:1 format, you would get a smaller look on the screen. Using anamorphic lenses on the Panaglide was quite tricky. The slightest listing side to side would accentuate the faulty movement greatly, especially on the big screen. So, I had to be very careful. Anamorphic lenses were much bigger and heavier than a standard spherical lens which made the Panaglide a little harder to control.

What kind of challenges did this project provide and which scenes, sequences or locations were the most challenging, problematic, memorable, and fun to work on? Any technical issues and such? I know the camera dolly broke down during the filming of the first scene in Atlanta and Frank Ruttencutter [Camera Operator: Second Unit] discovered some lens flares that weren't seen during shooting, which the first unit also got for instance.

As for which scenes were the most challenging. I think actually the ones that were done outside during the middle of the night with a lot of Panaglide involved like most of John's movies with fires and junk in the streets and small places like train cars and corridors were fairly challenging. We encountered some horse-shoe shaped lens flares now and then in certain situations. If a light was close to the frame and hard to flag sometimes these flairs would show up but could not be seen through the camera lens during shooting. As we began to see a few of these flairs in dailies we became extra protective about keeping extraneous light from hitting the front element of the lens on the camera. It was sometimes hard to see whether a shot was in focus or just slightly out of focus in low light situations. Consequently, we would get a slightly out of focus shot showing up in dallies which was not detected at the time of shooting. Always a bummer.

How was your experience working with the cast and crew? How did the first unit and second unit collaborate for instance?

Working with the cast and crew on *Escape From New York* was a delight, but then again it was a delight on most movies and especially John's. It was a lot of fun rubbing elbows with the stars. Second units are mostly comprised of smaller crews which shoot scenes without main actors in them. Second units will often shoot things like explosions, car chases, scenery, helicopter shots etcetera. The duties between 1st and 2nd units were fairly easy to define.

Is it true that Mark Walthour [Gaffer] went to Hannibal, Missouri to see where Samuel Langhorne Clemens [Mark Twain] lived on a day off with a crew consisting of mostly camera men? If you joined as well, how was the experience?

I did join that motley crew that went on the trip to Hannibal, Missouri, which was comprised of Mark Walthour, Dean, Clyde Bryan [First Assistant Camera], Tom Marshall [Best Boy Electrician], myself, and a few others. Our one day off a week was a good time had by all. I learned some history, saw Tom Sawyer's house, and the white washed fence.

What's your favorite memory or memories of working on the movie?

I think, as for favorite memories, it is very hard to pick something, so I will just say that the whole movie was a favorite memory. I enjoyed every minute of it. I do remember an incident which I will probably never forget. The second assistant [camera] Steve Tate came running out to hit second sticks in the house of nuts [Chock full o'Nuts] scene and accidentally fell through the fake floor set up for Season Hubley's [Girl in Chock full o'Nuts] character to be pulled through by the crazies. I don't believe anybody was hurt, but it was funny. I think Dean coined the nickname Steve "Which way to the Basement" Tate.

What do you think of the movie personally and which shots, scenes, or sequences are you most proud of?

Personally, I enjoyed the movie a lot. Being a low budget movie, we had to use our imaginations to get the utmost production value due to money limitations. Working on *Escape From New York* was one of my favorite movies to do. Good directing, good writing, good acting, and fantastic camera operating. Ha, ha! Hard to beat. There is not really one scene or shot that I am particularly proud of, but I naturally liked the scenes that involved long Panaglide shots that I pulled off well. Those types of shots brought much satisfaction.

What are you currently doing and what do you enjoy doing in your spare time?

As I noted earlier, I retired in 2013. I was shooting second unit on *CSI: NY* at the time and when the series went down so did I. I enjoyed my career from start to finish being fortunate enough to work for Dean most of the time. Working under Dean was the greatest thing I could've asked for. He was always a complete gentleman and always had my back and when I needed a question answered he always did so exquisitely. In 2008 I became an ambassador for Westchester Golf Course while still working around three days a week on *CSI: NY*. Needless to say, I played a lot of golf. I retired from my ambassador duties in 2019. I still play many rounds through the year.

CLYDE E. BRYAN
First Assistant Camera

How did you end up being a first assistant camera?

I wanted to be in the movie business from the time I was a young teenager. Then I got interested in camera work because of special effects and stop motion animation, but I decided it wasn't for me, being locked in a small dark room for hours on end. I was better working around people, but I knew I wanted to be behind the camera. So, that was my goal. I moved out to California in 1975 and met Dean [Cundey] [Director of Photography] in 1978. We started working together after that and worked together for more than twenty years. Then we had almost a twenty-year break and I did my very last movie with Dean.

How did you get the job of first assistant camera on *Escape From New York*?

As I mentioned earlier, I was working a lot with Dean Cundey. I did not do *The Fog* with John [Carpenter] because the producers already had someone they wanted to use, which they did, and I went off and did some other work. Later on, they needed to do television pick-ups for *Halloween*. At that time, there were things they couldn't show on television, so they needed a few days to do pick-ups on that. We combined that with a few days of pick-ups on *The Fog* and that's where I met John. Because I was with Dean, he recommended me to come along on *Escape From New York*. The rest is pretty much history.

How did you, Ray Stella [Camera Operator], Doug Olivares [Second Assistant Camera] and Steve Tate [Second Assistant Camera] prepare for this project and how did you collaborate?

Ray Stella and I collaborated closely as we were the A camera team. We would have prepped the Panaglide at Panavision as it was a favored device of John Carpenter. Steve Tate was my 2nd assistant for the L.A. portion of the picture. As this was my first union movie, I feel sure Steve was introduced and recommended to me by Doug Olivares. Doug and I had worked on a number of non-union

L-R: Clyde Bryan [First Assistant Camera], Dean Cundey [Director of Photography], Isaac Hayes [The Duke], Mark Walthour [Gaffer], Ray Stella [Camera Operator]
(Photo by/Courtesy Kim Gottlieb-Walker)

films in the past. I'm sure I asked Doug to do the job, but he was already working and recommended Steve. Doug worked sporadically on *Escape From New York* when we used extra cameras. Jack Gary [Second Unit Assistant Camera] worked as my 2nd assistant on the St. Louis and Atlanta portions of the show along with George Mooradian [Second Unit Assistant Camera].

What kind of challenges did this project provide and which scenes, sequences or locations were the most challenging, problematic, memorable, and fun to work on? Any technical issues and such?

Some of the more difficult and time-consuming things were the scenes that we shot on the streets in St. Louis for the streets for New York. Those were big night exteriors. Sometimes you saw several blocks in both directions during a shot like when Kurt discovers the empty pod in the middle of the street and the helicopters land. Because they were so big, we would go out when it was a couple of hours before dark and start working. The electricians and grips would start working and set dressers would close down the streets and start putting down all the debris and setting the fires. The special effects people were setting the fires. Then they'd start lighting and you couldn't finish the lighting until it was completely dark and, all of a sudden, it was so big.

I remember one time walking to the electric truck. A fella who became Dean's gaffer on a few pictures and his best boy on several pictures, a guy named Tom Marshall [Best Boy Electrician]. I walked through where the trucks where and I walked down to the truck and Tom was sitting there. It was big semi-trailer and every shelf was empty and he was working on a small lamp, like a 1K small incandescent lamp rewiring the plug on it because they needed that light. Every light that had been in that truck was out on the street working and that was the last light that we had, and Dean wanted to use it somewhere and he had to fix the plug so it would work. That's how big some of those shots were of the streets and we all had our own jobs to do. We all had so much to do. I'm sure there was toe-tapping and people going, "How much longer?" Dean is one of those people who can plan so far ahead. When he would light a huge street like that, once that was lit, everything else was pretty simple. So there was not a lot of time spent on individual shots. It might take, you know, two to three hours to get started, but once we got started that was pretty much slamming through the night.

The other scene that comes to mind is the control room where Tommy Atkins [Rehme] and Lee Van Cleef [Hauk] are talking to Kurt on the radio. That was a big set and I remember it taking a while to light, but then John came in and came up with a plan. He and Dean figured out a way to shoot an entire scene in one shot. I remember that day specifically because we worked up until lunch, then we stopped because we had shot today's work. John and Dean had worked out a way to shoot the entire scene in one long take so there was no coverage. We did that one shot. We got it perfect and we all went home that day at lunchtime. You remember those kinds of days because they don't happen very often.

The premise of the picture was that New York City had no electricity in it. There was no incandescent lights. There were no free lamps or anything like that and things had to be lit by fire, so we shot the majority of the picture right open on the lenses, the anamorphic lenses. We had a couple of anamorphic lenses that we put on. It was a Panaglide then but would be a Steadicam now.

It was 1/3 lenses and I remember that we actually pushed the film on stock because we didn't have enough light to get to 1/3, so for me the whole picture was extremely challenging. There were very low light levels, which meant there were very little focus levels as well. There's scenes like in the cab. Even though we shot that stuff on poor man's process, we were actually on the street. I had to be able to pull focus on the dialogue to keep the different people in focus as they spoke because I couldn't hold people in the front seat. Even if we shot at an angle, I could only hold focus on one person at a time. I had to change focus as the individual spoke, so the whole thing was quite challenging for me because we shot so wide open.

Anamorphic is a more difficult medium to work in, focus-wise, because now you have the depth and feel of a 50mm lens instead of a 25. I can't think of one shot. I just remember there were a lot of difficult things that I had to maneuver through. I was lucky to have Ray with me because he's an excellent operator, but he also has an excellent eye to be able to see what will work in the frame, which may sound strange but that is a quality not all operators have. So between Ray and Dean, myself, and John coordinating how to make the shots work in a fire lit, low level looking show I don't think there were any easy shots. Let's put it that way.

How was your experience working with the cast and crew?

I remember a lot of fun and a lot of hard work. Everybody was on the same page. We had an excellent AD [Assistant Director] staff and technical crew. There were always laughs. I don't remember any tension on that show. If there was tension, it was probably between some of the actors and John possibly, but not anywhere between the crew and John that I can recall. I can tell you an amusing story about the helicopters as a side note. Lee Van Cleef was definitely afraid of helicopters and would not fly. He was never in a helicopter that left the ground because he refused to do it. If you watch the picture closely, you see him kind of step out of the helicopter. I'm trying to recall exactly, but he was never in a helicopter. John wanted to land the helicopter for him to get out and he refused to do it, so if there was any actor tension, that might have been one. He was not gonna do it. "I'm not going up in a helicopter," so they cleverly cut around the fact that he was never in the air.

Kurt is one of my favorite people that I have worked with. I think we did five pictures together and I think I did five or six with John. That was my complete first picture working with John and then John and I became fairly close. I mean, on the operational lines of course. We did go out and socialize together and so on. Kurt as well on that picture and on *The Thing* and on the pictures after that as well. Kurt was always a friendly type and in St. Louis I'm sure we went out more than a couple of times. There's not always a lot of fraternizing between the cast and the crew but it does happen. The only one I can remember is Kurt. Everybody else, we just came to work and worked together and had a few laughs and whatever and then everybody went their separate ways. There was a fairly large group of guys that went out. If you notice in the end of the credits there's a thank you credit to a place called PT's, which was actually a strip club just across the river in Illinois I think. I know that a lot of guys went there with the actors.

How come you were chosen to be in the theater scene as a trumpet player in the band consisting of Nick Castle [Co-Writer] on piano, John Carpenter on guitar and kazoo, Dean Cundey [Director of Photography] on sax and Barry Bernardi [Associate Producer/Location Manager] on violin? And how was the experience filming this scene and collaborating with Low Moan Spectacular [Dancer] for instance?

That was in the Wiltern Theatre in Los Angeles, which is at Western and Wilshire Boulevard. It has since been completely renovated and is now a live music stage thing. It was an old movie theater and completely run down. There wasn't much we had to do to make it look like it had been unused and not taken care of. I don't know how long it'd been there, but it was empty. They were talking about a band and I'm not sure if it was Dean who started the conversation or John, but we started talking about how all of us played instruments when we were in high school in bands of one kind or another. I'm assuming that John said, "Why don't we all get in costume and dress up and we'll be the band?" and that's sort of how it all fell together. I played trumpet from the time I was in elementary school until I got out of probably my first year in college. All of us chose the instrument that we had played in school and they didn't record us because we sounded pretty bad. It was our chance to be in the picture. In those days it was kind of looked at like, 'Oh, this will be fun. This will be our [Alfred] Hitchcock moment where all of us can be in the movie and nobody will notice except us,' and now everybody seems to notice.

My interaction with them [Low Moan Spectacular] was keeping them in focus and stuff, so I don't recall very much about that. I remember that day.

You know, we shot a lot of things in the basement of the Wiltern when Kurt is going through and finds the carrier of the watch and has the attack, all the guys attacking in the dark hallways. All that was in the bottom of the Wiltern. I don't remember being there more than one day, so I'm assuming we probably did the stuff upstairs with the band and did our little performance piece and then finished the day downstairs with the fight scene and finding Buck Flower [Drunk] with the watch on. I could be wrong. It seems like we did everything in the Wiltern in one day and it would have made sense money-wise. We only had to rent the building for one day.

How did John Carpenter and Kurt Russell collaborate and were there ever any disagreements between them?

They had done several things together before. They knew each other. They were on the same page it seems like from the very beginning. They knew each other outside of work as well on a personal level. I always got the feeling that those two guys knew exactly where the character was going and what was gonna happen and there was almost a non-verbal communication between them about how things would work out.

Is it true that there were minor creative differences between Harry Dean Stanton [Brain] and John Carpenter since Harry liked to adlib etcetera?

Yes. Well, that's ok. That's alright. John Carpenter, like several directors I've worked for, is pretty particular in how things get done, but he's also not a stickler. If someone comes up with a better line or a better idea it may end up in the movie or it may not, but he won't say, "No, let's not do that." He would just say, "Why don't we do just one more and let's say what's written."

Did any performance surprise you?

Yeah. I don't remember the guy's name. One of the Duke's [Isaac Hayes] henchmen. His main guy [Frank Doubleday] [Romero]. That was so over the top. It was like watching a performance out of *Blade Runner*. He was so good. He was always fascinating because we never knew exactly what he was gonna do. It was so original and so spellbinding. That was the performance that surprised me the most.

What's your favorite memory or memories of working on the movie?

Oh, man. That's the kind of question that when they say, "What's your favorite movie that you've ever worked on?" I can never do that. I can never answer that. *Escape* was my very first picture as a union member. I actually got my days qualified to join by doing that movie, so besides it being a picture that I still look back on with great respect and joy in watching it, it was the beginning of a long career for me that led to a lot of different things. Going to St. Louis and shooting on those streets was a memorable shooting and in the old train station [St. Louis Union Station] [Grand Central Station], which again now it has been completely refurbished and rebuilt. Again, it was like the Wiltern Theatre. It was a place that when we said we wanted to shoot there they were like, "Why? It's a heap, you know. It's all rubble." "Yeah, perfect." The scene in the ring was inside that train station. I mean, there's just so many memorable things.

We actually went to Atlanta for a few days. We shot scenes that aren't in the picture. We shot in the metro transit and in the airport before either one of them were open to the public. That was like the stuff that you see now in *Westworld*. It was so futuristic. It was a great joy to do that and to be able to be in those places before they were open to the public. That was pretty special. I can't pick out one thing that is my favorite. When I watch the movie again, I can probably tell you a story in every showing. We took the production van and drove out to Hannibal and toured Mark Twain's Hannibal and went to the cave and did all that stuff. That was pretty memorable. I think it was a Sunday because, if I remember correctly, we worked six days a week when we were in St. Louis. On Saturday at midnight, it became expensive for us to work. They always pulled the plug by midnight on Saturdays.

What do you think of the movie personally?

I like it. I always liked it. I actually liked the ending of that picture as well because, unbeknownst to me, that was a perfect John Carpenter ending. As I did more and more pictures with him, I came to understand that John doesn't like pictures that have endings. It has a close, but it doesn't really have an ending because it's so perfectly nihilistic that he is walking away tearing the tape up listening to Cabbie's [Ernest Borgnine] music. I liked the movie. I still get joy out of watching it. I'm still very proud that I was part of it and I still recommend it to people because I think it's actually an entertaining movie. A lot of people get a kick out of Kurt. He may have modeled his voice after Clint Eastwood but Kurt's Kurt.

What are you currently doing and what do you enjoy doing in your spare time?

I retired three years ago from the movie business. I'm still involved in the union and I'm a national executive board for the camera guild. I spend some time teaching at the Georgia Film Academy in the last year and just finished helping them make a video about how I go back to work in the time of television. I'm gardening. Traveling. Not so much anymore. Waiting. Doing lot of reading and relaxation. Watching a lot of movies.

How was the experience reuniting with John Carpenter, Dean Cundey and Ray Stella at the 28th Annual ASC [American Society of Cinematographers] Awards celebrating Dean getting his Lifetime Achievement Award?

That was quite a night. I was pleased to be asked to be there as well and sat at the table with Dean and John. There were several picture of us taken that night together. Some of them trying to emulate or copy pictures that were taken during *Escape From New York* and I was really happy that John decided to speak for Dean and I thought that was great. It had been several years since I've seen John at that time. That was a great night and a great night for Dean but it was also really exciting to have John be there and be a part of that. The time before that that I've seen him he had shown a print. His personal print of *Big Trouble in Little China* at the ArcLight in Hollywood. We got to spend about 45 minutes or so afterwards talking and reminiscing and catching up because we hadn't seen each other in quite a few years.

CHRISTOPHER HORNER
Assistant Art Director

How did you end up being an art director and production designer so early on in your career?

I studied architecture and environmental design at UC Berkeley up north near San Francisco. Among other things I had studied a lot of architectural history. Very useful for film design. My father, Harry Horner, was a well-regarded film and theater designer. After graduation, with his help, I was offered a summer job at MGM working on a film called *Winter Kills* as a set designer doing drafting under production designer Robert Boyle. I found I really enjoyed the work and instead of going to graduate school I decided to stay in Hollywood.

For several years I worked as a draftsman and then as an assistant art director, then art director, and then as a production designer myself. In the early 90s, I had an opportunity to direct some commercials in Paris and my career took a new turn in France. Obviously, it's very helpful to have a talented father who can make introductions but at the end of the day, like anything, you have to be able to do your job. I worked for about fifteen years in Hollywood.

How did you get the job of assistant art director on *Escape From New York*?

You know, I don't exactly remember. I think I met Joe [Alves] [Production Designer] either on another production or through a mutual friend. I think I went in and interviewed for the job. Joe at the time was primarily looking for a draftsman and I had been drafting for a long time and now was looking for the next step in my career. The production was low budget, five or six million dollars. There was a lot to get done for the available money. I think I got hired at a little bit better than a draftsman salary, but not as much as a normal assistant art director. I think they saved a little money doing it, but it gave me the credit, which is really helpful when you're starting out your career. Joe was very kind about that. We enjoyed each other's company and I worked hard doing a lot of things in addition to drafting.

How did you, Joe Alves, Marv Salsberg [Construction Coordinator], and CLOUDIA [Set Decorator] prepare for this project and how did you collaborate?

I think Joe hired me not long after he himself was hired. I think there was probably only about six weeks of pre-production, maybe seven. Not a lot of time given the scope of the film. We had to work pretty fast. Joe would give me a rough sketch of something or he would occasionally even say, "Come up with an idea for this." Then I did the more detailed construction drawings to be used by the construction team to build from. We didn't actually have a lot of built sets. We were using locations for the most part, adapted for John Carpenter's and Joe's vision for the film and always with the budget limitations in mind. For example, for the lobby of the World Trade Center, which we shot at CalArts [California Institute of the Arts], I had to go and measure the location's floor plan. I think I did that with Marv or someone from the construction crew. We went out there and measured it so that we could make a precise drawing to know where to place things. CLOUDIA and the set dressing crew brought in a lot of trash to scatter around to turn a pristine modern space into a real dark and dingy one. Trash cans, old cars, and stuff like that. I don't even remember where we got it all from. There wasn't a lot of stuff in that location before we filled it up. It was pretty open. Obviously, it's a public building so you have to be careful where to put things. There was a lot of graffiti in that particular set. A lot of the crew pitched in with spray cans and we all got a little crazy. I think even Joe may have come and done some. Some CalArts students too, I believe. That was a really fun set to do.

Before that, everything was measured and I would basically draw up a plan so that Joe and John could block out how and where the action would be done and what we needed to bring in. That's the kind of thing that I did. I would measure and work a little bit with Marv and sometimes with Joe. Obviously, he was the designer, so he had the overall look of the film and overview things to be concerned with. He did a lot of the basic conceptual design, but then he handed it off to me and I would help make sure it happened along with the construction, paint, and set decorating team. Our art department crew was very tiny. It was really just Joe and me and then CLOUDIA had her crew as well, but her crew was more just physically moving stuff, renting stuff, working with the property department. Like I said, the budget was always really tight. There was a basic crew but additional workers were engaged and released as per the demands of the shooting schedule and the particular sets being worked on. I didn't get to go to St. Louis for that part of the shooting because it would have meant another hotel room for me, meals, and plane tickets. I basically did what Joe asked. I truly was his assistant, helping to ensure things got done. Sometimes also working on the finish of things with Ward Welton who was the paint supervisor. I sometimes coordinated also with Roy Arbogast who was the special effects supervisor who had worked with Joe on *Jaws* and *Close* Encounters [*of the Third Kind*]. Ward too. He and Roy were good friends of Joe. They had worked together a lot. Roy would do things like the landing of the glider on the World Trade Center. He did the rigging for that and all the physical effects. There was a lot of coordination. There was a graphics consultant named Arthur Gelb [Graphic Designer]. Joe sketched out the logo for the U.S. Police Force and I think Arthur worked on that too.

What kind of challenges did this project provide and which sets or scenes were the most challenging, problematic, memorable, and fun to work on?

Most of the sets themselves were fairly straightforward, though sometimes time and budget limitations made things difficult. The sets involving mechanical or other special effects such as the WTC rooftop glider landing and some of the bridge sequence in St. Louis presented some extra complexities, but Joe and Roy knew what they were doing. I think one of the most difficult things was getting permission to use locations like the Sepulveda Dam [Liberty Island Security Control Exterior]. I was relatively young, so in terms of getting things negotiated - that wasn't my job at all. I know that it was a challenge to get like the interior of the Art Center College of Design in Pasadena where we did all the stuff for the interior of the U.S. Police Force [Liberty Island Security Control]. That was a challenge because we had to bring in a lot of set dressing into a big room that they had. I don't even remember what the school used it for. A large display area, I think. It had catwalks, metal walkways around it, and you look down into this very large space. It was a great location, but we had to completely fill it up with electronics and things that looked like computers, so that was a big set dressing job. I mean, I think it was a big challenge too for CLOUDIA to get that put together and everything loaded into that room and all the electricity and light working. Big boxes of blinking light and that kind of stuff, so all that stuff had to be rigged. That was a challenge, as I recall. As for the World Trade Center rooftop, just the rig just to make sure that it worked and that it stopped at the edge.

Sepulveda Dam. That also was a challenge. I think we had limited time where we could be there. Setting up those bunkers and shooting at night presented certain challenges, but that was a fun sequence. We had helicopters out there at night. Those were all basically night shots. There was another scene I remember shot at the Wiltern Theatre [Theater Interior] as I recall. There was like this wacky vaudeville show where they sing "Everything's Coming Up Roses" ["Everyone's Coming To New York"]. That was another dressing job. I think the remote locations were probably a bigger challenge. I talked to Joe all the time when we were doing it but I was in L.A. and he was in St. Louis, so I just don't remember what those were. As I recall, in St. Louis there was some shooting on a bridge [Old Chain of Rocks Bridge] [69th Street Bridge] and that had to be rigged and I think that was a significant challenge. I can tell you that it was a significant challenge to get everything done. I think this is one of the reasons John and Debra [Hill] [Producer] hired Joe because he had experience with [Steven] Spielberg's *Jaws* and *Close Encounters*. *Jaws*, I believe, was a pretty tight budget. I think we actually had to do a lot more on *Escape From New York*. They had different challenges on *Jaws* because they were shooting on water but the budget on *Escape* was just a huge challenge. I mean, there's a lot of locations and a lot of sort of quasi-effects. There are some video effects and it had a pretty big cast. Tribute to Joe, he got a lot for the money as far as the look goes.

How involved were you in creating the Liberty Island Security Control bunkers, Air Force One interiors, Air Force One escape pod, World Trade Center rooftop, Chock full o'Nuts, and Grand Central Station gladiator ring for instance and how were they constructed?

The bunkers, Joe just designed that. We just wanted something that looked sort of ominous and we had this very nice metallic matte black paint that Ward Welton came up with. It had a little bit of a shine to it, so at night there were some helicopters and some light reflected on it. It wasn't glossy but a really subtle satin finish that gave the whole bunker complex a highly "machined" and techno-future look. They were supposed to be metal.

The plane interior before it crashed was probably a mock-up. We probably rented that. There's a couple of places in L.A. where they do mock-ups for airline commercials but honestly, I don't have a specific memory of how we did that shot. The after-crash plane and crash site, that was Joe who conceived that.

I don't remember what the origins of the egg-shape [escape pod] were, but of course Joe designed that too. I did have to draw the interior so that it could be built. It was bright orange and it had a pneumatic door that lifted up. There was a seat that Donald Pleasence [President] had to be fitted into if I remember correctly. There was some electronics, like homing equipment and that kind of thing. The concept for it came from Joe but might have also come from John. He was fairly specific in terms of how he wanted to shoot that scene.

Regarding the WTC roof, we had some aerial photos I believe for basic research. I also believe we kept some detail from the real building's edge for the shot of the glider almost going over. Otherwise, we took a lot of liberties to make the set visually convincing but workable for the effects and reasonable in terms of cost. Luckily, the sequence was at night which made things easier from a set design point of view. Darkness is very useful both visually and also to hide certain things. The "rooftop" was built on an area which was in real life an airfield on the Indian Dunes property. I don't remember specifically but my guess is working with Joe and Roy Arbogast, the head of physical/special effects I mentioned earlier, would have been key in making this work as per John Carpenter's needs. The glider was attached to a motorized cable rig so that as many repeatable takes of the landing could be done as needed.

The Chock full o'Nuts set was something we built out in Indian Dunes. Funny that I had largely forgotten it because that one had to be designed and drafted and constructed and finished. Along with the USPF [United States Police Force] bunkers this was one of the few actual sets constructed from scratch. It tells you how long ago it was. That's what set designers do. I know I drafted all of that, but I just don't remember the set that well, nor the scenes it was used for.

For the St. Louis sequences, it's likely that I had some minor drawing to do. Mostly I think Joe and the location manager found their location and brought in whatever was needed for filming. I don't think there was a tremendous amount of drawing to do on those. I don't remember having done it anyway myself. Joe probably did some just on location. Quick sketches with some dimensions and stuff. If you build a set like the Chock full o'Nuts set, it's not like architecture where you have everything detailed and engineered to last, but it's detailed enough so the construction crew can come and they see how to cut things, what the finish is gonna be. Everything is measured out. It's precise. With a set like the lobby of the World Trade Center or the bridge in a location, sometimes things get moved around at the last minute. You have a stand-by construction and paint and set decorating crew that's just on set to arrange things directly for the camera or the shot. There was a fair amount of that on this movie just because so much was location.

How was your experience working with the cast and crew?

John and Debra were friendly with everyone and certainly things were friendly with Joe and everyone on the paint, construction, and decorating crews but I wasn't part of the brain trust of the movie. I was one step removed, so in one sense I was very much an employee. John Carpenter, who I didn't have a lot of direct dealings with, seemed a pretty relaxed person. I don't have a huge memory of John, but he just seemed like a nice guy who was really enjoying his work quite a bit. Debra Hill. Just a lovely person and capable person. Unfortunately, not with us anymore. They did their best to take care of the crew. They were fairly inclusive and made the whole production team feel like they were grateful for the work everybody was doing. It was a nice working atmosphere.

John shot pretty fast and Dean [Cundey] [Director of Photography] lit pretty quickly too, so things moved along at a good clip. I mentioned this guy, Roy Arbogast, who lived and had his workshop not too far away from Indian Dunes. He was just a very talented guy who could basically make any kind of physical effect. He built the different sharks in *Jaws*, for example. An incredibly capable, talented and soft-spoken person. Ward Welton also had huge experience. When you're doing paint, there's paint and then there's paint you know. If you're just covering a wall with wallpaper or paint or whatever, that's one thing. But if you're doing like exteriors with bricks and you're trying to age them, he had a lot of experience with that kind of work. Aging surfaces is a real art.

CLOUDIA was really good and a very capable person. She too had a relatively small crew except on days when we were shooting in places that needed a bigger on-set crew. Marv was a funny character. He was in a tough position as was the art department because you're spending money, building things and bringing in props and doing all of these kinds of things, sometimes on the fly. The art department is one of the first places you go to cut budget, so Marv was always trying to get things done at a budget price so that we would stay on budget. Productions generally don't scrimp on the camera department, maybe a little bit on the lighting. You know, the camera people get pretty much what they say they need because that's what's going to show on film and talented directors of photography tend to be somewhat regarded as "magicians."

A big star or several big stars, that's going be where a lot of your money goes. In this case. Kurt was a star, but not yet as big as he later became. Isaac Hayes [The Duke], Harry Dean Stanton [Brain] etcetera. Larry Franco was the line producer. He was working for and with Debra Hill, but he and Alan Levine, the production manager, were key people who made sure everything got done. Alan was in charge of executing the budget. Actually, getting the bills paid so basically, he was the one who was the "bad cop" because that's his job but a nice guy. Larry was a really good guy too. Larry went on to do a lot of other films as did Debra and obviously John too. Joe was a nice man, definitely. He directed *Jaws 3* a few years later and he hired me as one of the art directors on that one. On *Escape,* it was fun meeting Isaac Hayes. Kurt was around the production office sometimes as he was friendly with John and Debra. He seemed to be a pretty regular person. The cast, they all seemed like really good people. Working on lower budget movies, everybody sort of gets to know each other and that's a really fun thing. I didn't stay for the entire shoot. I was on probably a total of maybe four months, something like that. At my level, they let you go when your specific work is done. They want to save the money and maximize what will actually show on the screen, but it was a really good experience. Like those nights we were doing the Sepulveda Dam. Everybody when we're not shooting or on a break, we gather around the craft service where they have food and hot coffee. A nice memory.

Is it true that the only part of the production that went over budget was the production design as mentioned by Debra Hill [Producer] in a vintage article?

Actually, I didn't know about this or that Debra said it. If true, I think there were a number of sets and locations that may have been more expensive than originally planned rather than any one single sequence. I was not privy to many of the budgetary details, but as mentioned earlier, the art department is very easy to point the finger at when budget cuts are needed or when there are cost overruns. It's possible too that the overall budget was underestimated in the early planning and that more complexity was added or needed later, which simply cost more. My guess is that cost overages were a combination of several factors and not just the art department spending too much.

What's your favorite memory or memories of working on the movie?

Working closely with Joe and Roy and Ward because it was relatively early in my career and this was a real learning experience with people who really knew what they were doing and were fun people to work with. For me it was the people and the experience of making the film.

What do you think of the movie personally?

Honestly, I have to admit I was a little bit of a movie snob at that point in my career. I thought *Escape* was good for what it was trying to be. An irreverent, dystopian, and exciting action movie. I gave it my best, but I worked on some other films where I was much more emotionally attuned to the subject matter. This was an action film and I just preferred other genres more. I actually didn't expect it to do as well as it did. I mean, it did really well, becoming a cult classic film over the years. I'm the one who underestimated what it was while I was working on and how difficult it actually is to make any kind of film well. I learned a lot on this movie.

What are you currently doing and what do you enjoy doing in your spare time?

Just as I was starting to achieve some success as a production designer, I had an opportunity to go overseas and work as a director. I moved to Paris and did commercials, music programs, and documentaries. The documentaries took me full circle back to my university days. My degree was in architecture and environmental design. I had always been interested in the environment and concerned for the health of the environment and the future of the planet. I made a film for French television called *The Disappearing of Tuvalu: Trouble in Paradise* with my partner about a tiny island nation called Tuvalu, which is in the middle of the South Pacific and is really on the front lines of climate change and its effects. This island will most likely not exist in fifty years due to sea-level rise. It's just a really interesting place populated by generally very kind-hearted people who eventually will be forced to move. It's one of the smallest countries on the planet and it's about a thousand kilometers north of Fiji, so we made this film there about what people were thinking about climate change. It's just a very interesting experience and I started to do more work in the environmental arena. My wife had stores in Southern California that sold sustainable products. Sustainable building material, home wares and things like that. I did a fair amount of work with her and have been involved in a variety of "green" business ventures.

I live in Santa Barbara, so a lot of what I like to do is oriented around the nature that's available in California. I do a lot of still photography as well. Just a lot of hiking and beach walking with my wife, our dog, and our friends. I like bike-riding and playing tennis as well. Those kinds of things, which I'm so grateful for.

CLOUDIA REBAR
Set Decorator

How did you end up being a set decorator?

I saw my first Broadway play at age eleven and was hooked on theater. I wanted to pursue lighting design. In the course of studying lighting at Hunter College, we had to create a set design to light and I then fell in love with creating sets. I studied theater design all through school and passed on my graduation ceremony to start working at the American Shakespeare Festival Theatre in Stratford, Connecticut. I was then accepted to study in England at the prestigious Slade School of Fine Art. While there, at the end of the year, I met a young Italian film student, Marco Bellocchio [he later became an important Italian director], who told me of the government film school of Italy. That same week I saw [Federico] Fellini's *La Strada* in London, packed my bags, and moved to Rome. I HAD to be in the country that produced that film! My Italian was limited, but I managed to pass the three-day entrance exams and was accepted at the Centro Sperimentale di Cinematografia in Rome.

At the end of the year, I met the renowned film production designer John De Cuir [*Cleopatra, The King and I, South Pacific, Hello Dolly*]. He mentored me for a year and then gave me my first film working with him on *The Honey Pot*, which was directed by Joseph Mankiewicz. I've since worked with Billy Wilder, Sam Peckinpah, Brian De Palma, and many other interesting directors.

How did you get the job of set decorator on *Escape From New York*?

I got a call from Joe Alves [Production Designer] to come and do *Escape From New York*. I had not known him before that project.

How did you and Joe Alves [Production Designer] prepare for this project and how did you collaborate?

My normal twelve week prep on the film was actually only two weeks due to scheduling, so it was quite a challenge. Once I've read the script, I break down the character information into symbols. Colors, shapes, textures, etcetera, that then guide me in every subsequent decision on the thousands of things that can go into making up a set. Being totally present in each moment of all the selections is driven by the symbolic aspects from the character analysis.

Can you give us an example or examples how you used the symbolic aspects to a character in a set or scene in the movie? Anything with Snake Plissken, The Duke [Isaac Hayes] or Hauk [Lee Van Cleef] for instance?

In analyzing Isaac Hayes' character, the edginess and brutality influenced my choices in his office in terms of colors, shapes, forms and textures that I used there. With Lee Van Cleef's office, things were more regimented. Snake Plissken never had his own environment. He was always on the move.

What kind of challenges did this project provide and which sets, scenes, or locations were the most challenging, problematic, memorable, and fun to work on?

It was a very small production, so every department head was working all together out of one room with their team and only two telephones. To be able to concentrate for even five minutes without interruptions was the biggest challenge. It all came together though.

    I remember being asked to provide a twenty-foot U.S. flag at 8 PM on set for 6 AM the next morning and begging a Santa Monica gas station to loan us their flag for our morning shoot, which is evident in the exterior shots of the command control [Liberty Island Security Control]. One of my favorite sets was the World Trade Center lobby which we shot at CalArts' [California Institute of the Arts] lobby in Valencia, California. All the St. Louis shooting was done during the worst heat wave on record there. We trashed the city downtown every night from 7 to 11 PM, shot 11 PM till 5 AM, cleaned up all the debris by 7 AM for St. Louis rush hour traffic to roar through, repeating this for thirty nights.

    The Chock full o'Nuts coffee shop and street was a moment I'll not forget. It was supposed to shoot in two weeks way out in the dessert [Indian Dunes]. I drove out there in the 117-degree heat just to look at the location and got a call that it was shooting at six o'clock that night. I had to phone in all the set dressing orders, including a full restaurant kitchen just from memory of what was available at various prop houses and restaurant supply store, then truck it out to the desert and dress it in hours in the sweltering desert heat.

So much of it was seat-of-your-pants instant decisions on site, improvising so much that one had no option but to be totally in the moment. This is most likely why, whenever anyone asks me which was my favorite film experience of the many films I've done, I always reply *Escape From New York*.

Were the mannequins and pinball machines featured in the scenes where they held the President [Donald Pleasence] in captivity at the Grand Central Station found at St. Louis Union Station or were they brought in by you or your team and who came up with this idea?

I found the mannequins there during the location scout in an abandoned storage area, probably left over from a shop. I brought the flags and the pinball machines. They were in a rubble pile. The building had been abandoned for decades and was full of fabulous treasures to use.

Were the bed and drying clothes in Brain [Harry Dean Stanton] and Maggie's [Adrienne Barbeau] lair [New York Public Library] [Hoose Library of Philosophy], which the script doesn't mention, a choice you made and if so, can you remember why you did this interesting choice?

It was the dangerous aspect of the world they live in that would mandate it being too hazardous to go out into the world unless absolutely necessary. I wanted it to look like they lived there. Set decorators have a lot of freedom to interpret what the characters would do and choose to have in their spaces. When you consider approximately five hundred items could be decided upon, shopped for, trucked to the location, unwrapped, dressed into the room, and shot for usually one day, then the whole process in reverse to get the item off rental quickly. EVERY room of every set is an empty canvas for a set decorator to express who that character is in the twenty second master shot in order to give that character history and context before the actor gives it voice. Rarely are there scripted requests for set decorating items unless there is action or a story point requiring them in the scene. The rest is the set decorator's imagination and creativity hard at work.

What's your favorite memory or memories of working on the movie?

Standing beside Roy Arbogast, our amazing special effects [coordinator] man, in total awe in the middle of St. Louis at night watching the 747 [DC-8] burning to the ground before we remembered it was a rented plane and wasn't supposed to burn THAT much. It was quite astonishing to watch.

What do you think of the movie personally?

I love the film and the experience. When one considers WHEN the film was made, before digital CGI and computer effects, it's quite remarkable. I've done several John Carpenter films and loved working on them all.

What are you currently doing and what do you enjoy doing in your spare time?

When I'm not making films, I'm teaching metaphysics and thoroughly enjoying life. As a professional member of the American Society of Interior Design, I'm enjoying Europe with design friends several times a year, especially for fashion and design weeks in Paris.

ARTHUR GELB
Graphic Designer

How did you end up being a graphic designer?

Before coming to Hollywood, I was the creative director of a New York ad agency and an award-winning designer of graphics. I came west with the intent of a career change into the world of film as an art director on a movie starring John Ritter. On that project, I fortuitously met Albert Brenner, the production designer who hired me to provide the myriad graphics on *Hero at Large*. That led to a sixteen year career as the first credited "Graphic Designer."

How did you get the job of graphic designer on *Escape From New York*?

After seeing a notice in the trade press that *Escape From New York* was in pre-production, I interviewed with Joe Alves [Production Designer] and my portfolio impressed him enough to have him give me the job. At that time, there was no such job title as graphic designer in the business. Joe's alternative to hiring me would have been the production illustrator or the studio sign shop and they would have only been able to provide a finished piece of art to a design that Joe could provide.

How did you prepare for this project and how did you collaborate with Joe Alves [Production Designer] and CLOUDIA [Set Decorator]? Any sources of inspiration and such?

I was given a script along with the instructions that I was free to design anything that I felt would help to establish an ambience of realism to the then future time period of 1997. Both Joe and Cloudia had much more important responsibilities and relied heavily on my judgment.

How did you come up with the designs and how long did they take to make?

In 1981, I was not yet a skilled user of the computer. My training allowed me to create a hard copy on illustration board the old-fashioned way by hand. I was responsible for all the designs and, where required, I used the services of a studio illustrator for the finished art. In the real corporate world, a project of this kind would have been given a time frame of several months for preliminary sketches and meetings, but time and budget constraints in the movie business demanded this project be completed within two weeks.

Which design or designs for the movie are you most proud of?

Unquestionably, designing packages for legalized marijuana, although they never appeared in the film. However, the symbol of the USPF [United States Police Force] presented an interesting challenge. The turning of the most popular city in the nation, perhaps the world, into a prison camp demanded a special symbol. Was this a subtle way John Carpenter was warning us of possible things to come? The eagle has been used by authoritarian regimes throughout history as a symbol of power and dominance. I wanted to keep the symbol of the American eagle for the same reason, but added a cruel touch, I believe, in the eyes.

The United States Police Force Signum
(Image Courtesy Joe Alves)

What's your favorite memory or memories of working on the movie?

Escape From New York was the third project of 150 that I worked on over a period of sixteen years. I really enjoyed meeting Joe Alves. Unfortunately, as is the condition of independent productions, you rarely make long term relationships or get to work with familiar faces.

What do you think of the movie personally?

While it was very well done and the production values were terrific, I am not a fan of that genre.

What are you currently doing and what do you enjoy doing in your spare time?

The day that I drove through the front gate at the MGM lot led to a sixteen year career that dreams are made of. It's been more than twenty years since I aged out of the business and I'm still playing with crayons. I, along with my daughter, design and build children's playhouses.

STEVE MATHIS
Flicker Box Technician

How did you end up being a gaffer?

I started as an electrician with Mark Walthour [Gaffer], who I knew from college in Oklahoma, and Dean Cundey [Director of Photography] on a movie in Santa Fe in 1976. I worked as an electrician and best boy with them through *Back to the Future*. At that point, I was offered a job as a gaffer [head electric] on a film and took it. Since Dean's gaffer was Mark, I had to move on.

How did you get the job of flicker box technician on *Escape From New York*?

I had worked on both *Halloween* and *The Fog* with Mark, Dean, Debra Hill [Producer] and John Carpenter. We were much like a loose family. They wanted me to be on *Escape From New York,* but I wasn't in the union. Dean lived across the street from an actual JPL [Jet Propulsion Laboratory]/NASA [National Aeronautics and Space Administration] engineer. They were farting around and came up with a design for an electronic dimmer to control the various firelit scenes in the movie. This is way before this kind of stuff became standard on sets and some thirty years before LED [Light-Emitting Diode] lights and DMX [Digital Multiplex] control. This dimmer used an electric eye to read the flicker in an actual firelight and dim the lights attached accordingly. The result was the first [that I know of] natural firelight made with dimmers. Dean, Debra, and John came up with the idea to call the dimmer a "Computerized Light Modulator" or "CLM" aka a Flicker Box [nicknamed by Larry Franco] [Producer/First Assistant Director].

Dean then called the IATSE [International Alliance of Theatrical Stage Employees] and asked them to supply a union member to run the CLM. Dean reckoned they couldn't even spell it, much less supply anyone who could run it. The union proposed the builder be allowed to run it and Dean named me the builder [the real guy had a real job]. This was during the actors strike of 1980 with ninety-nine percent unemployment in the union. I made *Escape From New York* and joined the IATSE in 1981. When the film came out, I was as surprised as anyone that my credit was flicker box technician, even though that is, more or less, true to the story.

How did you, Mark Walthour [Gaffer], and Dean Cundey [Director of Photography] prepare for this project and how did you collaborate?

Dean and Mark started prep way before me. I didn't join them until the first night of shooting in St. Louis when I walked around the corner to set, saw a real honest to god airplane plopped down in the middle of a main street, and thought, '*Wow. I really am on a big movie.*'

How was the computer light modulator utilized for the movie and which scenes or locations were the most challenging, problematic, memorable, and fun to work on? Any technical issues and such?

The actual dimmer was a blue and white metal box, about a foot square and 10" tall. It had a pocket for a 50A stage plug [light plugged into this]. I would find the best spot to hide the dimmer relative to where the firelight was supposed to be. Then I would run the electric eye and cable out to either a real fire being seen on screen or a purpose-built fire off-screen. The eye would "read" the flickering firelight and I would set the levels of the movie light [using controls on the CLM] to match the needs of the scene per Mark or Dean.

The biggest issue was setting the eye in a place that couldn't be seen in the shot but where it could accurately read the part of the fire that matched the scenes needs. I remember using these in St. Louis for the first time and being nervous. After all, I was the "builder" as far as everyone else knew, but Mark, Dean, Debra and John were concerned. If it fucked up, I certainly did not possess ANY knowledge of how to make it work again. Luckily, it worked perfectly.

How was your experience working with the cast and crew?

Escape From New York had a great cast. Looking back, I wish I hadn't been so new and shy so I could've talked to Ernest Borgnine [Cabbie] about *The Wild Bunch*. Or Lee Van Cleef [Hauk] about *The Good, the Bad, and the Ugly*. I remember Lee had really bad knees, so a lot of scenes minimized walking fast. Ray Stella [Camera Operator] operated a Steadicam [Panaglide] shot at night in the old train shed in St. Louis that still remains one of the best operated shots I have ever seen.

What's your favorite memory or memories of working on the movie?

Escape From New York was my first real large-scale film. It was also John, Dean, Mark, and Debra's first big movie. John and Debra ended up paying a lawyer to force the IATSE into recognizing my days on the film as qualifying for union membership. I owe my career partially to those two and their loyalty. Like I said, we were family on *Halloween*, etcetera. Dean, Mark, and I worked together through *Back to the Future*. I worked again with John on reshoots for *The Ward* some thirty years later. It was really fun to sit down at lunch and pick up where we had left off some three decades earlier.

My favorite memory would have to be rounding the corner on my first day on the film and seeing that plane planted on the street in St. Louis. I knew I had arrived when saw a set bigger than anything I'd ever worked on before.

One last anecdote. We were shooting at Sepulveda Dam [Liberty Island Security Control Exterior]. I had just parked and was walking with a bunch of the electric crew to set. John walked by, pulled me out of line, and took me up in a Huey [Bell UH-1 Iroquois] helicopter along with Mark and Dean and we circled the [San Fernando] Valley for a bit and landed and I went on and joined my crew. Because of the strike, the crew consisted mostly of unemployed gaffers. They were all amazed that a lowly lamp operator not only knew the director personally but went up in a chopper with him rather than run cable. They treated me like one of them after that.

What do you think of the movie personally?

Escape From New York was ahead of its time. I also remember John saying to me much later that there was a better film in there somewhere. I would agree that it has all the parts, but the editing wasn't as tight as it could've been. Part of me thinks that may have been intimidation on John's part, but I don't really know. He did say that to me though. I liked it. A forerunner to *Blade Runner, Road Warrior, Radioactive Dreams*, etcetera. One of John's best along with *Halloween, They Live*, and best of all, *The Thing*, which I wanted to work on, but the union would not let me.

What are you currently doing and what do you enjoy doing in your spare time?

I just finished three seasons of *Reservation Dogs* including acting in seasons two and three. It was shot in Oklahoma where I live now. Before that, I did a small movie called *Minari,* which was nominated for best picture. Also shot in Oklahoma. I have also been teaching at a local college. I never worked with Dean or Mark after *Back to the Future* or Debra ever again. While it lasted, we were a loose knit family. All of us started under thirty. We didn't know any better. It was as fun as it gets on those films.

KEN CHASE
Makeup Artist Supervisor

How did you end up being a makeup artist/supervisor?

My experience started in television with shows like *The Wild Wild West* and working on films like *Planet of the Apes*.

How did you get the job of makeup artist supervisor on *Escape From New York*?

The production manager recommended me.

How were some of the makeup created such as Romero's [Frank Doubleday] for instance and did you have any sources of inspiration?

I don't remember any of the characters other than the main one. Oh my, now I remember. I used to enjoy making character teeth and made the teeth. That was really fun, but I don't recall whose idea it was. Probably John Carpenter.

What kind of challenges did this project provide and which actors, scenes, or locations were the most challenging, problematic, memorable, and fun to work on? Was it a hard job considering the many extras as prisoners in the movie for instance?

I suppose it was, but I had help. The filming was mostly in St. Louis during one of the hottest summers on record. Luckily, filming was at night.

How was your experience working with the cast and crew such as Low Moan Spectacular [Dancer] for instance?

Sorry, no recollection. I worked with Kurt Russell several times and had much fun with him. Always happy and nice to be with.

What's your favorite memory or memories of working on the movie?

I had ordered a tattoo for Plissken's chest and a schedule change required me to paint the tattoo by hand as the tattoo wasn't going to be ready in time.

Was the tattoo chosen or approved by Kurt Russell or did you choose it?

The story indicated it was a snake. The usual routine was to have a pattern stamped on a special transfer paper. As I explained, it fell on me to draw the snake by hand with a marking pen. It was really hard keeping it from smearing.

What do you think of the movie personally?

Fun.

What are you currently doing and what do you enjoy doing in your spare time?

Woodturning, painting in oil, computer graphics, in particular digital painting with Photoshop and photography.

KIM GOTTLIEB-WALKER
Stills

How did you end up being a still photographer?

I majored in motion picture production at UCLA but had no contacts in movies or TV. I had shot stills for articles in the *Free Press* when my film school teacher did interviews, which included Jimi Hendrix. So, I went back to shooting stills for the underground press and for record companies. I met my husband during the formation of *Music World Magazine* in 1972. When that ended a year later, he became editor of *Crawdaddy,* later *Feature Magazine,* and did the first interview with John [Carpenter]. My portfolio landed me a job on a little low budget feature that was never released, but the script supervisor was Debra Hill [Producer], who went on to write and produce *Halloween* with John. She brought with her [on *Halloween*] all the crew members she had worked with as a script supervisor, including Dean Cundey [Director of Photography], Ray Stella [Camera Operator] and me.

How did you get the job of still photographer on *Escape From New York* and how come they chose Jim Coe [Stills] for filming locations outside of Los Angeles?

I had been part of John's crew since *Halloween,* so Debra asked me to shoot *Escape*. She knew they wanted to go "pro" as a union film, so she signed contracts with the crewmembers she wanted contractually committed to shooting *Escape*. When she signed her union contracts, they had to honor her previous legal contracts and allow us to work on the film even though we weren't yet in the union. It took thirty days working on a union film to be allowed to join the cinematographers guild.

I almost didn't get my thirty days because two weeks were spent shooting in Missouri, which was under the jurisdiction of the central region's camera guild, so she was forced to hire a local photographer while on location there. That was Jim Coe, who did a great job. There were still just enough days left when they returned to L.A. for me to get my thirty days. But the

FG: Kim Gottlieb-Walker [Stills]
(Photo by/Courtesy Kim Gottlieb-Walker)

union challenged the fact that she hadn't taken me to Missouri and hired a standby as proof that I'd been fired and was therefore no longer eligible to work on a union film. Debra fought this before a union arbitrator because she had been following the rules.

After a few weeks, she showed up on set with bottles of champagne to celebrate her victory. We held the wrap party on a Saturday night even though we had one day left to shoot on Monday, which would be my thirtieth day. The party was at a rolling skating rink where I broke my arm in three places. Debra took me to the hospital and stayed with me all night. I'm convinced it was the inspiration for *Halloween II*. I shot on Monday with my arm in a cast and on pain meds, but I got my thirty days! So, for Dean, Ray, me, and others, she was responsible for our careers in movies and TV.

How do you work with people to get the photos you want?

I try to establish a positive, friendly, supportive attitude. Letting my subjects know I'm there for them, to help promote them, to make them look their best. Sometimes little acting suggestions like determined, intrigued, flirty, dramatic, afraid, whatever is appropriate. On a set, the actors get used to the photographer always being there and the real pros know how to make the most of that relationship and will often pose off the set if there's good light. I try to have them see me through the lens as opposed to just seeing the camera to connect with the viewer, person to person. Sometimes I'll peek out from behind the camera to remind them they are relating to a person. Listening to what they are hoping for in the photos and trying for their vision of themselves.

What kind of challenges did this project provide which scenes or locations were the most challenging, problematic, memorable, and fun to work on?

I tried to make every shot count because film, unlike digital, is expensive! Much of it was shot at *very* low light levels. The shot of Kurt Russell inside the glider was lit by a single red bulb on the dashboard, so F1.2 at a 15th of a second with the Tri-X pushed to 2400 and holding my breath. The slightest movement would've rendered the whole shot a blur.

What's your favorite photo or photos and how many photos did you take?

My favorite photo of myself was from *Escape* posing with the rifle props with helicopters behind me! I shot about 6000 B&W frames and probably around three or four thousand color.

How was your experience working with the cast and crew?

I had already taught both John and Dean that if we were waiting between scenes, they should point to give me a usable shot. One of my favorite photos from *Escape* is where they are both on the camera crane spontaneously pointing in opposite directions. I loved the entire crew. Donald Pleasence [President] was a particular joy, a true pro who didn't mind striking an in-character pose off-screen or a comical reaction. Such a sweet man. He was the only one on the crew who had fought in a war [World War II] and had fired machine guns, so as the President of the USA firing the machine gun, he was right at home. That shot was particularly gratifying because there was no way to take a light reading from that distance and most of the illumination came from the firing of the gun itself, so I had to guess on the exposure. I was THRILLED when I got it back and you can even see the shells flying out behind him.

What's your favorite memory or memories of working on the movie?

The whole thing was a blast. but working with John was always fun. He was always good humored, loved practical jokes, never worked the crew over twelve hours and set a happy tone for the set with appreciation for every crewmember who was helping achieve his vision.

What do you think of the movie personally?

I loved it! And it helped Kurt make the transition from teen actor to action hero.

How come you decided to release a coffee table book called *On Set with John Carpenter* in 2014? An essential purchase for Carpenter fans with even more *Escape* stories!

England's Titan Books published *On Set with John Carpenter* covering *Halloween, Halloween II, The Fog, Christine* and *Escape From New York*. It is still in print and has an edition in Japan. They also published *Bob Marley and the Golden Age of Reggae* which has international editions in French and Russian.

What are you currently doing and what do you enjoy doing in your spare time?

Now in my 70s, I've become a novelist. My first book is loosely based on my early career in the 1960s and 70s both as a hippie journalist and a photographer for music companies and on movies but reimagined as a romance novel. It's called *Lenswoman* and my agent is currently seeking the right publisher for it. My second novel was written during the pandemic and takes place in Florence and England during the late 15th century. Titled *Caterina by Moonlight,* it was inspired by Sandro Botticelli and the Medici, who play important supporting roles.

EDDIE SURKIN
Special Effects

How did you end up being a special effects technician/coordinator/supervisor?

Very simply. Roy Arbogast [Special Effects Supervisor] and I had been friends for probably fifteen years before the movie. We'd both worked for Universal Studios where we did *Jaws* and *Jaws 2* together. Whenever he had a movie that he wanted someone to supervise, he would call me. I did a lot of movies with Roy and then, later on, I did movies for myself. We did *Jaws*, *Jaws 2*, *Return of the Jedi*, *Escape From New York,* and many, many other ones. I've known Roy for many, many years and I've known Kevin [Pike] [Special Effects] [Uncredited] for many years too, but Kevin came much later in the game. Kevin didn't get into the special effects into probably twenty years after I was an effects man. Roy and I started about the same time and we worked for Universal Studios for many, many, many years. We worked under a great supervisor, a guy named Orn Ernest. He was just a brilliant man and a great teacher. He taught both of us. Roy went more into rubber work and breakaway effects. I went more into the big metal workings, explosives and big hydraulic mechanical effects and electronics. That was my main thing. When people wanted things to be controlled on the set, they called me up because everything was always electronically or hydraulically controlled. Roy and I have been friends for about forty-nine years or so. He's a great guy.

How did you get the job of special effects technician on *Escape From New York*?

Basically, my experience. We don't work all the time. When we finish a movie, everybody is reading notes. This guy is available, this guy is available. Roy was friendly with John Carpenter. As soon as he got the movie, he immediately called me up and said, "Do you want to do this movie with me?" I said, "Sure," because I'd just come back from South America from doing *King Kong* with Dino De Laurentiis. I took *King Kong* on a road show to Argentina and Brazil and I'd just come back. He heard about it and called me to do the movie for him and I said, "Fine."

How did you, Pat Patterson [Special Effects], Gary Zink [Special Effects], and Roy Arbogast [Special Effects Supervisor] prepare for this project and how did you collaborate?

We'd have meetings and then we'd decide who's going to do what. You got to have a team that prepares. I think I was on the movie for probably two or three months before the movie started. We prepared most of the stuff in Roy's shop. Then we took everything pre-ready to St. Louis. Then we had the water scene where they're swimming away from Manhattan, the bodies we blew up, and stuff like that.

What kind of challenges did this project provide and which special effects, scenes, or locations were the most challenging, problematic, memorable, and fun to work on?

The water scene to blow the guys up was very memorable to me because we were in the sea with explosives in deep water. It was night, so it was very difficult. That was actually done after the main movie finished. It was a second unit shot.

Another memorable scene was just before the taxi goes through the pile of cars. He makes the hole between the cars. He exits and one car pulled out. We had to shoot that with live arrows fired into the doors. Normally, we would shoot it down on a wire, but we couldn't shoot the car with a wire because the car was moving fast. I said to the stunt guy, "I'm going to shoot it with a bow and arrow." "There's no way you can hit the car." I said, "I can do it." I took a bow and arrow and I followed the car. When it got close, I shot it perfect.

Isaac Hayes' [The Duke] car with the chandeliers, I remember the first jump we did. It didn't sail through the air, so I told the stunt guys, "I want weight on the backside," but we didn't have any weight. It was twelve midnight and we needed to do the shot. I remember going to the side of the road and filling the trunk full of dirt because the engine was too heavy and it oozed on the first shot, but I put weight on the backseat and it went nicely. Of course you got to have everybody's agreement too. I got to talk with the stunt people to make it sure it was ok. They were a good team.

I want you to know that the entire movie was shot with fire, which I made. Every night I lit up the entire place with fires. There were hardly any lights. Everything was with fires. Only the stars were lit with light. Everything else was lit with fires. I had five guys with me. It was the hottest summer ever. People were dying in St. Louis. I remember never going to work with a shirt and just working all night long to keep the fires up. The set dressing crew would bring all the garbage every day at night. In the morning once we'd finished, another crew would take all the stuff off. Then at night we'd put it all back together. I burned everything that was flammable. If there was anything not on fire, it's because it wasn't flammable. I had fire bowls and propane bottles and all that stuff. It was a very, very tough shoot.

How did you manage to blow up the cab at the Old Chain of Rocks Bridge [69th Street Bridge] in two pieces?

I prepared this car at my shop. Basically, the car would come apart and back together again as many times as they wanted it to. We did this scene at least ten times. I made a system so that the car would come apart in two halves. I would pull it together and, with a small piece of explosive, we would take it apart. It's called a quick disconnect. On the bridge, we created a basket to fit inside a manhole cover. The basket contained an explosion. When the car came to it, we blew it up and took the car apart.

How was your experience working with the cast and crew?

I became good friends with Debra Hill [Producer]. I became very good friends with her and Carpenter. I remember having some great parties with them. I've done some other movies with her too. There's only so many people around, so we keep going around and around seeing each other in different things.

What's your favorite memory or memories of working on the movie?

One big spectacular shot was when they catch Snake Plissken and they bring him to the headquarters. I think it was called the Sepulveda Dam [Liberty Island Security Control Exterior]. That was a pretty exciting night with a lot of work.

    I remember the stunt crew one Sunday morning. We worked so hard. Sunday morning was the only time you could sleep. They called me in and woke me up about ten, "We're gonna go see the arch. You're coming with us." I was so tired. They dragged me up there. We had a great Sunday. It was the only Sunday off we ever had. I remember it very well.

What do you think of the movie personally?

I love it. It's my favorite movie. I've done almost two hundred movies in my life and that is probably one of my favorite movies of all time.

What are you currently doing and what do you enjoy doing in your spare time?

First of all, I own a lot of properties now. I became a well-to-do person. I have a lot of properties and I have to manage all the properties. I have properties in California and Florida. I have a couple of yachts. One in California and one in Florida. I maintain them and enjoy them. When I'm available, I do explosions for other movies just as a cameo. The next three days I'm gonna be doing explosives. On Friday I'm flying to Florida for the Portland Boat Show. It's one of the biggest boat shows on earth. I'll probably spend eight days in Florida taking the yacht around. We might go to the Bahamas. We'll see. I work hard. I save my money. It's what I do now.

TOM THOMAS
Transportation Captain

How did you end up being a transportation captain/coordinator?

I was a studio teamster driver for eight years working at different studios and, later on, in independent film. These are films funded by major studios but not under the studio banners, which allowed for hiring away from studio seniority or studio regulations. My first captain job was in Arizona on a Kirk Douglas movie called *Posse*. One of the production assistants was Joel Douglas, Kirk's son. He was slated to be the UPM [Unit Production Manager] on an upcoming film with a relatively small budget. Alan Falco was the transportation coordinator on *Posse* and was asked to coordinate this new film by Joel, but the money offered was lower than the going rate. So, Alan recommended me for the film. Joel then offered me the coordinating position while I was taking him to the airport. I agreed, of course, since that was what I was told to do. As it turned out, the film was *One Flew Over the Cuckoo's Nest*. Actually, an easy film to do since it was mostly at one location - Salem Mental Hospital in Salem, Oregon.

I realized after I finished that I wasn't ready to move up to coordinating. The film went without any problems, but I didn't know enough about the politics of the business to be able to effectively manage the department. I went back to driving on various productions and watched and listened to how the coordinator I was working for handled and resolved different situations. After a couple years of watching, I felt ready to move up. Problem was, nobody knew who I was. As it turned out, a TV series was prepping and they didn't have a transportation coordinator. It was really busy and all the best guys were already working, so the production coordinator I had worked with on a previous production suggested me to the producer and I was asked in for an interview. I met with the producer and, while I was telling him of what I had done, he asked me if I could read. I said yes and he threw me a script and told me to find an office and get him a budget by the next day. That was my start with Jack Webb of Mark VII Limited. We did a number of movies-of-the-week for them and were always kept on the payroll in case something came up. Very boring. We did a series called *Project U.F.O.* and one of the first assistant directors I had been working with got a job as a UPM on an MGM film called *Pennies From Heaven*. Pretty big ass movie. Once I had a couple projects on my resume, it was at least easier to get in the door for interviews, sometimes with referrals and other times with a cold call. From there I did some movies for Paramount and a bunch for Disney. Through these projects I met more people in different departments and more producers. Eddie Lee [Voelker] [Transportation Coordinator] would refer me if he was busy as I would for him if I was unavailable as well as many other coordinators. Eddie Lee and I had the philosophy that while working for a studio we always followed house rules, kept an eye on the budget, and made sure the work was performed without any problems.

How did you get the job of transportation captain on *Escape From New York*?

I think Eddie Lee had a previous relationship with Debra Hill [Producer] or the production manager Alan Levine and, these guys, when they're happy they tend to hire the same people, Debra especially. She's really loyal to the crew, so she likes to go back and rehire people that she's worked with before because she knows exactly what to expect. I became captain. Eddie Lee and I worked together a lot through the years. Sometimes I'd captain for him and sometimes he'll captain for me. I was available. I usually coordinate but I was available and sometimes I don't want to coordinate, so he hired me to do the captain work. Pretty much work on the set. That's how I kind of landed the job.

How did you and Eddie Lee Voelker [Transportation Coordinator] prepare for this project and how did you collaborate?

Basically, how it worked... Eddie Lee worked days and prepped the next day or the day after that. Then he'd come to the set, open us up, then he'd go back and go to bed, then I would handle the rest of the night. He had stuff to do during the day and couldn't work that many hours and we knew how each other worked. Together we compile who is going to be driving on the show. He had his guys and I had some favorite guys and we ended up with a really great crew. Commitment was gonna be a lot of months and it was weeks and weeks and weeks of night work. John [Carpenter] is kind of nocturnal. He likes to work nights. I've done a movie for John since then, *Vampires,* and there were a lot of nights on that one as well. He just prefers working nights, I guess. Different look.

I don't know how much of this back story you know, but I'll give you what I have. The industry was going into an actor strike and we had a date that we had to ship the trucks by in order to start on time. Debra Hill was trying to make a sweetheart deal with the union, which is basically like, "We'll pay whatever you guys end up doing if you let us go on with our production," because they had already spent a lot of money. SAG finally said, "Ok. We'll make you a sweetheart deal." I don't think anyone does that anymore, but that's what was happening. I had to send the trucks. I stayed in L.A. Eddie Lee was in St. Louis doing the prep work. What we had to do was send the drivers and all the trucks to St. Louis. Every night when they stopped, they had to check in with me to see if they were gonna go forward to St. Louis or if they had to turn around and come back to L.A., depending on how she made the deal. The deal eventually worked out, but they would still call me every night and I'd say, "You're good to go. Go to St. Louis," so that worked out pretty well for everybody.

    Just after we got there, SAG went on strike and all the business in L.A. pretty much shut down, but we were all working, so that was good. I had to stay pretty much in L.A. and Debra Hill stayed there as well because she was the dealmaker. She was really great at what she did. After everybody left and we were all good to go, I think I flew there because there wasn't enough time for me to drive. It was supposed to be a four-day trip, but some guys made it a little quicker than that. Eight weeks at night, I think, and then we came back to L.A. and did more weeks at night.

How many trucks did you drive to Atlanta, St. Louis, Los Angeles, and New York [Liberty Island]?

I think we probably had ten to fifteen drivers that left Los Angeles. I mean, we had all the usual complement. We brought some set dressing with us and there was a vehicle or two we had to bring. It would be way different now because there's so much equipment available across the country, but at that time, there wasn't much available, so everything had to be brought. When we got to the hotel, there was a parking area we took all the trucks to and then we would take them to the location. Sometimes we had to move two or three times a day. We'd move the whole company to a different place. What we liked to do, if we could, was finish a location by five or six in the morning and then move the trucks to that afternoon's location. If something didn't get done, Eddie Lee had a move crew of guys that would come in and work days to just move the equipment around to where it was supposed to be when we went to work.

You talked about how they filmed in Atlanta and New York. We didn't have any part of that. We went from L.A. to St. Louis, did our filming, and then went from St. Louis back to L.A. to do the filming there. I don't know the progression of what they did because we had like six days to get from St. Louis back to L.A. and get set up. They may have gone to New York. If you go to New York, you wouldn't take our transportation equipment. They'd have their own. They are very territorial because it's their district, so when they did New York they would've hired local people, at least local transportation people. The first unit had nothing to do with New York and Atlanta.

What kind of challenges did this project provide and which locations and tasks were the most challenging, problematic, memorable, and fun to work on?

Well, St. Louis in general. It was really nice because the city pretty much gave us St. Louis, so we could go anywhere and park anywhere. The local officers that we had, they would let us just set up in the middle of the street. It was nighttime so they really didn't care, but they were very helpful in allowing us some parking areas that maybe we didn't have and could block off. Safety is always a concern. Everybody looked at that. The closer we can get, the better it is for everybody, so we always had a comfortable place. If there was a gap, we would take them back to our parking lot they had contracted for the run of the show and we'd stay there for the night, which is kind of standard procedure on movies. You work until seven o'clock in the morning, get back to the hotel, and be back at set at three o'clock in the afternoon, but you get into a rhythm after a while. It's not really a big deal.

There were some problems here and there. We had some local guys. Usually, when you go on location, you hire ten or twelve local drivers and they drive the vans. Those guys weren't really familiar with how the studios worked. We knew we were gonna work fourteen or sixteen hours and these guys that you pick up locally, they usually work eight hours per day. When you have a guy that's local, the first week or two are kind of difficult. Communication wasn't as good as it is now, so we had a light on the other side of the bridge [Old Chain of Rocks Bridge] [69th Street Bridge] and when there was something wrong, I had to get in the car and drive over there. I just couldn't get on the radio. That's kind of what it was and, if I left the set, somebody else would take my place and be sure that everything ran the way it was supposed to run.

It was difficult because it was nights. The crew worked extra special hard because it was night in St. Louis in the summertime. They all got along. Everybody laughed. It passes the tension when you get along with people. They helped each other out. When we got back to L.A., the filming here was pretty simple. We're familiar with the areas. Nights made it a little more difficult, but in general it became pretty simple. We're filming places downtown and the Sepulveda Dam [Liberty Island Security Control Exterior] area and we've all already been there, so we pretty much got around fairly easy. If there were problems and they didn't affect transportation, I didn't get involved. It seemed to be pretty smooth. I never really heard of anything bad that happened. It was a difficult show, but it was a lot of fun, especially when we got back to L.A. It was a great movie to work on. It was a really good shoot. It lasted a long time. I mean, I haven't worked on a movie since or even before that had as many nights. I've worked with John and we've done a lot of nights, but not that many in a row. In general, it was good work, especially since in L.A. there was no work because the actors went on strike. I don't think that strike lasted all that long. I think by the time we came to film in L.A., it was pretty much done.

I'll tell you of an incident we had. I don't know if people really remember, but it had to do with me and them. That's why I didn't really want to get into this because the movie isn't about me. We had a scene in the first week of filming, probably the first three days, where a car has to come around a curve, hit a pipe ramp, and roll to the right. They set up video village, which is where everybody gathers and watches the video reel of the shot. They set it up like twenty feet directly behind the ramp and I went over and said, "Listen, you guys are kind of in the wrong place. You're gonna have to move like thirty feet off in that direction away from where this is supposed to happen." And there was a lot of resistance. John wanted to be in line what the car was suppose to do. He said, "Well, it's ok because the car is gonna go over there." I said, "The car is supposed to go over there, but if it doesn't, the car is directly in line with the pipe ramp and you're only like twenty feet away." And they didn't want to move! I said, "Look, you're gonna have to move. This is like a safety issue." And it was kind of selfish on my part. There was no work in Hollywood and I didn't want to see the director get hurt and get us shut down. Then nobody would have a job. The conversation went on for a little bit and I know we had great stunt guys. I mean, we had the best stunt guys you could get out of Hollywood. Dick Warlock was the stunt coordinator and he's a great guy. He's always concerned about safety. He was setting up the shot with his stunt guys. If he had been standing where

I was at the end of the ramp talking to the video village people, he'd done the same thing I did. I said, "You got to move to this side," and John said, "Well, I don't want to move." I said, "You're gonna have to move because I'm not gonna let this happen with you guys sitting here." He said, "What if I fire you?" I said, "You have that ability. You can fire me, but you're gonna have to do it from over there. Not here."

So what John did, he had a prop guy get a whole new set of chairs and put them where I asked them to be, and he left the chairs that they had right where they were at the end of the ramp. They moved all the video monitors and all that stuff over to the right-hand side. Well, what happened, he hit the ramp dead center and the car went up in the air and came down and landed on the chairs that John had left there. It was pretty ugly. When they finally said, "We got the shot," John, Debra, and Dean Cundey [Director of Photography] came over and said, "Ok, you're the safety guy now. If you see something you don't like, you just tell us what it is, and we'll move wherever we have to move." I mean, literally it came down square on top above those chairs, which was where all of those folks would've been sitting. Not that anybody would've been hurt. Maybe they'd have gotten out of there in time. Nobody got hurt and we got to keep shooting, which was all our concern. Everything went pretty smooth.

We had another incident at the Union Station in St. Louis [Grand Central Station]. They were filming somewhere else, so I basically had base camp, which is all the production trucks and trailers. We were parked under a really bitchin' kind of glass dome that was part of the train station. Everybody was on the other side of the train station filming whatever they were filming. I had a guy standing there and, what happened was, the guy had a fuel truck. We had an old forklift that used gasoline and not propane, which is really more dangerous. He was fueling the forklift and there's a lot of static electricity. He didn't run a static line, which is what you would normally do. While he was filling it, he broke the grounding between the pump handle and the forklift itself and it sparked. A fire started inside the forklift fuel tank, which wouldn't have been a big deal, but he panicked. When he took the nozzle out, because there was a fire in there, he didn't take his hand off of the nozzle, so it was continuing to spray gasoline all over the ground, which caused that stuff to catch on fire. Gasoline isn't really an explosive, but the fumes are, so I kept yelling, "Drop the nozzle! Drop the nozzle!" but he was waving it around because he was scared he was gonna explode! He was putting a lot of gasoline on the ground.

The drivers we had there didn't really have a way to put it out and it was spreading. The gasoline was rolling over toward the effects truck, which is where they keep a lot of black powder because we had a lot of explosions and gun fire, so they had a lot of stuff in there we didn't want to get burned up. That could've been a pretty ugly explosion underneath the glass roof. Everybody was kind of running around, so I said, "Listen. Get brooms and start sweeping the gas away from the effects trailer." and I called for the water truck. It was on the other side of the set, but it never showed up. Not that it was gonna put the fire out, but I was hoping to get the water truck and the water to push the gasoline away from the trucks. It ended up, everybody did what they were supposed to do and finally everything burnt down and there was no gasoline left and the fumes were gone.

It was kind of one of those awe moments. Do you want to run and get the hell out of there before the place blows up or do you want to stick around and try to fix things? One of the guys said, "You should run." I said, "We can't get far enough fast enough, so let's try to deal with what we have here." Some people just kind of froze. It lasted five minutes. I remember Jeffrey [Chernov] [Second Assistant Director] beat it out of there pretty quick. He went back to the set. It was kind of ugly, but it went away quick and then it was over. I finally got somebody on the radio who said, "You guys need the water truck?" I said, "No. Not anymore. We're good. Don't worry about it." Little things happen and your appropriate people take care of what the problem is. It was a very interesting evening and nothing got damaged. We even used the forklift after we put the fire out. We just put a new cap on and went back to work.

How was your experience working with the cast and crew?

These guys were all low profile. Kurt and Isaac [Hayes] [The Duke] and all of those guys. What we would normally do is have four, five fifteen passenger vans that would pick up the crew and we had a bunch of stake beds so they could load what they wanted. We also had a sedan, and somebody would bring John wherever he wanted to go. He might discus the events of the day on the way to the location, so he might have the DP [Director of Photography] with him or the 1st AD [Assistant Director]. They were pretty casual about it. Nobody had any great demands. We didn't have a lot of cast trailers. John keeps things small, no matter how big the picture is. I mean, everybody gets trailers or whatever it is, the way it is now. At that time, it was pretty small. A honey wagon, a couple of tandem trailers, and everybody just got along. It was a great cast. They were really nice and seemed to be having a pretty good time. The cast got along really well.

Some of the locations in St. Louis were difficult, but they all seemed to work together. It was like, this is what it is and this is what we are. Let's get it done. That was the professionalism this cast had. We had a really great crew. Everybody busted their ass because night work is always harder. Just the fact that you can't see anything. It was really a busy show, and everybody rose to the occasion. They liked working for John. They liked working for Debra Hill, who was a genius at producing because she would figure out problems and solve them right away in a way that made everybody happy. They were all great people. Really easy to work with and, believe me, I've worked on movies where I've dealt with some real pain in the ass people.

Ernie Borgnine [Cabbie], he was a cut above. He liked to stay busy, and I've worked on other movies with Ernest Borgnine. He likes to stay busy, so he gets out and tries to help other people, so he was always great. I worked on a movie with him where he was a sheriff and between scenes, this is no kidding, he got out of his trailer and went over and started directing traffic because he just wanted to stay busy. He directed traffic for half an hour because he had his sheriff uniform on. Nobody really recognized him for what he was.

John Carpenter is a great guy to work with because he knows exactly what he wants and then we move on. We had a scene where Ernie Borgnine pulls up in a taxi cab in front of some building and he gets out of the cab and ran up the stairs and John said, "Ok. Print it. We're moving on." Everybody else was like, "Don't you want to do it again?" He said, "He drove up, he got out of the car and ran up the stairs. Is it something wrong with the camera? I mean, is there a hair in the lens?" and they said, "No." He said, "We already got this. Let's go somewhere else." A lot of directors won't do that. They don't trust one take, but John does that. If he sees what he likes, it's done. There's no sense going over it another ten times. I also did *Vampires*. We did that in New Mexico and working with someone in the past, it's gonna be easier for you in the future because you know what John expects. You know what he's after and he doesn't need limousines and all that bullshit. As a matter of fact, I picked him up at the airport in New Mexico in Albuquerque and I got a limo for him and John smokes. I told the limo guys, "Look. This guy is gonna smoke, so send me a car where they're gonna smoke." The freaking limo guys said, "No, no, no. I don't want you to smoke in my car." and John said, "Ok, no problem," so he rode in my pickup truck the forty-five miles to Santa Fe. I didn't give shit if he smoked in my truck or not. He's really a good guy. Brilliant.

Debra Hill. I've worked with her a couple of times and she was a master at people. If there was an incident of departments not getting along for some reason, Debra would stop production and get the principals involved that weren't getting a long. She'd put them in a circle and say, "What's the problem? Solve it right now. I haven't got time to do this," and they would get through their problems and we go on working and everything would be fine. It was a great loss for us when Debra Hill passed away. It was shocking and quick and horrible. We actually dated for a while. Nothing really heavy. Nothing really like, this is gonna go on for a long time. Let's just go out and have dinner and let's just have a good time, so we got pretty close. Losing Debra was losing a great mind in our business. She was really smart about how she wanted things done, how to solve problems. She was amazing. If I could pick the producer I wanted to work for, it would be Debra because nothing was ever crazy. She didn't let crazy happen. She saw crazy happening and she would put the blinders on it right away and solve the problem. Really smart. Great sense of humor. You wouldn't think she was the producer on the movie because she could've been one of the crew, which she used to be.

Eddie Lee was a great organizer and still is. Well, he is retired now, but he was a great organizer. We knew exactly what we're supposed to do, what was expected of us on that day and what happened at the end of that day if we had to make a move. As a matter of fact, I was a coordinator on *CSI: Crime Scene Investigation* that went on for fifteen seasons. I did the first thirteen and then I retired. Eddie Lee was my captain. He started on season six and he stayed till the very end, and he retired shortly after that. I retired after thirteen seasons and the last two were done by somebody that I trained or showed the way how to do the job. Eddie and I worked a lot and a lot of drivers that worked either for him or me, they were pretty much the same people. We shared people. If I had a group of guys or if he would get a group of guys, they were just as knowledgeable about what we're suppose to do.

I've worked with Jeffery Chernov from the time he was a PA [Production Assistant], assistant location manager kind of guy, all the way to where he was executive producer on some of the movies that I did and Eddie Lee did the same thing. We worked a lot for Jeffrey and he's really, really smart.

What's your favorite memory or memories of working on the movie?

When you're working nights and you put in a lot of hours, the job becomes the job. They took care of us, production-wise. Craft service had what we needed - coffee. Maybe a taco guy would show up and take care of the crew. In general, it was just a good time. I mean, you just deal with what you got to deal with. I think the whole thing was memorable in just the nature of the beast, what's it was about, how they filmed it. There was a lot of effects activity going on. It was a pretty big movie actually when I think back about some of this stuff.

What do you think of the movie personally?

You know, I look at movies differently than a lot of people. To me it's like, it's there to entertain. I don't care if it's politically correct. I don't care if this makes sense or maybe continuity was a little different from one thing to another. I don't really look at that stuff. It was entertaining. I've probably seen it twice and because, the first time, we probably had a screening. I watched it again a couple of years after that just so I could reflect back to who did what, where, and when, and why and how and what it looked like. What we had to go though and what the crew had to go through to get something accomplished. It entertained me for whatever the length of it was, but I don't critique movies. I'm just glad that people make them so it keeps people working.

What are you currently doing and what do you enjoy doing in your spare time?

Well, I retired in 2013 or 2014 and I kind of did that so somebody could move up into my position because he was ready. I did some traveling which was good for a while. I restored seven or eight cars of my own cars. I had been working on other peoples stuff. I quit doing that like a year ago because it was just too hard to get parts and get people to do things. Nobody really wants to get anything done unless you're a big money job and I usually do the most work myself and then that went away. Now I'm working on renewable energy stuff, so I'm working on some equipment that's more battery operated. Just lights, nothing big. More battery operated and basically to keep me busy. It might work. It might not work. It doesn't make a difference but right now I'm staying busy on a day to day basis trying to get these things compiled and put together.

A month ago I had lunch with Eddie Lee. He lives in South Carolina now, but he was in town visiting his daughter. We had lunch with a newer guy that's a friend of ours, Joel Marrow who's head of like Marvel transportation. We all sit around and talk about how it used to be like and the stuff that they've done over the years, the changes that they've made, the amount of paperwork that has to be done. Far more safety cautious. My daughter is a dispatcher for the studios and one of my sons, he's like a director of health and safety for Netflix on the east coast, so they kind of stayed in the business and are doing it really well. I get information of what's going on and, like I said, some of us are older guys, we sit around and shoot the shit and talk about the way it should've been and what's wrong with the guys now. They don't take any pride. I started in 1966 and we all had this pride in what we did because we were in a special place in a special business with some special people. The friends you make, you may not see for two years but then you'll see them on another show and you work with different crews.

What we notice now is people don't really have much pride in what they do. They don't really feel like it's this special job for them anymore. They just want the money, which is kind of unfortunate. A lot of guys do the job. We had to have different qualifications when we did it, but it gets so busy that they started picking guys up that weren't really quite ready but they get the job done. Maybe not in the way that some of the old guys would've done it, but they all get the job done. It would be more difficult now I think to do that movie, *Escape From New York*. It would be more obstacles involved and there would be more safety concerns involved. Larry Franco was the 1st AD and the 1st AD is usually the safety officer on the set and he was really good. Larry was a really good 1st AD. He's moved up obviously to producing and stuff. He was really good at getting groups to do what John wanted them to do because there were a lot of group shots as you've seen for sure in the *Escape* movies.

I actually started to prep *Escape From L.A.* at Paramount because I was originally gonna do that, but I was wrapping another show. We have these random drug tests that they make us do, which is fine, but I got hung up on the set I was wrapping and I thought the drug place closed at eleven. They closed at ten and I got there right at ten o'clock and the guy wouldn't open the door. I said, "I got to get this done." He said, "No. I'm closed," so that's what happened. No matter who I told, whatever I told. If you missed the test, you get suspended for six months. Debra basically wanted me to move to like an associate producer position so I wouldn't be considered a teamster. I didn't like that idea. Paramount didn't like it at all. The unions were like, "No, you can't circle and bent this thing." I said, "No. I get it. There's no problem." I ended up working on some of the picture cars on a contract thing. Kenny Searl ended up doing the show. He's another good guy. It was a totally different kind of show. It was bigger in some sense. *Escape From New York* was done as an independent basically. I was on the show for about a month and I just arranged picture cars for Ken. It was an interesting job. It was a very interesting job. Transportation is like the second biggest budget on a show below the line. Sometimes construction is a little bit higher but the transportation usually cost more. On a movie like *Escape* where you're working the hours that you're working there's no place to trim. There's no place to tighten up because there's a lot of equipment.

GEOFFREY RYAN
Production Assistant

How did you end up being a production assistant and location manager?

I started off house painting. I landed my first job in film after painting the house of a high school teacher I really respected. He recommended me to a producer who did industrial, Army, Navy, and Marine films. I agreed to paint his house for $80 per week if he'd teach me film and he did. Then later, because I had family in the business, I got a bit of a kickstart into dramatic films. It was a great help that I had some background from the first film jobs. That's how I got into film. As to the specific jobs, that's a long boring story.

How did you get the job of production assistant on *Escape From New York*?

I was friends with Jeffrey Chernov, the second assistant director, but it was Larry Franco, the producer and the 1st AD [Assistant Director], that gave me the shot. I will always be grateful to those two.

How did you collaborate with the cast and crew and what tasks did you do?

Everything. I prepared the initial call sheets and production reports, called actors to and from the set, set background action. I even doubled for Kurt on one night of second unit filming.

What kind of challenges did this project provide and which scenes or locations were the most challenging, problematic, memorable, and fun to work on?

It was tough but I loved it.

How was your experience working with the cast and crew?

I loved it.

L-R/FG: Jeffrey Chernov [Second Assistant Director],
Geoff Ryan [Production Assistant]
(Photo by/Courtesy Kim Gottlieb-Walker)

What's your favorite memory or memories of working on the movie?

Those are not memories for public consumption.

What do you think of the movie personally?

I always loved it.

What are you currently doing and what do you enjoy doing in your spare time?

Working on reshoots of the Nicholas Sparks movie *The Choice*. I play guitar and have written some songs.

DONALD P. BORCHERS
Avco Nominee

How did you end up being a production associate for Avco Embassy Pictures as well as a producer and director?

I went to the University of Notre Dame. At school, my junior year summer job was working as a tour escort on the beaches of Hawaii for Cartan Travel, a wholly owned subsidiary of Carte Blanche credit card company. The VP I reported to was Robert C. Aagard. I graduated from Notre Dame one semester early, so while my classmates were completing their last semester, I was applying to grad schools. After eight months in Hawaii doing five island tours, I enrolled at USC to obtain my MFA [Master in Fine Arts] in film. I settled in on campus attending my first lecture. About a half hour or so into the lecture, I was confused. It was a simple confusion. I raised my hand. The professor told me to put my hand down. I didn't. He said I could ask questions to teaching assistants at scheduled tutorials. I kept my hand raised. He then asked me what it is that I didn't understand. I said I didn't understand why he spent more time explaining why he won't answer my question than it would have taken him to actually answer my question. He still didn't want to hear what my question was. That bothered me, so I explained to him that I took a full-time job and worked for eight months to pay cash for my tuition for this semester. He then suggested that I could get a full refund from the registrar, so I walked out of class and did.

Ironically, six years later I became an adjunct professor, teaching budgeting and scheduling in the Peter Stark Producing Program at the same school. Then I called Robert C. Aagard, who I knew to have transferred jobs from Cartan in Chicago to Carte Blanche in Los Angeles. I met with him in search of employment. Bob was a great guy. In Chicago, he lived on an old speakeasy. It still had the underground tunnels. In L.A., he had an equally funky place in Silver Lake. Bob didn't like the rush hour traffic and always enjoyed a cocktail, so he spent time after work in the lobby bar. The building was a double high-rise on South Wilshire, a few blocks west of the Ambassador Hotel [where [John F.] Kennedy got shot]. It was mostly occupied by companies owned by The Aviation Company [Avco]. Carte Blanche was wholly owned by Avco. Also officed in the building was Avco Embassy Pictures. A couple years earlier, Joseph E. Levine had sold his Embassy Pictures to Avco. After I called Bob, we met after work at his lobby bar. He sometimes would play the bar game using dollar bill serial numbers with the treasurer of Avco Embassy Pictures, Roger Burlage. Having been to such establishments in my life, I knew to keep dollar bills that had strings of the same number. I played this game with Bob and Roger and made a few bucks that night. While Bob said he would find something for me ASAP, to make sure I could keep food on the table Roger suggested that I take a job as a junior accountant, preparing outside producers' profit participation statements. I presented myself to work each day with a proper dress shirt and a very skinny black tie. I wore my shirt unbuttoned at the top two buttons and the tie was tied at the third button. Definitely a "look." I lived in Hollywood. I was going for a "look."

After about four or five months, there Debra Hill [Producer] came in to complain to Roger Burlage that she did NOT need to pay for an accountant out of her budget for *The Fog*. She explained that she had produced *Halloween* with no accountant. She had a checkbook. When people needed to buy things, she wrote a check. Roger was explaining to Debra that, as the treasurer of the company, he was going to make his opinion clear to Bill Chaikin that Avco Embassy should NOT finance this picture without an accountant. Debra looked away to regroup for her next offensive and saw me sitting there separated, in her eye, from a group of accountants because of my then sense of fashion. And, believe it or not, like the title sequence for Marlo Thomas' *That Girl Debra*, pointed at ME to Roger and said, "Okay, if it's THAT accountant. He looks like he could fit in with us." And just like that I was the production accountant on *The Fog*, but that's another story.

A fond memory I will share before moving on. Debra Hill didn't pay for dedicated drivers. Trucks were driven by someone from the department that used the truck. She took turns with her AP [Associate Producer] and others to pick up and drop off the actors at the airport. One day she asked me to pick up Janet Leigh from SFO [San Francisco International Airport]. On the day, twenty-two year old me had never seen a Janet Leigh movie. Suffice it to say, she was pretty upset with me after waiting thirty minutes and getting paged over the intercom by me to connect at SFO. I opened the front car door and she walked right by to sit in the back of a compact car. Yup, she was pissed. After a few minutes, she needed a restroom. I followed her instincts, "Exit here. There's a Baskin & Robbins there." I parked. Did you know Baskin & Robbins doesn't really have a public restroom? Janet and I found out by experience. However, I needed to make points. I proclaimed that the famous screen star Janet Leigh was in their presence and if their employee restroom was clean, she would be availed to put it to good use. When we returned to the car, she sat in the front seat but was still silent. The move must have been more for leg space. Hmm. How could I be forgiven? I remembered from my Cartan tour days how much I loved to eat shrimp cocktail and drink Olympia Beer at Fisherman's Wharf so, without asking, I just drove us both there and parked. I left the motor running and said I needed to run a quick errand and would be back in a few minutes. I went off and came back with two fresh shrimp cocktails and two cold Oly's. Her face beamed. We got out of the car and had our first conversation. She talked about working with [Alfred] Hitchcock.

In high school, I joined Junior Achievement. Through JA [Junior Achievement], I produced an on-air radio show on Sunday mornings at WLIR in Long Island, NY. Through JA, I participated in a fundraising skit for donors at the Waldorf Astoria. It was produced by an off-Broadway producer. The more I learned about her job, the more I wanted that for my career. At Notre Dame, I enrolled with the focus of being a movie producer. I graduated with a BBA [Bachelor of Business Administration] in business administration with a major in finance and a minor in theater arts. When I worked for Cartan Travel, I met Bill Busse [Busse Bread, South Bend, IN]. Bill and I were having a conversation at dinner over a glass of wine in early 1978 at the Kauai Surf. He's many, many years older than me and, on this night, his words spoke wisdom to me. He was ruminating about the lack of fairness in the world. The absence of justice and the example was white privilege. Somewhere in his pontification I heard that "A young white man has an advantage over the rest of the world. A young white man can report to a master of his craft and volunteer to work for free for six months and the master will teach his craft in return."

On *Vice Squad* I met the late, great Sandy Howard. I made him what I like to think of as the Bill Busse offer. Sandy agreed and let me work on his desk for free for six months. After that, I got paid to be associate producer on location in Mexico for *Triumphs of a Man Called Horse*. From there, Roger Burlage hired me to run production for New World [Pictures]. After I produced *Angel* and *Children of the Corn* as an in-house VP, it was decided that I have a separate production company. In 1984, I started Planet Productions Corp. [which I ultimately wound down in 2012]. Through Planet, I produced three more movies for New World. Then they brought in Steve White and the first thing he did, no surprise here was clean house.

I wanted to own my own movie. I chose *Grave Secrets*. My business plan was to make a scary Halloween movie that was intentionally not R-rated, so grown-ups could have a Halloween experience at the movies. Since I financed it myself, money was tight. Basically, I took on multiple jobs including director to save the cost of labor. All the accredited producers worked for credit only.

How did you get the job of Avco Nominee on *Escape From New York*, how involved were you in the production and what exactly did you do?

By this time, as an executive at Avco, I had developed a working relationship with Lindsley Parsons Sr. He was the completion bond guarantor on *Escape From New York*. Avco had financed and distributed a few movies in between *The Fog* and *Escape From New York*. All productions now required that each check [written to pay the expenses of the production] must have three signatures. One each for the producer, the completion bond representative, and a representative from Avco. In contract negotiations, Avco wanted to make it clear that the producer could not hire their cousin to be the representative from Avco. The producer was equally concerned that someone with an axe to grind against the producer was not chosen. The solution was that Avco would nominate this person and the producer would then approve it. Since it was left to the attorney drafting the PFD [Production/Finance/Distribution] agreement, the person nominated by Avco was referred to in the agreement as the "Avco Nominee."

After the production, I left Avco to work on *An Eye for an Eye* as a second assistant director. I thought it would help my resume to get a screen credit on *Escape From New York*. Debra Hill had me speak to Larry Franco [Producer/First Assistant Director]. Larry and John [Carpenter] were taking their very first steps to move on without Debra. I asked Larry to give me a screen credit, but there was no legal obligation for me to receive credit. Larry said he thought he could make that happen, so I asked for a credit as Production Associate. He gave me credit as Avco Nominee. Lindsley Parsons Sr. and Avco had me do this on both *The Howling* and *Vice Squad*, but this time I negotiated upfront for onscreen credit and as production associate. I signed each and every check on behalf of both the completion bond company and the distributor/financier. I read daily call sheets and production reports to monitor the "on schedule" status. When status fell behind, I would discuss catch-up strategies with Debra Hill, which were mostly me listening and reporting back to my two bosses. And I would read script supervisor reports and attend dailies screenings to compare. There were no variances.

Were there any issues between Avco Embassy and the production company?

Not really. The Avco financing formula worked like this. Have each sales team estimate best case, worst case, and most probable case. Sales teams would be domestic theatrical, foreign sub-distribution, and ancillary. Using this forecast, deduct average distribution costs for this size picture then deduct ten percent as a contingency for future unknown expenses. The number that's left is the approved budget at Avco. I think of it as the Roger Burlage formula. The question at the time, as I recall it, was not did Avco approve Debra Hill's budget but rather, could John Carpenter make a movie for this? Well, that's how *Halloween* got made. They knew the budget first. As I recall, John brought Nick Castle [Co-Writer] back after they knew Avco's number and there was a further script revision that, amongst other things, addressed any budget issues. On the day, I recall Embassy Pictures was being groomed for sale by the parent corporation who wanted to divest. They understood that the company would have far less value if it wasn't currently active and profitable. To that end, the ongoing business plan was to use the Roger Burlage financing formula and to submit the new project, genre, track record of director, writer[s], producer[s], and star[s] and then, on a case-by-case basis, the parent company would finance or not. Joan Rivers' *Rabbit Test* was also financed for distribution in this fashion.

Was anything too costly to pull off?

Yes, there was a small plane needed for use. Debra Hill had calculated that the cost of buying and selling would save thousands from the rental price budgeted. I pointed out that there was no capital expense provided for in the cash flow with a subsequent credit for sales of merchandise to be taken in the future to net out the capital cost. Debra got really, really mad at me and rented the plane.

Did anything go over budget?

Nothing went over budget. That was really my principal responsibility.

Did you have to negotiate with any of the actors? There was an actor strike going on at the time and a settlement between the production company and extras regarding low wages that had to be accommodated for instance.

I have no recollection. Regarding extras, in the year of production, the SAG basic agreement did NOT cover extras or bits. Our production manager, Alan

Levine, was very savvy. For the crowd sequences, he did deals with organizations who provided their members. Low wages? This type of trade is NO wages. Not low wages. I can't recall how the non-crowd extras were cast and paid. I have no recollection of an actors strike.

Is it true that was the largest budget Avco had provided for a movie at the time?

Everyone who worked for Bill Chaikin was inherited from Joe Levine, so not for them, but for Bob Rehme and his new tenure, yes.

What kind of challenges did this project provide and which scenes or locations were the most challenging, problematic, memorable, and fun to work on?

The opening sequence [deleted] was originally a chase in the underground metros. A travel unit was calendared to shoot this in Atlanta. On the day, the Steadicam [Panaglide] was lost in transit. John Carpenter had to abandon the storyboards and re-design coverage on sticks.

How was your experience working with Avco Embassy, Robert Rheme [Former President of Avco Embassy], and Debra Hill [Producer], etcetera?

At Avco, an entry level person needs an opportunity. I was entry level, so this was my opportunity. I made the most of it, then moved on. On *The Howling*, we shot on location. To save money, Mike Finnell doubled up the crew in hotel rooms. He intentionally doubled himself to lead by example [and save money]. I was doubled with Finnell. He noticed that I had lots of free time, so I drove the car for the second unit driving sequences.

Bob Rheme was singularly the least impressive movie executive I have ever met in the business. We all used to joke about him being in the "clean desk" club. You see, most of us at the time had a bunch of piles of papers for different things in progress. Not Bob. He delegated everything important, then spent his time micromanaging details that most CEO's [Chief Executive Officer] would delegate.

After my high school experience, Debra was my second producing mentor. Debra taught me how to physically produce a film. Perhaps if I knew more going in, I could have learned more. An empty mind can only be filled so fast. On *Escape From New York*, I was kind of stapled on to Debra Hill.

James Cameron [Director of Photography/Matte Artwork: Special Visual Effects] was running Roger Corman's special effects shop on this show. Their "stage" was in a converted industrial space with LOW ceilings.

How involved was Avco Embassy in the production?

Not really at all.

How was Debra Hill as a person and do you have any other fond memories of her you'd like to share with us?

A real down-to-earth normal human being. After the *The Fog* had wrapped but before *Escape* started, Debra Hill hired me freelance to do the full charge bookkeeping for Hilltopper Productions, the company that she owned with John Carpenter. At the time, she was living in a split-level single on Hilltop Drive in Hollywood with an awesome scenic view. She shared the place with a record executive named Michael Arciega. I would later hire Michael to package the licensed songs for my movie *Angel*. At the time, I did the books on her living room couch table. I sat on the floor, so I didn't ruin my back pasture by sitting on the couch. I recall one day in particular, after I had put in a few hours work and Debra returned from running some errands, that I suggested she could do well to invest in a housekeeper. She then began a tirade of teasers and taunts at me regarding my standards of cleanliness and such. She started to say over and over again, "Donald Borchers thinks his shit doesn't stink." You probably had to be there, but it was pretty fuckin' funny at the time.

On one afternoon in the office of Roger Mayer at MGM laboratories, I learned more things that would be helpful in my future than I even realized. John Carpenter had a relationship with MGM labs and on behalf of New World. I had just negotiated an exclusive distribution deal with CFI [Consolidated Film Industries] labs for release prints with no guarantee of upfront lab work. John negotiated for the upfront lab work for *The Fog* to be done at MGM. On the day, Debra took all of the unpaid bills, the checkbook, and me as the second check signer, renegotiated the outstanding balance with Roger Mayer, and paid in full by check on the spot. The outstanding balance was tens of thousands of dollars and she got more than twenty percent knocked off. Brilliant! Discounts can be negotiated and taken after the fact for the promise of immediate payment of cash. Did you know that cash flow mismanagement is the principal cause of small business failure?

When I worked on *The Fog*, I was rewarded by being allowed to observe John Carpenter and Tommy Lee Wallace in the editing room. The price I paid was doing the munchies runs to 7-Eleven and such. Both John and Debra liked to drink cola soft drinks, but here's the thing. John only drank Pepsi and Debra only drank Coke. No compromise. Both had to be purchased.

Debra had the unlisted phone number for Ma Maison [Wolfgang Puck was head chef]. When she heard my mother was coming to visit me, she insisted on making a luncheon reservation for us there. It was a brilliant day. Jack Lemmon was two tables over.

What's your favorite memory or memories of working on the movie?

The wrap party. Isaac Hayes [The Duke] performed. Also, the helicopters in in the streets of St. Louis in the middle of the night was pretty awesome.

What do you think of the movie personally?

Love and adoration.

Was Avco Embassy surprised that this movie became a modest box office hit?

Not in the least. *Halloween* was monster and *The Fog* was huge for us. Our foreign sales team was excellent and so were their sales numbers. If the film was never released theatrically, we had profit and on the day, it was more than rare when a theatrical release didn't make P&A [Purchase and Assumption] back. This film had provenance that would guarantee disaster would never occur.

What are you currently doing and what do you enjoy doing in your spare time?

I own the *Children of the Corn* IP [Intellectual Property]. I bought it out a few years ago. The Argentine tango, which is on hold for at least one more year due to Covid and writing. In 2020, I have completed two spec [speculative] screenplays, an action comedy and a crime drama, which I plan on bringing to the market after the holiday season.

MARIO SIMON
Driver

How did you end up being a driver/transportation captain/coordinator?

I did a small movie in my local neighborhood that needed someone to handle picture cars, some stunt work, and work on the engines. I started to build a reputation after that. I did picture cars and drove anything they asked me to. I eventually was in charge of transportation at MGM and also Disney, then just ventured off on my own as a driver/captain/coordinator.

How did you get the job of driver on *Escape From New York*?

I bumped into Tom Thomas [Transportation Captain] and Eddie Lee [Voelker] [Transportation Coordinator] and he said he was looking for driver/mechanics for picture cars.

How did you and drivers Joe Benet, Bobby Benton, Rod Berg, Steve Boyd, Mike Connolly, Chuck Hauer, Dick Lee, Wayne Roberts, Wayne Williams, Eddie Worth, as well as Tom Thomas [Transportation Captain] and Eddie Lee Voelker [Transportation Coordinator] prepare for this project and how did you collaborate?

I also drove a ten ton, but I was mainly the mechanic on the picture cars to keep them running. Specifically, the Cadillac and the taxi.

Is it true that you are the owner and designer of the Duke's [Isaac Hayes] 1977 Cadillac Fleetwood Brougham? If so, how did you come up with the design, why was a 1977 Cadillac Fleetwood Brougham chosen for the movie, where did you obtain it, how long did it take to construct and were more than one Cadillac used?

Yes, I was the owner of the Cadillac and helped Roy Arbogast [Special Effects Supervisor] on some of the design. I purchased the car in Hollywood and bought it specifically for the film. We actually had two Cadillacs. As I remember, it took about four weeks to get both cars identical in things such as paint, interior, and design.

Is it true that you, Isaac Hayes, and Debra Hill [Producer] were sent to Detroit, Chicago, Pittsburg, Washington, New York, and St. Louis on a publicity tour in the Cadillac? If so, who came up with this idea and how was this experience?

Yes. I went on tour with both Isaac and Debra. The publicity tour was great and a lot of fun. It was organized by the marketing department. The only issue was keeping Kurt and Isaac out of sight from fans and autograph hounds. Ha, ha. But I mostly spent my time working on the car and keeping it in mechanical shape.

Is it true that the Cadillac was parked illegally outside the premiere party at the New York, New York club and got a ticket?

Yes. The car did get a ticket. Ha, ha.

How was your experience working with the cast and crew?

Great people. I went on to work with Debra on later films. I went on to work with Debra, John Carpenter, Eddie Lee, Dick Warlock [Stunt Coordinator/Stunts], Tom Thomas, and others later on. Back then, you developed business relationships. If you did a good job, they would take you on to the next show! I had a great time, but again, being new, I kept my nose to the grindstone and wasn't completely aware of what was going on around the production.

What happened to the Cadillacs after the publicity tour and is it true that Isaac Hayes wanted to buy it?

The second car was just a mock-up they used on stage. After the production ended, I kept the car for about a year. It was just sitting and rotting. I eventually sold it to another movie company, but the name escapes me.

What's your favorite memory or memories of working on the movie?

My favorite memory working on the movie was visiting Washington, DC with Debra Hill and Isaac Hayes as we attended a Motown show with many of the current popular acts at the time.

What do you think of the movie personally?

I thought the movie was good. I actually very rarely watch movies. I think this one would be great as a remake considering the condition of our nation today in the U.S.

What are you currently doing and what do you enjoy doing in your spare time?

Right now, I am just trying to maintain my health after forty-five years in the business of long hours, no sleep, and bad eating. Ha, ha! But I had so much fun and made great friendships. In my spare time, I always have a vintage Hot Rod to work on. Sadly, I'm losing my eyesight. I cannot do much of that anymore but I'm waiting for that person to create a bionic eye!

SHARON TUCCI
TalentPlus: Extra Casting [St. Louis]

How did you end up being the founder of TalentPlus?

I transitioned from in front of the camera to behind the scenes in 1977. My curiosity led me to become the 1st AFTRA [American Federation of Television and Radio Artists]/SAG agent in St. Louis.

How did you get the job of St. Louis extra casting agency on *Escape From New York*?

Reputation, I hope.

How did you prepare for this project and how did you collaborate with Pegi Brotman [Casting] and Jeffrey Chernov [Second Assistant Director]? Is it true that around 600 people auditioned and that 150 extras were chosen [30 Gypsies, 28 Broadways and 55 Prisoners]?

At least that many people showed up at my studio. Lots of bikers with tattoos and chains. They bragged about their prison records and hoped that would give them entitlements. And it did!

How was your experience working with the cast and crew?

It was super fun. My first experience with a major production. Since it was shot during the night, I was able to spend more time on set.

Did any extras stand out? Such as Al Coleman being Isaac Hayes' [The Duke] body double. I know St. Louis Post-Dispatch writer Jeff Meyers was also cast as a Crazy.

Al Coleman looked amazing as his body double and he lived that dream and told stories for many years afterwards.

What's your favorite memory or memories of working on the movie?

The fighting scene in the boxing ring with all the prison crazies surrounding [Grand Central Station] [St. Louis Union Station], it was the highlight. The green rooms had dozens of trash can lids filled with look-alike dirt for the extras who lived in the sewer systems to smear on their faces. I could only recognize them by their teeth when they smiled. I was on set quite a bit since it shot at night. The sets were pretty interesting.

What do you think of the movie personally?

When it came out, I was excited with the finished product and was amazed at the locations. St. Louis did a great job posing as Manhattan prison.

What are you currently doing and what do you enjoy doing in your spare time?

I am still agenting. Spare time? Doing some traveling but always scouting for the next new star.

R.J. KIZER
Project Supervisor: Special Visual Effects

How did you end up working for Roger Corman early on in your career?

I was first hired by Roger Corman at the recommendation of Mary Ann Fisher [Producer/Liaison: Special Visual Effects] [whom I had met at a party hosted by one of my NYU classmates in Venice, California] in May of 1979 to do a recut on a monster fish movie that was filmed in the Philippines by Charles B. Griffith and produced by Cirio Santiago. Corman was the overall producer. He and Griffith were having some kind of argument over the final cut of the film, so I was hired to work directly with Corman and do Corman's cut of the film [which was the cut released to the theaters]. I wound up getting hired as second film editor for *Battle Beyond the Stars* and, during the troubled post-production of that film, I got to know many of the visual effects people. When *Escape From New York* happened Jim Cameron [Director of Photography/Matte Artwork: Special Visual Effects] was the person who had the original contact with Joe Alves, the production designer. Jim then set about convincing Roger and Mary Ann that effects crew from *Battle Beyond the Stars* should do the job because there wasn't any work on the immediate horizon coming from Corman. But we did know that there was a film called *Planet of Horrors* [filmed under the title *Quest*, test screened as *Planet of Horrors*, initially released as *Mindwarp: An Infinity of Terror*, retitled *Planet of Horrors* and finally released as *Galaxy of Terror*] that might be happening sometime in 1981. *Escape From New York* was perfect for keeping the "old gang" together and employed until then.

How did you get the job of project supervisor of special visual effects on *Escape From New York*?

Though Jim Cameron was the person who was the original contact between *Escape From New York* and New World, Jim was not a very good "company man." Both Roger and Mary Ann wanted someone else, someone they felt who would mind the budget and the schedule. Chuck Comisky was the original supervisor of the effects department for *Battle Beyond the Stars*, but once that project was

R.J. Kizer [Project Supervisor: Special Visual Effects]
(Photo Courtesy R.J. Kizer)
(Publisher's Note: The blurriness is inherent in the image.)

over, he lit out for greener pastures. All the other key personnel had objections with one another, so I was put forward as a compromise candidate and that was acceptable to all the parties. That's how I got the position.

How did you, Mary Ann Fisher [Producer/Liaison: Special Visual Effects], and Aaron Lipstadt [Associate Producer: Special Visual Effects] prepare for this project and how did you collaborate?

We did not have a strong hierarchical management structure. Mary Ann was in charge of managing New World's [Pictures] Venice facility/studio. She was in charge of the negotiations to lock down the contract with John Carpenter's company, Slam Dunk Productions. Once that was achieved, the administration of that contract was left to Aaron Lipstadt and myself. She was not involved in much of the day-to-day activities. Aaron was the link between myself and Mary

Ann. I was in charge of managing the day-to-day activities of the units creating the various special visual effects for *Escape From New York* [creating schedules, adjusting personnel to meet workload requirements, coordinating operations between different units, leading discussions on how best to achieve certain shots]. Aaron would handle the administrative roles of payroll and general property operations and make sure we were adhering to the general shape of the contract. But it was all very loose. Aaron and I were in the same office room along with the project bookkeeper and scheduler. Everything was very informal. Aaron would be present for any of the shot design discussions and sometimes Mary Ann would be present as well. It all depended on her schedule, but she did not want us to wait for her availability. Aaron would update Mary Ann on the status of things with respect to *Escape From New York* and she would report to Roger Corman [who owned the company].

I remember there were days when there wasn't much for me to do. Once everyone had their marching orders, they were busy executing them. I would lend a hand to them whenever needed. Basically, my job was to make sure work was getting done and to liaison with John Carpenter and the film editor. What sold Carpenter on using New World was Jim's proposal to use 70mm front screen projection background plates with anamorphic 35mm cinematography. Having done that, we now had to build a very large front screen made from the Scotchlite material, construct a 70mm process projector, and line up a movie lab to process the 65mm negative and make fine grain 70mm positives. The screen we finally managed to build hid enough of the seams to get by. The projector was Austin McKinney's [Director of Photography: Special Visual Effects] project. He found a 70mm movement and a chassis and, using C-clamps and 2" x 4" pieces of wood, managed to jerry-rig a perfectly operational projector. The lab was Metrocolor on the MGM lot. Luckily, one of MGM's screening rooms could run 70mm, so that became our screening room for checking out our 70mm prints. All the work down at the New World effects facility used the cover title "Prisoner of Venice."

The work occurred between late July and early December of 1980. The Screen Actors Guild went on strike starting July 21 and ending October 23 of 1980 [94 days. Their second longest strike so far]. This strike shut down the entire motion picture and television industry in Los Angeles. Film laboratories were operating only two days out of the week. Because New World had landed the *Escape From New York* project, it was one of the only effects houses actually working during the time of the strike. This generated a lot of resentment among the visual effects community. New World's work on *Escape From New York* was for twenty-one weeks. It started on July 28 and ended December 19, 1980. There were twenty-two shots contracted.

What kind of challenges did this project provide and which visual effects, scenes or locations were the most challenging, problematic, memorable, and fun to work on?

From August 7 through August 11, Jim Cameron, Randy Frakes [Camera Assistant: Special Visual Effects] and myself went to New York City to take reference photographs. We went with both a 35mm SLR [Single-Lens Reflex camera] and a rented 5" x 4" negative Speed Graphic camera [the kind that newspaper photographers used in the early twentieth century]. We might have also had a 2" x 2" negative camera, but I can no longer remember. We barely got hotel space for Jim and Randy because the Democratic National Convention was happening between August 11 and 14. I crashed at a friend's apartment in Manhattan. I do remember that we were on a very tight budget. We had very little spending cash. I also remember that we missed our original outgoing flight because Randy was late getting to the airport. We found another flight on another airline, but it might hauling our gear and luggage several terminals away. In New York, our task was to take photographs for the Central Park shot, reference photos of the World Trade Center, reference photos looking out from the rooftop of the WTC and reference photos of the Brooklyn Bridge. The large-format camera obtained fine grain images suitable for significant enlargement.

On top of the World Trade Center, we were confronted by Port Authority representatives who demanded to see our shooting permits. They claimed that the view from the observation deck was copyrighted by the Port Authority of New York and New Jersey [the owners of the World Trade Center]. This controversy was triggered because we had the Speed Graphic camera on a very solid, professional tripod. Clearly, we were not tourists taking holiday snapshots. I kept the guard occupied with a cock and bull story of our being art students at Cooper Union, that the large camera was taking a slide for us to project on the large wall of the auditorium as a guide for our proposed mural showing New York City after it had been abandoned by humanity sometime in the dim, dim future. Jim was quickly and quietly taking as many photographs as he could. Eventually the guard got too suspicious of my story and ordered us off the observation deck. Luckily, we had taken a good amount of large-format photos. Prior to the guard's arrival, I had taken some general reference photos with my 35mm SLR camera. One thing we

L-R/BG: Jim Cameron [Director of Photography/Matte Artwork: Special Visual Effects], R.J. Kizer [Project Supervisor: Special Visual Effects], Ken Chase [Makeup Artist Supervisor]/FG: Unknown, Randy Frakes [Camera Assistant: Special Visual Effects], William Arance [Production Assistant: Special Visual Effects] [Uncredited], Austin McKinney [Director of Photography: Special Visual Effects] (Photo Courtesy Ken Hanis)

noticed as soon as we walked onto the observation deck of the WTC was that the whole premise of landing a glider on the rooftop was physically impossible. The North Tower had the huge TV and radio antenna on top of it. The South Tower [where the observation deck was] had a rooftop covered with air ducts and pipes and motors for air conditioning and elevators. Plus, there was the observation deck itself that went all around the South Tower. Well, it's only a movie.

How did you manage to create the visual effects on such a modest budget and is it true that John Dykstra who was approached prior to you and whose bid was too high consulted and provided you with ideas?

Not that I am aware of but Cameron was always going off the reservation, so he might have talked to Dykstra. Truthfully, it was the only way we knew how. We didn't have an optical effects shop, so all the techniques we employed were geared to multi-pass, original generation effects. We were more influenced by the Lydecker brothers and their work for Republic Pictures than by anyone else. We didn't have a proper matte painting department. While working on *Escape,* we were buying equipment from Doug Trumbull's operation which had just gone out of business.

How was your experience working with the rest of the New World Special Effects facility team such as Bob Skotak [Matte Artwork: Special Visual Effect] [Supervisor: Special Visual Effects] [Uncredited], Dennis Skotak [Director of Photography: Special Visual Effects] and Jim Cameron [Director of Photography/Matte Artwork: Special Visual Effects] for instance?

Working with Bob and Denny was always pleasant and interesting. Jim was challenging, but I felt he was the most creative of the bunch and had the best eye in terms of shot design. By the way, the facility was the old Hammond Lumber [Company] yard on Main Street in Venice, California, south of Rose Avenue and north of Abbot Kinney Boulevard. There's no trace of it left anymore.

What do you think about Jim Cameron getting too much credit on things he didn't do on this movie such as painting the Central Park/Manhattan skyline and being involved in the graphic displays miniatures/effects?

Of course, that is what everyone believes. Print the legend as the old saying goes. The images of the buildings are actually photos he took in Central Park in August of 1980. They were cut out and mounted on a sheet of glass. Our shot was not, strictly speaking, a matte painting. It was a glass shot, a much easier "sell." As the sun traveled across the sky, Jim would use a pencil to shade in shadows on the images to better match the shadows on the ground. For me, the New York lamp post in the foreground is what sold the image. I do remember that when we showed the daily of the finished shot to Carpenter and Todd Ramsay [Editor], they were ecstatic. It looked so convincing. Todd was especially happy and saying to us things like, "We would wait for months to get a matte painting out of Doug [Douglas] Trumbull [for *Star Trek: The Motion Picture*] and they never looked half as good as this!" The graphic displays were done by a completely different firm and we had no contact with them. That's why their wireframe display of New York does not match up with our miniature New York. They assumed the Snake Plissken glider was approaching the World Trade Center completely from the north. We mapped a route informed by my reading of the script as heading to New York over Liberty Island approaching the financial district from the south, turning westward [once well over the city] then turning southward towards the Towers.

What's your favorite memory or memories of working on the movie?

One of my favorite memories was when I went to a screening room in the Van Nuys area where Carpenter screened his dailies. I was there to show some completed shots and tests to Carpenter and company. One of the shots was a POV moving over New York harbor heading towards Battery Park at the southern tip of Manhattan. The first time the assembled looked at it, they loved it. "How did you do the water," they all wanted to know. I wouldn't tell them, but they kept after me. Dean Cundey, the DP [Director of Photography] kept suggesting all these different methods. I kept saying I didn't want to tell them. Finally, Carpenter demanded to know, so I told him, "We painted the water area glossy black and when the paint was tacky, we rolled a roller brush over it all to stipple the finish. As the camera moved over the area the stippled surface would reflect the back and side lights differently creating the illusion of moving water." This was a Skotak idea that they brilliantly executed. Carpenter then insisted on running the shot again. Now he was unhappy. He could see how the trick was done, but he honored his original response and did not say that we had to do the shot again. He "bought" the shot and we moved on. That experience fixed my mind to never tell the director how something was really and truly accomplished. Always make up something more involved and more complicated.

What do you think of the movie personally?

I was unhappy with the finished movie. First, I was flabbergasted that they dropped the whole opening scene of the robbery. Yes, it was too long, but it could have easily been trimmed and maybe incorporated into the opening titles. Overall, I found the pace of the film to be way too slow. It doesn't bother me so much now, but I do remember at the time that I was disappointed with the slow pace.

How come you wrote *Report on the Special Visual Effects in Escape From New York* for the Academy of Motion Picture Arts and Sciences?

The report is what the Academy requests from every show that is eligible to be considered for nomination. I don't know if what I submitted was what the Academy committee wanted, but we were chosen for the "bake off" screening, so I guess it came close enough. I remember with all the other films, there was a bit of discussion among the assembled. After our reel was screened, the silence was so thick you could cut it with a plastic knife. Remember, that summer-fall the town was crippled by the devastating SAG strike. All the effects houses lost work and money. Except New World. We were "shunned" by the community. Oh well. Only three films are nominated for the Academy Award and there were 12 films in contention. They were [in the running order for that bake off screening], *Dragonslayer, For Your Eyes Only, Raiders of the Lost Ark, Outland, The Great Muppet Caper, Clash of the Titans, Escape From New York, Superman II, The Incredible Shrinking Woman, Wolfen, History of the World-Part I,* and *Heartbeeps.* The screening occurred on the evening of February 2, 1982.

What are you currently doing and what do you enjoy doing in your spare time?

New World couldn't maintain its effects facility. It was largely employed doing visual effects for Corman movies and a few other independent films. By 1984 or 85, it was gone. The Skotaks opened their own facility. I believe it was called 4-Ward Productions. Cameron went on to direct and produce his own material. As for the others, I don't know where they went. By that time, I was chasing work elsewhere. Nowadays I'm working mostly as an ADR [Automatic Dialogue Replacement] editor. I was admitted to the sound branch of the motion picture academy in 2008.

BRIAN CHIN
Miniature Construction

How did you end up working for Roger Corman early on in your career?

An FX team that worked on a Filmation live action TV series formed the beginnings of Roger Corman's FX studio for his proposed *Battle Beyond the Stars*. I had contacted them earlier, but they were not immediately hiring. Several months later I called again, and a very commercial DJ voice answered the phone. This was Budd Lewis, a famous comic book writer who was doing storyboards on the Corman project. He was extremely positive and said I should come down and join the gang in the Valley. "Yeah, we have the Skotaks." Budd Lewis said. Bob Skotak [Matte Artwork: Special Visual Effects] [Supervisor: Special Visual Effects] [Uncredited] and Dennis Skotak [Director of Photography: Special Visual Effects]. "They're 60s radicals who've mellowed out." I had read about the Skotaks when they had crew-cuts in fan publications and decided to pack up the car and move to Los Angeles like the *Beverly Hillbillies*. I settled in with a writer friend who worked for Disney and went over to this little studio in a corrugated tin shed. There I met the Skotaks, Budd Lewis, and several others who were the founding members of the Corman FX facility. They convinced their boss to hire me and within days I was working for $250 a week and my association with the studio lasted till it closed.

How did you get the job of miniature effects supervisor on *Escape From New York*?

When *Battle Beyond the Stars* finished, Corman had an existing FX crew, motion control system, and model shop slated for upcoming New World productions. In the meantime, a few projects were brought in from outside, mainly *Escape From New York*.

How did you prepare for this project?

I was asked to get the required models built on a six-week schedule. With me was Tom Campbell [Engineer: Special Visual Effects], who would do all the electrical and mechanical work on the miniatures. And because of the short schedule, two more builders were hired. Gene Rizzardi [Miniature Construction] [Uncredited] and Bruce MacRae [Miniature Construction] [Uncredited].

How was the Manhattan miniature model constructed and how did you, Bob Skotak [Matte Artwork: Special Visual Effects] [Supervisor: Special Visual Effects] [Uncredited], Dennis Skotak [Director of Photography: Special Visual Effects], Steve Caldwell [Camera Assistant: Special Visual Effects] and Tom Campbell [Engineer: Special Visual Effects] collaborate?

The Corman group provided shots from the viewpoint of a glider flying over Manhattan with its streets and buildings. The miniature was set up on the concrete floor of the FX stage and filmed by the Skotak unit. Several of us worked on the little buildings and I contributed a number of them. They were roughly constructed from scrap cardboard and existing boxes. Photo books of Manhattan architecture provided much of the window patterns and textures, which were photocopies pasted onto the blank cardboard boxes and quickly toned with color pencils. Balsa and cardboard strips simulated the mid-century columns and cornice detail on many of the buildings. One of the more difficult structures to quickly recreate was the circular fort at Battery Park at the southern tip of Manhattan. The glider passes over this recognizable area of the island, so it had to be done right.

Is it true that, in order to make an accurate Manhattan, you photographed a map of it and projected the negative in a slide projector on a wall and made the foundation out of plywood? Also, is it true that you hand-colored black and white Xeroxes and put them on some of the buildings due to the lack of color photos?

The base of the miniature Manhattan were large pieces of plywood cut to shape and laid out on the concrete floor of the shooting stage. I do not recall if a map projection was used in cutting out the plywood contours since the FX crew did their own miniature work on the shot and built much of the buildings themselves. I did join in and worked on a fair number of the buildings, especially the early 20th Century ones with their columns and cornices and the ring-shaped fort at Battery Park, which was not so easy to make. Using black and white Xeroxes colored with crayon for the window and surface detail was a conscious choice and not because we lacked color photos.

L-R/BG/Stairs/Row 1: Sara Nelson [Production Accountant: Special Visual Effects], Tom Campbell [Engineer: Special Visual Effects], Dr. Ken Jones [Elicon Camera operator: Special Visual Effects], Steve Caldwell [Camera Assistant: Special Visual Effects], Anthony Randel [Lab Liaison: Special Visual Effects]/BG/Stairs/Row 2: William Arance [Production Assistant: Special Visual Effects] [Uncredited], Robin Thomas [Production Secretary: Special Visual Effects], George Dodge [Director of Photography: Special Visual Effects]/BG/Stairs/Row 3: Gary Wagner [Gaffer: Special Visual Effects], Phil Thomas Jr. [Production Assistant: Special Visual Effects] [Uncredited], Brian Chin [Miniature Construction]/FG/Ground/Row 1: R.J. Kizer [Project Supervisor: Special Visual Effects], Steve Elliott [Rotoscope/Elicon Camera Operator: Special Visual Effects], Charles Skouras III [Production Manager: Special Visual Effects], Austin McKinney [Director of Photography: Special Visual Effects], Aaron Lipstadt [Associate Producer: Special Visual Effects], Stephen Barncard [Motion Control Designer: Special Visual Effects]/FG/Ground/Row 2: Mary Ann Fisher [Producer/Liaison: Special Visual Effects], Julia Gibson [Elicon Camera Operator: Special Visual Effects], Dennis Skotak [Director of Photography: Special Visual Effects], Bob Skotak [Matte Artwork: Special Visual Effects] [Supervisor: Special Visual Effects] [Uncredited] (Photo by/Courtesy Kim Gottlieb-Walker)

215

Top and Bottom: The Manhattan Miniature Model
(Photos Courtesy Bruce MacRae)

From photographic books on NYC architecture and from our own hand drawn images, we created a variety of window patterns photocopied on plain paper then cut and pasted onto the paper boxes, which were our buildings. If we tried using color photos as some suggested, we might have had a glare problem and glue problem with thick photo paper. So doing it the simple way is usually better especially as the Manhattan miniature was a night shot.

How was the Jet Bell Ranger miniature constructed and how come you chose Gene Rizzardi [Miniature Construction] to build the Air Force One and Gliders, Tom Campbell to build the Huey helicopter and you to build the Jet Bell Ranger?

The Huey helicopter was adapted easily from a large plastic model kit. Tom Campbell put in the working blades and searchlights. The Bell Jet Ranger was another matter. The model kits of this helicopter then were too small for our purposes, so I scratch built a fiberglass model about twenty inches long. Some of the detail parts like the skids came from the Huey helicopter kit. Tom Campbell installed working rotors and searchlights.

For Air Force One, we bought a travel agency display model Boeing 737, gave it a 50s rudder and a stubby fuselage to match previously filmed live-action footage. Only the side facing the camera was detailed and painted, especially around the presidential seal as the camera pushes in on it. We found a seal from a book in the Santa Monica Library and turned it into a decal to stick on the plane. Tom Campbell rigged up the flashing position lights and the bright interior lights blazing through the cockpit and side windows. Those interior lights had to be so bright. It was hard preventing light leaks through the paint job as the camera pushed in real close on the miniature.

For the glider landing scene atop the World Trade Center, a local hobby shop had exactly what was needed: a flying scale model in foam of the real thing in kit form with an eight-foot wingspan. Wingtip skids were added to match the real live-action glider. The concrete foundation of a yet-to-be constructed sound stage was decked out with appropriate miniatures to represent the rooftop of the World Trade Center and the large glider model was flown in on invisible wires in a very convincing effect. A second glider model was built for the shots using motion control. Gene Rizzardi and Bruce MacRae worked on this scratch-built resin cast model, which had about an eighteen inch wingspan. One time the motion control camera ran amuck and pushed in inexorably on the fragile resin glider mounted on its support pylon. The programmer typed more commands to stop it, but the camera came closer and closer until finally it pressed up against the delicate model, splitting open the spindly resin fuselage. Luckily, the damage was not as bad as it appeared and the model was repaired. The third model of the glider was a tiny balsawood miniature with a wingspan no more than four inches long. This was used for a straight down shot as the glider teeters over the edge of the WTC roof.

What kind of challenges did this project provide and how long did the models take to make?

The challenge was providing realistic camera-ready models that looked like their true-life prototypes. Several models required silicon molds and resin casting. An exacting process that had to work perfectly the first time on our limited six-week model budget. Fortunately, all was built and camera-ready on time.

How was your experience working with the New World Pictures special visual effects facility team?

I enjoyed my time at New World Pictures FX. The crew started together on *Battle Beyond the Stars* and continued through several years with the projects getting smaller over time till eventually everyone was gone on other endeavors and all that was left was the motion control track and the studio that was built from an old lumber yard. The FX crew was a colorful eclectic bunch, much interested in filmmaking with a cynical delight for low-budget exploitation cinema. In that regard, *Escape From New York* might be considered a cut above the sort of projects we would normally have done.

What's your favorite memory or memories of working on the movie?

The time we worked on *Escape From New York* was relatively short. The three FX units did their assigned shots, the model shop provided miniatures, and the administrative staff coordinated activities. The studio was quiet and orderly. Once an attorney came to take my deposition in an unrelated court case. The lawyer looked a bit bewildered standing there in his three-piece suit with briefing books under arms as this big robotic camera crane did its motion control maneuver around him. Finally, we were invited to the *Escape From New*

York cast and crew screening seven months later. The program folder was white with gold print with all our names printed just as they appear on the credits.

What happened to the models after the movie was finished?

When FX production wrapped up Corman came down to the studio and saw the Manhattan miniature being demolished. "I want every little bit of this to be saved." he told the studio manager. "We can reuse it for our own productions." As Corman was saying this, the crew pushed brooms across the Manhattan miniature, sweeping buildings, landscaping and accumulated dust to throw in the garbage. Except for a few of the exceptional buildings, the Manhattan model disappeared with the end of production despite myriad claims of original models on the internet.

As for the helicopters, about five years after the production I saw my rubber molds of the Jet Ranger at another FX shop, probably acquired with the closure of Corman's studio.

I have seen internet photos of that Air Force One model. I don't know who owns it now, but the plane's nose is not the original one from the film. I had the original nose and kept it in my toolbox for years after the production.

What do you think of the movie personally?

It is a good movie and I don't mind saying I worked on it.

What are you currently doing and what do you enjoy doing in your spare time?

As the projects at Corman's FX studio got progressively smaller, I began the transition to art and storyboard work for the television animation studios, which abounded in Los Angeles. Aside from a few live-action movie storyboards, TV animation composed the rest of my career in Los Angeles. Today I am retired and have a collection of plastic model airplanes and tanks that I expect to build someday.

TOM CAMPBELL
Engineer: Special Visual Effects

How did you end up working for Roger Corman early on in your career?

High school graduation in Indiana came just when the Vietnam War was ramping up. It was a very stressful time waiting for your draft number. I shocked my parents one day coming home to tell them I'd signed up for three years in the Marines. I just wanted to get it over and on with life. I learned much over there and returned with the G.I. Bill [Servicemen's Readjustment Act of 1944] allowing for some schooling, which was my opportunity to "Go West, young man." Two years in motorcycle school followed by jobs in a number of shops. Roger had purchased the Hammond Lumber [Company] with the intention of turning it into a special effects facility. I was in need of work and a neighbor, Paul Vlahos, said I should speak with Chuck Comisky as he was putting together a team to do special effects for *Battle Beyond the Stars*.

Work would begin in a space in the San Fernando Valley while the lumber yard was being converted. I asked Chuck what he needed. "Someone to help build spaceships and install lights and motors." "I can do that." I heard myself say, not knowing what sort of things were ahead. Maury Shallock had been hired as model shop supervisor and I was to assist him with structural and anything electrical, motors, lights, control panels, etcetera. I was trained as a motorcycle mechanic and many of those skills were utilized.

How did you and Brian Chin [Miniature Construction] prepare for this project and how did you collaborate on the miniature helicopters outside of working on the Manhattan miniature model?

The helicopters kept me busy, installing lights and motors. The Bell Jet Ranger was sculpted by Brian Chin. It's been years and I don't remember if the two helicopters used the same parts or not. I have no idea where we sourced the Huey [Bell UH-1 Iroquois] kit, this being forty years ago.

How were the models constructed/filmed, what kind of challenges did this project provide, and how long did they take to make?

The Huey was a kit that I installed bearings, mounts for photographing from various angles, and lights and motor to actually power the rotor if need be. They had hand built armatures providing multiple mounts for filming specific shots from different direction.

Motor speeds were variable and propellers easily removable. Neither actually flew. The Elicon's iron track allowed for camera movement. The Elicon was used primarily for miniatures with foreground and matte passes, which were later bipacked into background shots on site. The model mover where the models were mounted also had movement options. A foreground pass would be shot and a duplicate movement for a matte pass. Special pin registered rack over Mitchell cameras were used, which were old Army or Navy cameras. A color pass for a shot would be made against black and not developed. Then the exact same shot with no light on the model against a white background, which was developed to see the black model with a clear background. Special bipack magazines allowed for the two films to run through the gate at the same time. The black matte blocked the helicopter image while the camera photographed the background.

Once developed, the foreground and background came together. It was a very painstaking process, but without opticals and on one piece of film. Any problems and the shot was trash. We also used a huge front screen and had a custom front screen projector built. I actually got to pilot the glider into New York on wires and stuck the landing on the only take. So cool! The buildings were set on the stage floor and I remember putting in the streetlights using grain of rice lights.

How was your experience working with the New World Pictures effects team?

Many of us started together on *Battle Beyond the Stars*. A small group of us were working on *BBTS* [*Battle Beyond the Stars*] when Jim [Cameron] [Director of Photography/Matte Artwork: Special Visual Effects] came to interview. We were shown his student film and asked to vote if we should hire him. Many months later, I was working on his camera unit with Alec Gilles and Jim came back from a long lunch where he had secured funding for *Terminator*.

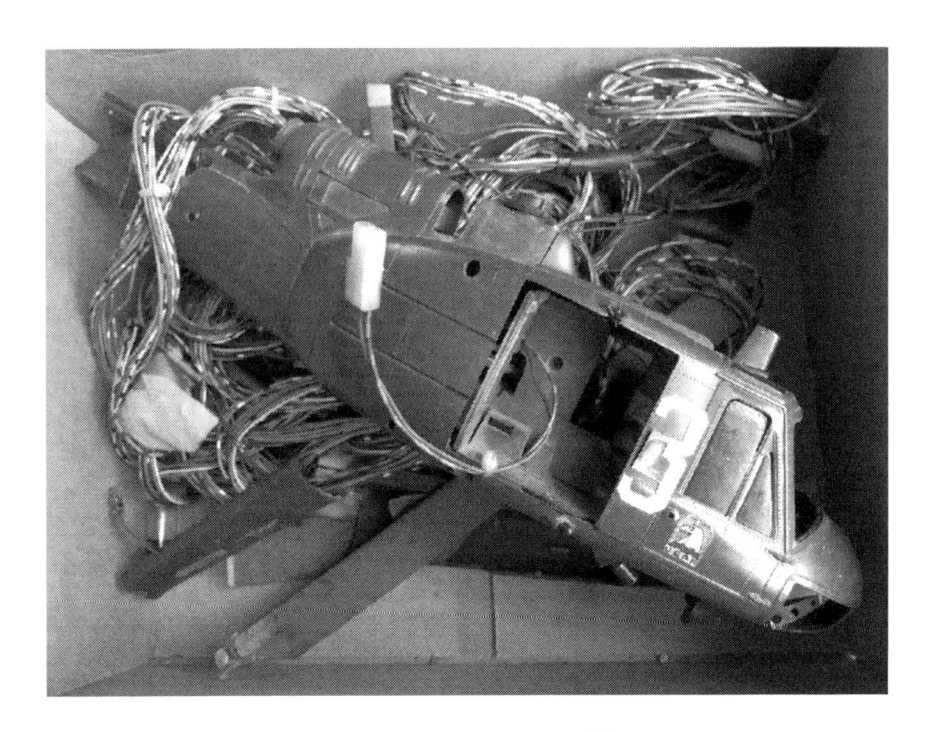

Helicopter Miniature Model
(Photo Courtesy Tom Campbell)

What's your favorite memory or memories of working on the movie?

I enjoyed being the roving engineer, working with the miniatures, and then photography. The friendships with many continue to this day. Hard working creative people that did what was needed, doing the most with the least.

What happened to the models after the movie was finished?

I'm guessing New York was scrapped as it was a huge miniature using the floor of the entire stage. I have one of the helicopters that is in a state of disrepair. I pulled it out of a trash can after we wrapped.

What do you think of the movie personally?

I enjoyed the movie considerably. We watched daily screenings of our shots, but seeing it all put together was a treat.

What are you currently doing and what do you enjoy doing in your spare time?

A brief stint at the bus company as mechanic with benefits left me looking for other work. Taking an acting class, learning to be a director. I was working with a woman whose boyfriend, also an actor, got a gig. She asked if I wanted to take his place. I ended up being a test driver for BMW engineering department for eleven years based out of Los Angeles. I became the lead driver, training others and driving prototype vehicles. After approximately a million miles and eleven years, it seemed time to give it up.

Around 1998, I moved to Illinois, took classes at a community college, worked in the print shop as a student worker, later doing graphics for special events, eventually laying out the college catalog. During this time, I became involved with a local theater company, Limelight Players, with artwork, eventually getting to direct *Picasso at the Lapin Agile* along with creating publicity materials. I also became involved with Special Olympics, helping coach, driving to events, chaperone for dances, and driving the van state games for several years where dorm life could be quite interesting. Big dance at the end, the highlight of the event for many. I was lucky to retire from Southwestern Illinois College before severe downsizing. I knew I needed to stay active to help manage my agent orange related diabetes, multiple joint replacements, etcetera. I went on a website called *Fitness Singles* and met a woman from St. Louis. We hit it off and have been able to travel, bike, and enjoy life. I've been living in St. Louis for a number of years now in an old craftsman home we rehabbed. I enjoy seeing my old friends from the Corman days whenever possible. I've been lucky.

STEVE CALDWELL
Camera Assistant: Special Visual Effects

How did you end up working for Roger Corman early on in your career?

This is a weird one. Actually, I worked on a film up north in Northern California where I lived. I happened to be an apprentice carpenter and the production crew was really cheap, so they had me building things. The assistant director came to me and asked if I could build this camera jib arm because the movie was called *Swim Team* with Buster Crabbe. They were doing a lot of swim team shots where they had a Chapman dolly alongside the pool, and they wanted the camera down at the pool level to dolly along while the swimmers were in the pool. Of course, I said, "Sure." I guess they had looked into it. To bring one up from Hollywood was $800 a day to rent and they wanted it for a good two or three weeks, for most of production. I told them, "I can build something," and I built this monstrosity on the back of the grip truck out of two-by-fours and all thread.

Basically, the key people came from L.A. Everybody else, it was really a scam. It was an acting school trying to get people to sign up for their acting classes and you would be in the movie. Well, they brought up just the key people. The key grip, gaffer, camera, first assistant. The rest of the people that were working as a grip or electrician were just local people. So, these guys would come out the grip truck and every time they looked at the thing, they walked away shaking their head because they're Hollywood people. They don't deal with two-by-fours and all thread. After the third day I said, "Ok. I'm ready. Let's test it out." We went in the back, we were at the pool, put it on the Chapman dolly and the thing worked. One of the most exciting moments in my life at that point. The key grip came up to me, "I just got to shake your hand." They were looking for a grip/electrician to join their crew, and after that evening, they went to the AD [Assistant Director] and said, "The person we want is Steve Caldwell." So I got in tight with the Hollywood guys for the remainder of the shoot.

At the end of that, they said, "Why don't you come to L.A.? You'll probably make it working on films." I went home, packed all my carpenter tools, a sleeping bag, and a suitcase. The grip truck driver offered me a place to stay and I headed to L.A. Three days after I was there, they were just getting ready

L-R: Steve Caldwell [Camera Assistant: Special Visual Effects], Dennis Skotak [Director of Photography: Special Visual Effects], Bob Skotak [Matte Artwork: Special Visual Effects] [Supervisor: Special Visual Effects] [Uncredited]
(Photo by/Courtesy Kim Gottlieb-Walker)

to start shooting on *Rock 'n' Roll High School*. See, the movie up in Northern California was *Swim Team*. It was not a Roger Corman production, but they had rented Roger's grip truck, so the grip truck driver worked for Roger. After I got there. they needed some lights set up in the main hall of the school they were shooting at. They assumed since I knew carpentry I knew electricity too. Of course, I said, "Sure. I can do that." Then I went to a library or a book store and bought a book on electricity and how to make it work, then went back. The grip truck driver had a side business of building sets and he had this little commercial spot. Basically, a shop and an office type of commercial thing. I was living above the office in the loft. He came to me and he said, "They need some lights," and I said, "Ok. Yeah, I can do that."

225

So anyway, I did that and, lo and behold, it worked. The key grip was looking for another grip and offered me the job, so I went on to *Rock 'n' Roll High School* and that was a Corman film. Then after that, I worked on *Lady in Red* as an electrician. Since I was able to hook up lights, everybody thought I was an electrician. Then Chris [Brightman], the grip truck driver, was basically trying to pursue his set building business. He wanted to get out of grip truck driving, so I kind of got handed the grip truck. We did not have a production at that time. I was supposed to go up and work on *The Fog*, but I sprained an ankle and I was on crutches for six weeks, so I missed that gig. When I finally got back to L.A., I was working with the owner of the grip truck and just going through lights in between projects. Cleaning, fixing.

How did you get the job of camera assistant of the special visual effects on *Escape From New York*?

At that time, that's when the miniature builders had been working on models for *Battle Beyond the Stars* for a little bit. They needed some lights because they were getting ready to start shooting some test footage and what not. Well, I had the light. I was the grip truck driver, so I delivered the lights down to Santa Monica where they had set up a little store front to build the models and start work. Bob [Skotak] [Matte Artwork: Special Visual Effects] [Supervisor: Special Visual Effects] [Uncredited] and Denny [Skotak] [Director of Photography: Special Visual Effects] had been asking for somebody to help them. I just happened to be there, so they offered me that, so I never really drove the grip truck as a grip truck driver. I never had a chance. I was basically Bob and Denny's third wheel starting on *Battle Beyond the Stars* in Santa Monica and then we moved to what was Hammond Lumber [Company] once upon a time. Roger Corman had bought Hammond Lumber, a lumber company to build his "visual effects studio." Then we moved over there and worked on *Battle*, did all of that, and then *Escape* kind of followed right after that.

How did you and Randy Frakes [Camera Assistant: Special Visual Effects] as well as fellow Manhattan miniature model builders Bob Skotak, Dennis Skotak, and Tom Campbell [Engineer: Special Visual Effects] prepare for this project and how did you collaborate?

Randy, too? Okay. Jim Cameron [Director of Photography/Matte Artwork: Special Visual Effects] went to New York and took a bunch of pictures of sides of buildings in Manhattan. It was Randy and Jim's job to enlarge those. I had given them to Bob, Denny, Tom, and myself for the building of Manhattan because Manhattan was basically blocks of wood with enlargements glued on. I don't think it was all cardboard or wood, probably both. There were mock-ups, but the final I'm not sure. High-tech miniature work. For Manhattan, that was it. It was just kind of the four of us. There were some other model builders. You had the Air Force One, the glider, and where the glider lands on top of the World Trade Center. Somebody built the larger top of the World Trade Center because we literally brought in a good size glider that basically came in on wires. There was another shot there with Manhattan where you see the glider. I think it kind of comes from above and dips down and then goes into the streets. That glider was maybe five, six inches because we used some of the same miniatures that we built for Manhattan. We used those for the shots where Snake Plissken is starting the glider flight into the World Trade Center. There were a couple of different sizes, so there had to be other model builders working on those things.

Basically, Bob was the artist. Bob would look through the camera. He had final say on design and what to put where, how to set up the shot. Denny was definitely the camera man. He would adjust lights and what not. I did everything else. I set up the lights. I did all the rigging. I did pretty much everything else. I was camera assistant because I was always loading the camera too, but Randy and Jim, they were in a dark room with an enlarger and that was about it. At the end of the day, Bob, Denny and I, we'd get a stack of enlargements and we'd be in the back. Oh God, sometimes nine, ten o'clock at night, trying to put these and ninety percent of all these enlargements were wrinkled. Bob and Denny would always complain. Complain, complain, complain.

So finally, one day I went into the enlargement. It was basically an oversized closet with an enlarger in there. I go in and there's Randy and there's Jim and there are enlargements scattered all over the place. On the floor, everywhere. I had come to find out what Randy and Jim were doing, their priority. They were writing *Terminator* at the time. That's what the two of them spent most of their day doing, writing *Terminator*. The obligatory enlargement, "Oh quick. We better do some enlargements. Bob and Denny are gonna need them," and they were crap. I mean, we're back there trying to smooth out enlargements and getting frustrated. That's pretty much most of what they were doing on *Escape*

From New York in the early end. At the back end. Jim did have some large front projection shots that he was in charge of on the stage, but in the early end they were more concentrated on writing *Terminator*. As it turns out, it worked out for them very well. I was there when Jim first got hired on *Battle Beyond the Stars* and I saw his portfolio. I knew he was gonna go someplace. He's a very, very talented guy. A complete dick, but very talented.

On *Escape*, when I went into that room and saw all the enlargements, I basically just read them the riot act. I said, "Do you realize the hours that Bob and Denny and I are spending because of your lack of caring and your crappy work?" I said what I had to say and I left. Well, he followed me around the studio for about forty-five minutes, "But Steve, but Steve, but Steve." I turned on him and said, "I don't care. Get your shit together because all you're doing is making harder work for us." I turned around, walked away, and he'd follow me, "But Steve, but Steve, but Steve." Before that day, Jim Cameron looked down his nose at me and thought I was a nobody. I was just another minion in the cog. After that, he respected me and would listen to me. Bob and Denny would never say anything. They would never say anything against anybody. I'm in Texas now and I don't care. I don't burn any bridges you know. Twenty years ago when I was still in the film industry, I probably would have kept that to myself. The bottom line is that Randy and I, we never worked together. We never did anything together. I was the camera assistant working with Bob and Denny and he was supposedly a camera assistant working with Jim.

What kind of challenges did the miniature model of Manhattan provide and how long did it take to make?

I was leaning towards a couple of weeks. I mean, it was pretty crude. How long does it take to cut a four-by-four and glue stuff to it? We did use a pamphlet of Manhattan. I think some of the buildings in the front were a little bit more detailed. The World Trade Center was. God, I can't really remember. It was only maybe four feet tall and then basically we built the Manhattan miniature for the approach shots on. You've been to a lumber store before where they actually have lumber in it? They had this one big, huge room where you knew they had all the lumber stacked around there, forklifts moving it around and what not, so we used that. That was kind of the main studio part. It was the biggest room we had, so we set up in there.

When Air Force One comes in, you can see the water. Well, the concrete in this area, I don't know if they finished it or what, but it was very rough. When we were first going in there and figuring out, "Ok. If we set the dolly here and we put Manhattan there and we put 10K there," this and that and the other. Someone asked, "What are we gonna do for water?" And I looked at the concrete floor and I ran my hand over it and it's like, "Oh my God. I don't know, but I think this might work." Bob and Denny were going, "What do you mean? What are you talking about?" I said, "We paint this floor black and there is enough roughness and there were swirls." It was just the way the concrete was. I said, "I'm betting the farm this will look like water," and they kind of looked at me and said, "Are you kidding? No. No way. No way." I said, "Yes way. Paint it black. Let's do a quick test." So, we painted a section black, put a back light on it, put a blue filter over that, and ran a test. Sure as shit, it looked like water. Bottom line is, the water on the approach shot was literally the concrete that was there just painted black and it worked beautifully. I mean, I couldn't believe it. Then of course, we built the front edge of Manhattan with little miniature trees and all that stuff. I think they had the wall there at the time. All those miniatures you see in that shot, those were all literally pieces of wood with enlargements glued on.

Is it true that in order to make an accurate Manhattan you photographed a map of it and projected the negative in a slide projector on a wall and made the foundation out of plywood? Also, is it true that you hand-colored black and white Xeroxes and put them on some of the buildings due to the lack of color photos?

Yes, that sounds about right. You know what? I think, for the most part, I think you're correct. I'm trying to remember but yeah, they did not have a color enlarger, I don't think. I think you're right. I think it was just black and white. I mean, it was pretty crude because none of these buildings you got that close to. It was just a flat surface. It was an enlargement, but you're right. I think it was just like colored pencils or something so the black would still get your dark lines of like ratlines and what not from the black and just fill in with kind of a reddish brick color.

What kind of other challenges did this project provide and which special visual effect scene or scenes were the most challenging, problematic, memorable, and fun to work on?

It was actually a very fun project. I'm sure you probably know the movie pretty well, probably better than I know the movie. There's a shot where they're looking for some escaped guys down at the river. The Brooklyn Bridge is in the background and you see this helicopter come in and then they turn on the light on the helicopter. The light hits the water and then the helicopter comes up over the rocks and flies off. That was one of the more interesting shots. We had the Elicon, which was a computer-controlled camera. Any of the shots you see with Air Force One or the helicopters, those were what was called bipacked. They would shoot multiple takes, multiple latency of Air Force One or the helicopter. Then we would have to put it in this bipack with the matte and run that through where we would be shooting our miniatures. For that, the helicopter was one of those elements that was shot on the computer camera. We had that as an element. Also the bipack of the latent helicopter. Then the rest of that scene was rocks in the foreground. We had a couple of beam splitters on that shot. I had these rotary tables. They used them in like metal working, so they're in very fine increments and very smooth moving. Then we had a front projection of the water. The Brooklyn Bridge was just a matte painting in the background. Then we had the helicopter light that turns on and off, that was actually the computer-generated miniature shot. Then we had a front projection with water and light hitting in it.

When the light went off of the water, I had a light above that we turned on manually and pulled, so it kept looking like the light came off of the water onto the rocks. That was one of the most difficult shots that we worked on. Bob and Denny didn't really understand movement. They're great with still shots. There were some shots in *Battle* that were basically supposed to be still shots, establishing shots, and I would ask them, "Can I make it move?" And they would kind of look at me and say, "Well, if you can, we don't care." So because I hate static cameras, I would add moves into some of these shots that we had. I was kind of in charge of figuring out how to make it move. I opened my big mouth. I got to figure it out, so I did all the rigging, all the engineering, all the, "Ok. This goes here. This goes there. We got to be at this point." That shot took eight hours to shoot and what was it? Maybe a twenty second shot, if that?

We had so many things that had to be choreographed perfectly so we would basically take one frame, I would move the rotary table a certain degree, and then move this a certain degree, whatever. The first time we shot that shot, I put the matte in backwards on the bipack, so in dailies the next day you had the helicopter coming in from the left and you had a matte coming in from the right and they crisscrossed and went off-screen. Oh shit. It never made the cut. It just made it into the room with all my co-workers looking at it and giggling, "Steve made a mistake, Steve made a mistake." That eight-hour shot was dumped in the crapper, so we did it again. This time, I loaded the matte properly and this is the actual shot that's in the movie.

If you watch through where the helicopter has its light on and when the light goes off, I was off by one frame. Either I left the light on the foreground one frame longer or I turned the light off one frame too soon. That'll give you something to look for, but at twenty-four frames a second, nobody's ever gonna see it. I'm the only one that notices it because Bob, Denny, and I would go to the Moviola after dailies and look at everything frame by frame to make sure that there wasn't anything most people would notice. Once you blew it up to the big screen, something might be there. I went to Bob and Denny and I said, "Oh, I fucked up again. The light goes off one frame too early or vice versa." I forget which way it went. They said, "Ah, nobody has noticed it. Shut up." We did not want to spend another eight hours shooting this shot for a third time. That by far was the most involved.

Let's see. I had two rotary tables. We had a front projection projector for projecting screen. We had on set lights. We had blinking lights on the wall that we had to, "Ok. On three frames, off." There was just a whole pile of notes and stuff that had to be double checked and triple checked as we're shooting it. Normally, we did stuff at a quarter frame, a quarter second exposure and we would just slow everything down as far as movement. You know, scale the move down so the movement would look natural and normal, but on that one there were too many variables with what was going on with the foreground and this and that. The wall lights blinking and all that other stuff. We chose to just do it stop motion. That way we could keep track easier of when things needed to be turned on and when things needed to be turned off.

How was your experience working with the New World Pictures special visual effects facility team?

It was a great life. It was a lot of fun. When *Escape* was over, Bob and Denny and the guy with the toothpick, the head of the visual effects. He was basically a used car salesman. This guy was a piece of work. Seriously, he had been a car salesman once upon a time and now he's a visual effects producer. This

L-R: Austin McKinney [Director of Photography: Special Visual Effects], Randy Frakes [Camera Assistant: Special Visual Effects], Jim Cameron [Director of Photography/Matte Artwork: Special Visual Effects]
(Photo by Abe Perlstein / © Abe Perlstein)

tells all about him. He was bringing people through to meet and work on the models or the set or the other. Bob, Denny, and I had this cornered off area where we were starting to do test shots and stuff of some of the models. He brought this somebody, I don't know who he was, but he was introducing him to Bob and Denny because he thought Bob and Denny were the crème de la crème. They were the best and I knew what he was doing. I just stood in front of him as he was leaving our area. I knew he wasn't gonna introduce me to this guy, "Oh, and this is just Steve." I became "just Steve" to all my co-workers and we all laughed about it. I was "just Steve," so he ended up taking Bob and Denny to this other guy that was starting up a visual effects company. I think they were doing *Jaws 3* at the time. Well, Chuck [Comisky], he really didn't like me. He liked Bob and Denny. He didn't like me because I spoke up. I was the facilitator. I had a mouth. I wasn't the guy he could push around, so I ended up staying at New World. At that time, it was called New World Visual Effects and Julia Gibson [Elicon Camera Operator: Special Visual Effects] and I kind of ran the thing. She was the head producer in the front office and I was the director of photography in the back and did *Android* there and I think a couple of other little things.

What's your favorite memory or memories of working on the movie?
All in all, it was a pretty fun production. What was kind of fun was, I mean, here we're working with wood and enlargements and I kept thinking, "Really, Bob. Is this really gonna work?" "Oh yeah. It'll be fine." We did a lot more stuff on *Battle Beyond the Stars* before. That's where I got into some crazy camera moves when they weren't necessary and had made my *2001: A Space Odyssey* shot. I don't know why. I don't know how. Engineering and rigging and all that type of stuff just came very naturally to me. I think it's just from playing out. You know, just being a kid. I used to build lots of models. I really don't know, but Bob and Denny had no engineering or rigging. They just couldn't grasp the progress to a certain degree, so that's what I did and I enjoyed it. It was like being a kid. Here I'm being paid to play with models.

I look back fondly on calling Jim Cameron out and having him bawl for a moment because, at that time, it was like everybody idolized him. You know, I screw up also. That whole show went really nice and it was just like I told my wife earlier. The cast and crew screening was at a big theater in Hollywood. Every one of us got these, and I still have it, these big pamphlets that John

Carpenter had made with all the names of all the cast and crew and gave one to everybody. I had only been in the film industry for maybe four years or so and *Escape* was kind of the biggest deal I ever worked on, especially with the cast and crew. It was a nice event. It was like, A-ha, I made it.

What happened to the models after the movie was finished?

I do not know what happened to a lot of them. I'm sure Bob and Denny held on to a few of their favorites. Probably most of them just got trashed. Dumped in the trash dumpster.

What do you think of the movie personally?

Actually, I thought it was a really good film. I thought it was really cool. I mean, it is a cult classic. I have my copy here at home and I think I have a VHS and no way to play it. When you're working with visual effects, you just don't know. You're working on such a tiny portion of the movie. What we're doing really has nothing to do with anything in a way that you can tell. I had the script and I did read the script and thought, "Oh, this is pretty cool." I really liked the idea of it. I think they should look into that now. Find an island and shove them all on an island and let them take care of themselves. The jails are overcrowded, you know. They'd cut down on a lot of tax dollars being spent. I really thought it was a very clever idea and the actors were very believable.

What are you currently doing and what do you enjoy doing in your spare time?

Bob and Denny had moved in with what was called L.A. Effects and they were in England shooting *Aliens*, which Cameron wrote and directed. They called me and wanted somebody here in the [United] States, so I was hired by them thinking I'm gonna work on *Aliens* and big pictures and what not. Well, we did some odd jobs there. We did the opening for *Aliens* where you see the horseshoe ship, the mother ship from *Alien*. The company was run by even worse shysters and basically stuck us. They didn't pay us for months and months and months. That's when I decided I've had enough. I ended up moving up to Northern California and getting totally out of the film industry.

    I got my general contractors license and was doing that up there and then had a kid. Where we were was kind of remote. We ended up moving back to L.A. where I continued with doing some general contracting because we had the Northridge earthquake and there was money to be had fixing things. I carried on with my general contracting and then got very frustrated with these people that wanted to do these jobs.

By that time, Bob and Denny had formed 4-Ward Productions so I called and talked to Elaine [Edford], who was Bob's wife at the time. I kind of got back into the film industry that way and worked on *Hard Rain* for about nine months. I had worked with this model builder back at Corman's visual effects place named Ron Thornton and some of the model builders were talking about him. Ron and I were kind of friends at the time but, with me moving away for six years and got out of the business, we lost touch. I heard that he had just started a digital visual effects house. And I could see the writing on the wall. Miniatures were going away. Everybody was putting all their eggs in the digital realm basket.

So I met with Ron and he basically bought me a computer and gave me LightWave, which is the 3D program. We got a project [*Mystic Nights of Tir Na Nog*] coming in about six months. I was remodeling his kitchen and then going home and working on LightWave on the computer he bought me until they got the project in-house ready to go. Finally the kitchen is done and I'm up to snuff on LightWave and he brings me into the studio and has me messing around with it. He could tell something was wrong. "What about compositing," he asked. I started working on After Effects and three days later I was actually compositing shots. It all just came very naturally to me. That's kind of what I had been doing with the miniatures. Except now I sit with a computer in an air condition office not breathing in smoke and fog juice and dust and everything else you use in miniature to make them look miniature. I was there for a little over a year and a half.

That's basically how I got into the digital end. It's not what you know. It's who you know. That came so true. I worked for four companies that went out of business. I was starting to feel I was a bad token for a while there, but it wasn't anything I was doing. I was doing quality work. It was the politics. It was all the people in the higher echelon that wanted the fancy tables, the fancy chairs, the fancy monitors. They were just overspending to get the fancy and not worrying about the bottom line. That is, get the shot done in a timely basis. I worked on a lot of stuff at Custom Film Effects. I worked on, God, probably at least we were working on six, eight, ten movies a year. A lot of them were just little things. Remove a sandbag. We worked on *Chicago*. I had to take pimples off of Réene Zelwegger's face. On *The Devil Wears Prada*, we had to reduce the hips of Meryl Streep. We worked on a lot of big films doing goofy things. When Custom Film went under I reassessed my life and kind of just pulled the plug on it. I ended up getting a divorce and meeting the mouth that you keep hearing and moved to Texas and couldn't be happier.

I have fulfilled a dream, which a lot of people can't say, but it's hard work. A lot of abuse. That's one of Roger's things. You don't pay anybody much. However, I didn't go to any sort of film school or anything like that so there is a debt of gratitude towards people like Roger Corman for allowing people like me a position. It's not a real glamorous profession. Lots of long hours, and at the end of the four, six week shoot, you're exhausted, but it does get in your blood where there is an excitement to it. But it's definitely not glamour. A lot of these people that people look up to are complete assholes. Sometimes it's like, it's just a movie. I didn't cure cancer. I didn't do this. I didn't do that. I mean, since then I've built complete homes by myself that will be standing hundreds of years from now and people will enjoy them. That is more gratifying for me to a certain degree because it's a physical thing. A movie is entertainment. At the end of the day, it is. However, there is certain movies like this and others that you know there is pride. I'm very proud of what we did on *Escape*. It was a lot of fun. It really was and it was a good one. You walked out of the theater feeling. Ah, that was good.

EUGENE P. RIZZARDI
Miniature Construction [Uncredited]

How did you end up being an FX technician and model maker/supervisor?

When I first got into the business in 1979, I was inspired by those who went before me, especially Greg Jein. I thought he was a great guy to work for, so when I had the chance to lead a crew, I took it and tried to emulate his ways. I only worked for him later in my career [*Star Trek* TV shows and *The Blob*], but he was someone who I thought was a great leader. Although special effects is where I started, once you got into the union you had to fulfill certain requirements to become a special effects technician. I would say it takes a minimum of six years in the union before you can even attempt to be considered. You have to have had a prop shop rating for at least four years before you're eligible to apply. I always considered miniatures and especially the destruction of them, if required, to be special visual effects. No, not the CGI stuff you see today, but real miniature work that may be destroyed at the end of the shot. I was influenced by *Godzilla*, Gerry Anderson's TV shows, Sylvia Anderson's TV shows, and early sci-fi. They were so much fun and I thought I could possibly do that, but I never really tried to do this work till I moved to California in the late 70s and thought I should try to do commercials and movie work for a living. Trust me, it's not for the weak! But if it is in your blood, you will find a way.

How did you get the job of model maker on *Escape From New York*?

Like many of us at the time, I heard about this show going on and wanted to work on it. The supervisor knew of my work, so when I interviewed. I got the job. I think I recommended Bruce MacRae [Miniature Construction] [Uncredited] to join me.

How did you, Brian Chin [Miniature Construction] and Bruce MacRae [Miniature Construction] [Uncredited] prepare for this project and how did you collaborate on the Air Force One miniature and the three gliders in different scales?

Gene Rizzardi [Miniature Construction] [Uncredited]
(Photo Courtesy Eugene P. Rizzardi)

There was never any preparation before the job as far as I know. Maybe Brian would have more insight into that. We were given tasks and we had to build whatever we were given. Bruce and I worked as a team. Bruce would do most of the finish work and I would do the molding, making the parts and assembly. Bruce would do the paint and details. We were a great team. Tom [Campbell] [Engineer: Special Visual Effects] built the helicopter and I think I remember helping him with the mechanics, but I don't remember that too well. We were much more focused on building the gliders and the Air Force One.

How were the models constructed, what kind of challenges did this project provide, and how long did they take to make?

Most of the models were built from fiberglass, automotive body filler, and urethane foam. While we were working, we realized the molding material we were using was not really compatible with the fiberglass resins, so we had a lot of fixing to do. We probably had about eight to ten weeks to build everything. That included the three gliders, the Air Force One, the helicopter, and some of the buildings and the roof top where he lands. Air Force One started out as a display model for the airlines. There was a company we used to order these from for various shows we have worked on, so we were familiar with how they were made and used them from time to time. I was an R/C glider pilot, so making the gliders was something that was left to me to do.

How was your experience working with the New World Pictures special visual effects facility team?

We knew everyone from when we worked on *Battle Beyond the Stars*, so it was pretty easy to do the work. Bruce and I and Tom were left alone to get our job done. Brian would come and check on our progress from time to time, but for the most part we just made our models and whatever else they threw at us.

What's your favorite memory or memories of working on the movie?

Well, I have a few. One was the glider going over the water. The floor of the warehouse was painted gloss black and, because it was rough, it looked like water, especially the way the Skotaks [Bob] [Matte Artwork: Special Visual Effects] [Supervisor: Special Visual Effects] [Uncredited]/[Dennis] [Director of Photography: Special Visual Effects] filmed it. Another memory, most of the buildings were just Xeroxes over boxes. Since it was mostly at night, it did not matter that they were accurate. They just had to be there. Remember that model making is impressionism. If I make you believe you saw it, I am doing my job.

The one I really remember was Brian saying to me, "Stop doing what you are doing. You cannot polish Plexiglas." I was working on Air Force One at the time and cutting out the windows to replace them with long pieces of clear 3/8" Plexiglas that were sanded and polished to shape. Bruce would then paint the windows over that. Bruce and I also got in trouble because Bruce was well known to Brian because he was published in *Military Modeler* magazine and I was giving him direction on how I wanted certain things done. Please remember, we worked as a team and had worked previously together, so we knew each other's strengths and weaknesses.

What happened to the models after the movie was finished?

I am not sure what happened to the models. I had heard the mid-sized glider ended up at some guy's home but he passed away about 10, 15 years ago so I have no idea where they went.

What do you think of the movie personally?

I liked the movie. The only thing I would have changed is the Air Force One. I did not think an old viscount was the right plane for the conversion, but it worked and that is all that mattered.

What are you currently doing and what do you enjoy doing in your spare time?

I usually work on Nickelodeon's *Henry Danger* and *Game Shakers*. I build special props and run the set of *Henry Danger* and sometimes help setting up special effects or special props for *Game Shakers*. What does that mean? Well, the man cave has different things that work. Secret doors, elevators, gear doors, the couch and the up the tubes gags. I also provide wind and smoke as needed. I work with a team of people and we all solve the problems as they are introduced. We have a great team! I also work on *Face Off* from time to time usually doing smoke, fire or fog. What do I do for fun? Well, that depends on the time of year. I am usually working on my house or property and sometimes when I have the time I build garden scale trains for my own enjoyment or do photography.

BRUCE MACRAE
Miniature Construction [Uncredited]

How did you end up being a model maker?

Getting into the movie industry was a fairly long road. I got interested in building model kits when I was seven and never stopped. I'm still modeling to this day. In 1968 at fifteen, I discovered the IPMS [International Plastic Modeling Society] where I was astounded by the quality of modeling possible. People were turning "mere" plastic kits into museum-quality pieces. I found very talented people I could learn from, and they indulged me by answering all my questions. Within a few years, I was competing successfully in monthly and regional competitions. One day in 1978, I was displaying my scratch-built *Star Wars* stormtrooper at a show when I was approached by some people "from the movie industry" who asked me if I wanted to work on *Star Trek: The Motion Picture*. Naturally, I jumped at the chance. I wound up at BPMM [Brick Price Movie Miniatures] making props for the TV series *Project U.F.O.* and soon was building props for *Star Trek: TMP* [*The Motion Picture*], including tricorders, phasers, bio-belt buckles, and the like. Because of *Star Trek,* I was eligible to join the union, IATSE [International Alliance of Theatrical Stage Employees], Local 44 and that opened more movie industry doors.

How did you get the job of model maker on *Escape From New York*?

I got a call from Gene Rizzardi [Miniature Construction] [Uncredited] and he asked me to join him. I met Gene at BPMM in 1980 and we became good friends and have always worked well together. We both had different strengths, so we made a good team. He had stronger skills in construction, so I followed his lead. When it came to details like paint and finishing, then he followed my lead. In the many projects we worked on together over thirty years, we never knocked heads over how to do something. We would discuss all the ways to get the job done and then pick the best. It didn't matter whose idea it was, so we made a good workable team. Anytime I got the chance to work with Gene, I jumped at it. I was thrilled to get the call to join *Escape From New York*.

How did you, Brian Chin [Miniature Construction] and Gene Rizzardi [Miniature Construction] [Uncredited] prepare for this project and how did you collaborate on the Air Force One model and the three gliders in different scales?

No prep. You just brought your tool box, got your assignments, and barreled on.

How were the models constructed, what kind of challenges did this project provide, and how long did they take to make?

Gene's interview already answered this perfectly. There is not much I can add.

How come you have photos of the Manhattan model, which you didn't work on?

The Manhattan miniature photos I took while the crew was out to lunch. I often took photos of what I worked on, even when we were forbidden to do so. I understand that they didn't want photos flying around during production, but I was taking and keeping them for a time like this. I wanted a record of what I did and of what we did. I never leaked my photos. It wouldn't be professional and, after the movie was out, nobody cared about photos. I had to be careful and I was. I think movie miniature history should not be lost.

How was your experience working with the New World Pictures special visual effects facility team?

Gene had been there before on *Battle Beyond the Stars,* but for me it was my first time there. Gene and I had our own room. The New York stage/set was next door. Brian [Chin] [Miniature Construction] would check in on us but pretty much we were on our own.

What's your favorite memory or memories of working on the movie?

Gene's story on the, "You can't polish Plexiglas back to clear!" is my favorite memory. Gene loves working with Plexiglas. He can make it do anything. Stand up, sit, lie down, roll over, etcetera. We still laugh about it. After that, Brian let us do our thing and we got the job done right on time and they loved it.

One story I will tell is, we were working too well, meaning, we were going to finish at least a week earlier than our deadline. I told Gene, "When we

Top: Air Force One Miniature Model
Bottom: Glider Miniature Model
(Photos Courtesy Eugene P. Rizzardi)

finish early, they will be delighted and will pay us off. They will save two man weeks of labor and we both lose a week's pay." Gene says, "Hmmm you're right. We need to start taking two hour [unpaid] lunches." We got the models done right on time and no late nights. One of the more enjoyable jobs I had in thirty-three years in the industry.

What happened to the models after the movie was finished?

I have no idea. I never heard anything about them. I'd like to think some collector has given them a loving home.

What do you think of the movie personally?

I enjoyed it. I got to work with Gene, fun models, no pressure, and a mortgage payment. What's not to love? Seriously, it was a very fun action flick.

What are you currently doing and what do you enjoy doing in your spare time?

I moved to Las Vegas and worked at Bigelow Aerospace as a model maker for over five years. I'm retired now and loving it. I've gone back to building miniatures and dioramas like I did before the movies. I found the IPMS here and am competing again. I've taken seventy awards since I moved here. I enjoy posting my miniatures on Facebook and sharing my tutorial with many other miniature makers around the world. I've also been scanning my vast collection of photos that I've taken while in the movie industry and sharing them on my FB [Facebook] page and other movie FB groups.

JOHN C. WASH
Graphic Displays

How did you end up being a graphic display animator and effects artist/supervisor?

At the University of Southern California where I majored in cinema, I was originally interested in character animation. My artistic interests and talents, however, were stronger in the area of graphic design and typography. I gravitated towards graphic animation as a result. During my final year at USC, I worked on several graphic display shots for *Dark Star*, a film being made by John Carpenter and Dan O'Bannon in the senior production workshop. After graduating, I did further work on *Dark Star*, which was being expanded into a feature film by John and Dan. I worked on my first model shot, which was the Phoenix Asteroids. That was filmed with a bunch of Styrofoam spheres to which I had added craters. I dropped them in front of a high-speed camera mounted on its side to get the elements for the scene.

How did you get the job of graphic displays maker on *Escape From New York*?

John Carpenter and I stayed in touch after our time at USC. He called me in during prep work for the production and explained the sequence where Snake Plissken lands a glider on one of the World Trade Center towers. Budget constraints allowed only two or three photo-real visual effects shots for the scene, which were done by Bob [Skotak] [Matte Artwork: Special Visual Effects] [Supervisor: Special Visual Effects] [Uncredited] and Dennis Skotak [Director of Photography: Special Visual Effects]. To flesh out the scene Carpenter wanted a high-tech series of displays representing wireframe images to play on monitors in the glider and in full screen during the scene. Based on the work I had done on *Dark Star*, I think John trusted that I could accomplish those shots. This work was completed in time to be used as video playback elements during second unit photography. Once Carpenter had finished principal photography and was working in the edit room, he called on me to animate some additional shots that were needed to dramatize and enhance the film. Among them was an animated prologue scene, a graphic of the crash of Air Force One in Manhattan and a countdown clock showing the rapidly dwindling time limit for Snake to finish his mission.

John Wash [Graphic Displays]
(Photo Courtesy Mark Stetson)

How did you prepare for this project?

First, I needed to decide whether the models should be negative or positive in nature. I initially thought that white buildings with black edges would be easier to light evenly and that shadows would be less of a problem. It would be trivial to flip the polarity of the images during the optical printing stage. To test this hypothesis Mark [Stetson] [Miniature Construction] [Uncredited] and I built a small section of the model. His wife Leslie, a professional photographer, shot stills of that test model. To my surprise, the white buildings with black lines photographed with undesirable shadows so I committed to constructing black buildings with white edges. For cartographic and architectural research on the glider sequence, I discovered and rented a large book which was essentially a real estate map of Manhattan. It contained detailed maps of the city grid block by block and listed the number of floors of every building in the city. I used rough calculations to determine the average height of each block as we were going to limit the resolution of the full Manhattan model to one city block. Mark and I made a ground level template using chart tape and had it photographically enlarged and mounted on Masonite. The other shots I animated for the film were my own designs.

Why didn't you use a computer for the effects?

At that time, computer graphics were still in their nascent stage. Most of the computers used to do very simple animations were large expensive machines reserved for research work at large corporations and universities. In the instance of Plissken's glider sequence, I knew that a computer model of the island of Manhattan with hundreds, if not thousands of structures, would be beyond the capacity of any computer that existed then. For other shots that were two-dimensional in nature, using traditional animation tools was simply a matter of time and cost savings. Interestingly enough, there was one shot at the end of the glider sequence that I used a computer to animate. I believe it was the final shot I did for the film. During editing, Carpenter needed a visual that sold the idea of the glider skidding across the roof of the tower and nearly going over the edge. None of the models we had already built were suitable for this shot. However, I learned that Bo Gehring, another member of the Hollywood community of visual effects and graphic animation specialists had a computer system available that could do simple line animations and output them as sequences of plotter drawings. I animated the forward view of the rooftop on his system and shot the resulting artwork under an animation camera. That shot finished the sequence.

How did you make the graphic displays in the movie look computer-generated?

I acquired a good deal of experience in the mimicry of computer graphics on *Dark Star* and other projects. I subscribed to a magazine called *Computer Graphics World* and pored over the images printed in that journal. To get that unique machine-generated look I learned to think visually like a computer but without abandoning my artistic sensibilities. For shots other than the glider sequence, I used high-contrast black and white transparencies what were then called litho negatives and colored gels. These were photographed on top of a light box that was part of the animation camera. I learned lots of techniques to create the imagery I wanted, like using white Plexiglas for diffusion and combining multiple passes through the camera to achieve complex effects. Another trick common to graphic animators was called a slot gag where one piece of artwork remained static under the camera while a second piece was panned on top or underneath. I used that method to generate the waveform traces for the President's [Donald Pleasence] vital signs monitor.

When you heard that John Carpenter wanted multiple wireframe POVs as the glider flew into Manhattan, how did you figure out how to accomplish these effects?

I decided to build high-contrast models built to look like wireframe renderings. I worked with Mark Stetson, who had set up a model shop in his garage to build those models. Three models were constructed. A wide overview of Manhattan and two larger scale models. One of Park Avenue leading to what was then the Pan Am Building and the area around the World Trade Towers. Mark and I decided to represent the wide view model of Manhattan topography with a single rectangular prism for each block. This would give us a nice level of detail without being overly complex to construct.

The models were shot on a motion control system by Hoyt Yeatman and Scott Squires at Dream Quest. At that time, another garage operation. Five angles were shot for each portion of the sequence. Forward, rear, three-quarter right and left and down. These played on five small monitors mounted in Snake's cockpit. In addition, Carpenter played some of the animation full screen. Dream Quest came up with a nifty snorkel lens that allowed the camera to get very close to the models and even fly in between them as in the shot that flew down Park Avenue and did a steep climb to barely miss an impact with the Pan Am building. The miniatures were an asset when it came to shooting multiple angles. The movement of the motion control system stayed the same and what was required for each pass was a bit of lighting adjustment and a repositioning of the lens at the end of the snorkel.

Top and Bottom: L-R: John Wash [Graphic Displays], Kathy Iguchi [Production Assistant: Special Visual Effects] [Uncredited] (Photos Courtesy Mark Stetson)

Top: Mark Stetson [Miniature Construction] [Uncredited]
Bottom: Park Avenue Graphic Displays Miniature
(Photos Courtesy Mark Stetson)

I worked with an optical house. I believe it was called Modern Film in Hollywood where the footage was colorized and graphic overlays were superimposed.

What kind of challenges did the three miniature model sets of Manhattan provide?

The shoot had a lot of tricky requirements. The lighting had to be absolutely flat and shadowless. The high-contrast film stock we used was incredibly slow and long exposures were required to properly photograph the model. We couldn't use a lot of lights since the models were built with hot glue. Too much heat and the buildings would be dropping off the base! If I recall correctly, we were shooting with an exposure of between one and two minutes per frame at an aperture of f/22 for a large depth of field. At one angle in which the camera was shooting straight down on the top of the Trade Center tower, the roof of the tower was reflecting light back at the camera. Even though the design covering the roof was a matte black hi-con [high-contrast] photograph like the surfaces of the rest of the large models, I solved the problem by switching out the roof graphic with a piece of specialty paper covered with black flocking. It was like having a piece of black velvet atop the tower. It photographed flawlessly.

How long did it take to animate the prologue sequence for instance?

Although I was working on multiple shots simultaneously, I would say that the prologue sequence took about two weeks. I was working on my own at that point.

Is there anything you would've done differently in retrospect to any of your animations in the movie which are timeless and iconic by the way?

In terms of style, I think in retrospect that I would have pulled back a bit on the explicit modernism in the designs of the fonts and saturation of the colors. But of course, one might argue that in terms of the overall style of the movie, which embraces action and visuals that are in the realm of a graphic novel, the animated shots are an appropriate fit. One other thing that I wished I could have weighed in on was the orientation of the monitors in the glider cockpit set. I didn't see the actual set until the scene was being shot. At that point it was too late to make changes.

What's your favorite memory or memories of working on the movie?

Seeing the glider sequence cut together for the first time. It was a gratifying feeling to see how well the animation played in the scene given all the hard work our team had put into it.

Another interesting tidbit occurred after I read the script for the first time during pre-production. I suggested to Carpenter that the President wear a signet ring bearing the presidential seal on the finger that is severed and given to the authorities as proof of his captivity. It was fun to see that gag make it into the movie.

What do you think of the movie personally?

I still enjoy it immensely. I really appreciate Carpenter's sense of style, the character of Snake Plissken, and the concept of Manhattan being turned into a penal colony.

What are you currently doing and what do you enjoy doing in your spare time?

I'm on the verge of complete retirement right now although I have been doing short stints of VFX supervision from time to time. My most recent assignment was on-set VFX supervision for the pilot episode of the forthcoming Warner Bros series *Containment*. Other than that, I enjoy trail running with my dog, bicycle rides with my local cycling club, and shooting time lapse videos with my GoPro.

MARK STETSON
Miniature Construction [Uncredited]

How did you end up being a model maker, visual effects artist, and model shop/miniature/visual effects supervisor?

In 1977, I was continuing my studies in industrial design at Art Center College of Design in Pasadena, California. I also had a little over a year of professional training as an industrial design model maker at General Electric Company in Bridgeport, Connecticut. I went to see *Star Wars* on opening night at the [Grauman's] Chinese Theatre in Hollywood. I was blown away from the opening shot. I realized that I was looking at miniatures. I knew that I could make those miniatures and I had an epiphany that I could be pursuing that work instead of product design. A few months later, two of my classmates at Art Center, Christopher Ross and Tom Pahk, answered a job notice to work on miniatures for the upcoming *Star Trek* movie. A few months after that, I started pestering them and their boss Jim Dow to try to get on that crew. In April 1978, Jim hired me and my new career began. I ultimately worked for three different companies on *Star Trek: The Motion Picture* as I followed those models on their journey to the screen.

How did you get the job of model maker on *Escape From New York*?

I can't remember who recommended me to John [Wash] [Graphic Displays]. Perhaps it was Greg Jein or Pat McClung. I was working in set construction for a TV series when he called. I promptly quit that job and equipped a model shop in the garage of the house I was renting.

How did you and John Wash [Graphic Displays] prepare for this project and how did you collaborate on the wireframe computer graphics miniature model sets of Manhattan?

John worked very collaboratively and together we worked out the concept of the miniatures and how they were to be made. Then I bought the additional tools and built the fixtures we would need to accomplish the tasks. Besides

Mark Stetson [Miniature Construction] [Uncredited]
(Photo Courtesy Mark Stetson)

John and me, I hired an assistant, Kathy Iguchi [Production Assistant: Special Visual Effects] [Uncredited], the wife of one of the original Dream Quest Images founders Fred Iguchi. My wife Leslie was a working commercial photographer at that time, and she helped shoot the test model we built to verify the approach.

How were the three miniature model sets of Manhattan constructed, what kind of challenges did they provide, and how long did they take to make? John Wash came up the idea with using high-contrast lithographic line art glued to the models for instance.

I don't remember exactly. Probably five-six weeks. He started his career as a talented effects animator and had already accumulated extensive experience with photographic effects animation techniques. He also came up with the idea of rephotographing the footage on high-contrast stock to build contrast and try to take out as much shading of the shapes as possible to better simulate computer displays. That technique was used for the larger-scale model. For the small-scale model, John created line artwork of Manhattan and its streets and had it blown up to four feet by eight feet and dry mounted onto lauan plywood. I think a company called the Photo Blow-Up Lab performed the Photostat and dry-mounting work. Then I built some jigs to cut up 1/4" thick white Plexiglas into little shapes ranging in size from about 1/2"H x 1/2"W x 1/4"D to 3"H x 1/2"W x 1/4"D to represent each city block on the map with a generalized height. We spray painted all those thousands of blocks opaque black and then used a little Dremel router set up with some custom jigs to mill the edges off each of the blocks revealing the white plastic color beneath. That gave us our city block outlines for the wide view map. It was very tedious, but it worked well and it gave us a very consistent line thickness. We then hot-glued those shapes onto the dry-mounted line map.

How involved were you and John Wash during the filming of the models at Dream Quest and how were they shot?

John Wash and I were both involved in shooting the models at Dream Quest. Dream Quest Images had just been formed by a group of smart and talented guys who had been working for Douglas Trumbull [where I met them working on *Star Trek: The Motion Picture*]. There were seven partners in Dream Quest Images, if I remember correctly. Hoyt Yeatman, Scott Squires, Rocco Gioffre, Fred Iguchi,

Bob Hollister, and Tom Hollister. Hoyt, Scott and Rocco lived together in a rental tract house in a suburban neighborhood in Mar Vista and they were using that house as their headquarters. They were building a motion control camera rig in their two-car garage and writing software and painting matte paintings for demo projects in the house. John and I visited DQ [Dream Quest] to check the feasibility of shooting the miniatures with the motion control setup in the garage and then designed the tabletops accordingly. As you can see from the picture, the motion control rig worked best and the miniatures were easier to light when the tabletops were turned on their sides. That required some extra gussets and bulkheads in the models to screw them down. Final assembly of the larger-scaled models was accomplished in DQ's backyard outside the garage. I think John Wash mentioned the snorkel lens that was used for photography. I can't remember if that was a lens that DQ kept or if it was a rental. The snorkel lens was certainly a tool that DQ put to great use over the ensuing years. The tiny-scale model of Manhattan for the wide approach shot was assembled with just hot glue attaching the little acrylic building blocks to the tabletop. The sideways rigging under the hot studio lights in the confined space of the garage caused the little buildings to constantly fall off. The DQ stage crew took up the task of model maintenance once we had delivered the models and solved the basic rigging problems.

Bob and Tom Hollister were both experienced stagehands in the Trumbull organization, so they were quite adept at handling the miniatures. John Wash stayed close to the shoot throughout photography as the VFX supervisor responsible for creating the display graphics. He then, of course, took the footage and reprocessed it and added text graphics to it working from his studio in Hollywood. I went right into my next projects working for Greg Jein with Robert Short and David Heilman to build the first *Firefox* design prototype after which I started a design study mock-up for the Spinner for *Blade Runner*. The project that made my career. It was a busy little garage that summer in 1980.

According to IMDb, a model of the city was repainted and reused for *Blade Runner*. Since you were the Chief Model Maker for the movie, how much of this is true and how come that you used the models for *Blade Runner*?

Yes, that's true. We used the large-scale models as study models for shot planning with the main cityscape building set. Then we painted them black to use them as silhouette shapes to fill out the backgrounds of some shots.

Hoyt Yeatman [Motion Control Photographer] [Uncredited]
(Photo Courtesy Mark Stetson)

What happened to the models after *Blade Runner*?

At that point, they had become basically just black wooden blocks. They didn't have much value other than as last-minute space fillers. So, like many other miniatures, the effort and expense of storing them exceeded their immediate value and they were recycled or discarded.

What's your favorite memory or memories of working on the movie?

There were several. First, it was my first freelance miniatures contract which started me on my path of running model shops and my own business for the next fifteen years or so. I enjoyed meeting John and his family. We have remained friends since those days. I enjoyed working with John. We clicked well and we worked on many other projects together after that one. I also remember visiting the set with John while they were shooting at my alma mater Art Center College of Design [Liberty Island Security Control Interior] and seeing how locations so familiar to me could be used so effectively and look so different in the movie! I also visited Roger Corman's low budget VFX facility in Venice, California known as Hammond Lumber [Company] because it was housed in a defunct lumberyard. There John introduced me to the Skotak brothers, who were filming the night approach to Manhattan at the time. The exterior view that we were simulating with our computer displays. I saw some of the truly clever tricks the Skotaks were using for that scene like simply painting the concrete stage floor with glossy black paint to simulate New York harbor off the tip of Manhattan. Then I was very happy to have helped connect John with the talented group of guys who had just formed Dream Quest and who ambitiously shot the miniatures we built with a home-built motion control system in their garage!

What do you think of the movie personally?

I am a big fan of *Escape From New York*! In addition to its cult classic status, I think it is a wonderful cultural glimpse of the time it was made and a great satire. There is good chemistry amongst the cast and Kurt Russell's performance is iconic.

What are you currently doing and what do you enjoy doing in your spare time?

I spent the first fourteen years of my career as a model maker or supervising model crews, prop crews and creature crews. I had my own business, Stetson Visual Services, Inc. from 1989-1995 which specialized in miniature effects. Since 1995 I have worked as a VFX supervisor sometimes working directly for the movie studios and sometimes working for visual effects companies. For the last five years I have been working at Zoic Studios, a mid-sized VFX company that has studios in Los Angeles, Vancouver and New York City. I am the creative director of the features VFX division at Zoic Studios. Zoic is known as a powerhouse for episodic television work. The features VFX division is smaller than the episodic VFX division. I am currently supervising VFX for *Crouching Tiger Hidden Dragon: The Green Legend*. I haven't had much free time lately. When I do, I enjoy spending time with my family and our pets. I enjoy reading, listening to music, watching movies, watching motorsports, and when I get outdoors and past the chores, I enjoy skiing, diving and underwater photography.

JOHN L. HAMMONTREE
Special Thanks: National Guard of Missouri

How did you end up being military police?

I served four active-duty years in the U.S. Navy and, when I got out in January of 1970, I went back to college to work on a degree in criminal justice. I had stayed active in the Navy Reserve, but because of my interest in criminal justice, a friend of mine suggested that I join a U.S. Army Reserve military police unit, which I later did. While serving in the U.S. Army Reserve, I met an active-duty major that suggested that I go on active duty with the army. After considering military service as a career, I decided to do just that and this began my career in the U.S. Army Military Police Corps.

How did you and the Missouri National Guard get the job to be involved in *Escape From New York*?

I was assigned to a Missouri National Guard military police battalion headquarters at the time of the movie was shot in St. Louis, Missouri. We received a request to support the movie director by providing a platoon of military police officers in combat ready gear supplied by the movie company.

How did you prepare for this project and how was your experience filming?

A field hospital unit from the Missouri National Guard provided three Huey [Bell UH-1 Iroquois] helicopters for the event. There were approximately fifty guardsmen participating in a volunteer capacity, which also included the air crews of the helicopters. I believe they were paid $25 dollars each as extras in the movie. The set for the filming was the heart of St. Louis' downtown district. The movie company had turned the downtown area into an apocalyptic setting with destroyed old cars and debris everywhere. Smoke pots were used to create an even more ominous scene. This was the area the presidential pod had landed with the surviving President [Donald Pleasence] after the crash of AF-1 [Air Force One]. The mission of the guardsmen was to land in the helicopters about a block away from the downed pod and make a tactical approach to the area and extract the surviving President, take him back to the helicopters, and fly to safety.

This all created a problem the movie director had not expected. The downdraft between the buildings was so severe that the helicopter pilots didn't feel safe to try maneuvering in the located LZ [Landing Zone]. Rumor on set was that the copper crews were paid over $200 each if they would do it, so they agreed to the following. To minimize the danger, the helicopters would land in the downtown LZ empty of troops and equipment. They then shot the scene where Lee Van Cleef [Hauk], as commander of the United States Police Force, moved with the troops to the presidential pod where they found that the President had been taken by prisoners. The scene ends when one of the prisoners presents Van Cleef with the ring finger of the President as evidence that the President was in the possession of the prison population. At this time, Van Cleef and the MP's [Military Police] retreat from the area of the pod back to the awaiting helicopters. We boarded the helicopters and the pilots fired up the UH-1's. We lifted off the ground about fifty feet and then they settled back down on the LZ.

This was all filmed and gave the appearance that we were making a tactical landing. The troops got out of the helicopters and moved down the street towards the presidential pod. At this time, we had one injury with one of the guardsmen tripping over a box spring mattress in the street and breaking his ankle. After shooting this scene, we were treated to refreshments, paid, and released. If I remember correctly, it took most of the night to shoot the scene as I was pretty tired the next day at work. I don't remember how many takes were made, but the air lift up and down only took one try and the advance down the street as well. The scene at the presidential pod may have taken more.

Is it true that the scene started out with thirty men pouring out of the helicopters and into the streets but ended with only fifteen tired guardsmen left due to heat exhaustion, hard to see through helmets, a dislocated shoulder, and as mentioned a broken ankle? Also, was the guardsman who broke his ankle compensated in any way?

Well, there were ten men per helicopter for a total of thirty that participated in the shoot. Others were on hand to be used as extras as well but ended up not being used at all. As I recall, it was a platoon sized group which would be about fifty total. As far as the number that took part in the close-in shots at the presidential pod, there were probably only about fifteen, but that was all that was asked to participate. We did have one individual that received a broken ankle, but I'm unaware of any other injuries. It was terribly hot that night with all the equipment on, but I don't know of anyone suffering from heat exhaustion. The uniforms we wore were army surplus BDU's [Battle Dress Uniform] that had been dyed black. The helmets were standard black motorcycle helmets with dark tinted face shields. We didn't start the shoot until well into the evening [approximately 21:00 hours] and it lasted until after midnight so yes, the helmets were hard to see through in the dark. The weapons we carried were AR-15's with the forearm removed, so it exposed just the barrel of the rifle and had a flashlight taped to the barrel. The guardsman that received the broken ankle was put on workman's comp and received medical care through that state system.

How were the Huey helicopters you provided modified into the ones used in the movie? There's a goof in the movie where you can see one of the helicopters with a part revealing the original color only to be fixed in the subsequent shots for instance?

Ah yes, the black helicopters. The helicopters were the standard olive drab [OD] military colors when they landed at the site. The movie crew spray painted them a flat black using a special quick dry paint that is easily removed with high pressure air guns. Now remember, they were on the ground during most of the filming. The only problem came when we staged our retreat back to the helicopters and we took off as if we were leaving the city. The high press rotor wash blew the paint off most of the aircraft. The tail sections were again OD and had to be altered on the film. They corrected most of it but, as you said, you can catch a glimpse of the OD color if you watch closely. The United States Police [Force] emblem was only on the nose of the aircraft and that too came off easily with high pressure air. When the filming was over, the paint was blown off with the use of a compressor and air gun.

How was your experience working with the cast and crew? Is it true that Lee Van Cleef [Hauk] refused to fly in a helicopter and that John Carpenter himself flew up dressed as one of you and carried an AR-15 at one point for instance?

The cast and crew stayed pretty much to themselves. There was very little interaction between the guardsmen and them. I know that Lee Van Cleef did not go up in the chopper and to the best of my knowledge no other civilian was allowed in the choppers either.

What's your favorite memory or memories of working on the movie?

I would say the most memorable event for me was when we approached the presidential pod. I was the United States policeman to Lee Van Cleef's immediate right. Other than that, the way the scenes were shot kind of in a reverse manner was interesting and gave me a whole new perspective on how movies were made.

What do you think of the movie personally?

Well, I'm a Kurt Russell fan and back then Adrienne Barbeau [Maggie] was high on my list, so I got a kick out of seeing the movie. It's one of my favorites, but mainly because I was in it.

What do you think of having a police state as depicted in the movie by the United States Police Force?

Well, I have been all over the world and in countries where they have national police as opposed to local municipalities and state police. Trust me, you don't want a national police force. Our constitution doesn't allow for it to begin with, but in today's tumultuous times, who is to say that this couldn't change. The idea that one police organization would be responsible for control over the entire nation scares me to death. That's why we have the protection of the Posse Comitatus Act, which limits the use of military forces to police the states. The National Guard, when they are activated for riot control, they are under the control of the state governor from which they come from and can have police authority as a state police force. If federalized, then they fall under the control of the military and can no longer provide law enforcement duties only support to state law enforcement. Oh, I could ramble on all day about this, but it suffices to say I not in favor of a national police force.

What are you currently doing and what do you enjoy doing in your spare time?

I'm currently retired and live in Myrtle Beach, South Carolina with my wife and we enjoy the beach and nightlife of the city.

GINO LAMARTINA
Special Thanks [Uncredited]

How did you get the job of rental car supplier for the cast and crew on *Escape From New York*?

I hired a gal by the name of Valerie Abell. Her father was Walter Abell [Special Thanks]. He was director of streets and when the *Escape From New York* crew contacted him about doing the movie in St. Louis, Walter was in charge of that. They asked him if he had any references where they could get rental cars from and obviously his daughter worked for me and he called me. At the time I was with Horizon's West Rental Car. I was one of the operators of it so he called me and I was supplying the rental cars for them. I got to be involved with the people in that operation.

How many rental cars did you supply?

Close to fifty rental cars.

What kind of challenges did this project provide?

None whatsoever.

How was your experience working with the cast and crew?

I would go out and watch the filming at night like from midnight to six or seven when traffic in St. Louis started picking up. They filmed in a few places. They filmed at the Fox Theatre [Theater Exterior] which has been remodeled now. The old union station [Grand Central Station] at the time was under reservation. It was just very interesting to watch. The night filming was just amazing to watch. It was amazing to watch the production that goes on. The many takes that they did. Everything was precision and for somebody who comes from a retail, an automobile background it was just astonishing to see.

Eddie Lee Voelker was the transportation coordinator at the time for the movie. He and I worked very close. I became involved with Ernest Borgnine

[Cabbie]. Very, very affable person. He was just a character to be around. His stunt double was George Sawaya [Stunts]. Whenever they weren't filming they were hanging around my office hiding away. We had some good times there. Ernest is probably one of the most genuine down to earth people you'll ever run into. Just a neat, neat guy. We just shoot the boule all the time. I ended up introducing him to a friend of mine who owned a hotel, or several hotels in St. Louis. We were lifelong friends and we took Ernest and George out to Norwood Hills Country Club one day to play golf because Ernest wanted to get away from the set and get away from everybody else. We had an enjoyable time.

Lee Van Cleef [Hauk] was another one. I had very limited contact with him. I was with Adrienne [Barbeau] [Maggie] a couple of times. She's a wonderful lady. All the people on it. You think of movie stars these days and they're aloof and they're arrogant and this and that. Those people back then weren't that way. They were there, they had a job to do and they did it well and they were just humble people. Kurt Russell. I think it was just pretty much the beginning of his career. Just a neat, neat guy. He was a clown. He was a typical clown on the set. He was easy going. Fun to be around. Kind of a cross between I guess Bruce Willis and George Clooney. You know, just fun-loving people. Those are really the only ones I had really good contact with. In fact, Ernest. His wife Tova. She was doing a beauty line at the time. She was rolling out a beauty line. Skin care for women and Ernest went back to where he lived. I think it was L.A. at the time. Tova sent my wife her whole line of skin care products. That's how wonderful and genuine people they were.

Any special requests from any of them and such?

No, no, no. Whatever they needed, whatever they wanted, we gave it to them. Like I said, we were just in the transportation part of it. You know, if they had a day off shooting and needed an extra car, we just gave it to them because they did such good business with us. There was no prima donna request or any type of that stuff.

What's your favorite memory or memories of working on the movie?

Just being around the people. Just enjoying this thing with others. I was young at the time. Probably twenty-two or twenty-three years old. I'm sixty-one now. That's almost forty years ago. When you weren't star struck you were just happy to be a part of something. We were happy to be a part of that whole deal. It was quite an experience. It was a good experience for the city of St. Louis at the time too. You know, because we had a lot of stuff going on in the 80s here.

What do you think of the movie personally?

Well, I'm not a big science fiction type guy, but it was interesting. It was entertaining. Let's put it that way.

What are you currently doing and what do you enjoy doing in your spare time?

I'm currently still in the car business. I'm in the whole sale business. My spare time is fixing up my house. That's what my spare time is tied up in right now. It keeps me busy. I work about sixty hours a week. People say, "Why don't you start thinking about retiring?" I won't retire. I love working. It's something I've always done. Something I always do. What do they say? Find something you love to do and you'll never work a day in your life. That's the way it is.

RICHARD HESCOX
Pre-Production Ad Artist

How did you end up being an artist and a movie poster artist?

I always drew and loved doing art. I went to a good art college and graduated with honors. Being in Hollywood, film work was all around, so I just fell into it. I did poster art for *E.T.*, *The Dark Crystal*, *Swamp Thing* and lots of other projects.

How did you get the job to do promotional art before principal photography on *Escape From New York*?

I was doing film advertising illustrations at the time, and I would send my portfolio to all the ad agencies in town. On occasion, I would get a call to come in for an assignment. I was called to a company I hadn't worked for before. I don't remember their name now. They roughly explained the film to me. General story line was about all. They had a vague idea of the image they wanted. Snake squatting in front of a ruined but recognizable New York skyline with a suggestion of prison walls. It was pre-production, so there weren't any photos of the actors or sets to work from. They mentioned the eye patch, the snake tattoo, and they asked for a semi-futuristic big gun in his hands.

How was the art conceived?

I had full freedom to design the scene and the weapon and costume for the painting. The hair was just what my model had since they did not tell me any different. In terms of development, it was just to hear the details they gave me in one meeting. Do the painting, turn it in, and get paid. I have a vague memory that the art was initially done for an ad in *Variety* magazine to generate interest in the project before it got going. Maybe not even cast yet.

Did you know that your art was the inspiration behind the promotional pre-production photos of Kurt Russell as a long-haired Snake Plissken where his futuristic weapon was removed and a leather shirt was added?

All the other uses for the art were a surprise to me!

Top: Pre-Production Ad
Bottom: Pre-Production Ad [Close-Up]
(*Variety*)

Was this the only piece you did for the movie or did you have other drawings or ideas?

This was the only piece done.

How long did it take to make and what reactions did you get from it?

Probably less than a week. Hollywood always seemed to have short deadlines. Don't remember any specific reaction to it but they accepted it, paid me and used it so they must have liked it?

Are there any other anecdotes you'd like to share with us about the art?

My brother-in-law posed for the figure in my backyard. I changed the face from his, though.

What do you think of the movie personally?

Unfortunately, I never saw it.

What are you currently doing and what do you enjoy doing in your spare time?

Now I mostly paint personal paintings in the fantasy art genre and sell them to collectors. I was in computer game design for many years, but now I paint as I like without art directors.

FRANCIS DELIA
Pre-Production Portrait Photographer

How did you end up being a still photographer, screenwriter and director?

I grew up as a rock 'n' roll musician with my brothers and we were signed to RCA in 1966. The Bruthers resurfaced on compilations when the internet arrived with "Bad Way To Go" being recognized as a "garage punk classic." A Bruthers album was released on Sundazed Records in 2003. We never became the second coming of the Beatles, so I became a photographer and operated as a commercial photographer in New York in the mid-70s and got some cinematography experience. When a work opportunity brought me to L.A., I opened a studio in Hollywood with some friends where I took the photo of Kurt as Snake Plissken.

How do you work with people to get the photos you want?

It will always depend on the scope of the situation, your crew and the talent in front of the camera. "Previsualization" is always a key to getting what you want. Imagine what you want to depict then organize the troops to get it on film. Working with those in front of the camera is always a series of trials and errors. Some subtle, some more extreme. [See below for more details].

How did you get the job of portrait photographer of Kurt Russell as Snake Plissken before principal photography on *Escape From New York*?

My studio in Hollywood was very often hired to produce and shoot key art for movie ad campaigns. I was surrounded by a talented team that would build and help execute whatever was required for me to light and shoot. A boutique agency called B.D. Fox & Friends hired us to do the *Escape From New York* shoot.

How did you prepare for this project and how did you turn Richard Hescox's pre-production art for *Escape From New York* into reality? The skyscrapers depicted in his art were however missing in your photos. Were these originally going to be in the photos as well?

I'm guessing the prep took a day or two. Simply an arrangement of barbed wire, set smoke, lighting. Standard purchases/rentals were used to dress and/or light the set. I never intended to use skyscrapers per se but concentrated more on "mid-wife-ing" the birth of the character.

How was your experience working with Kurt Russell and how was Snake Plissken's initial look developed? In Richard Hescox's art Snake was suppose to be bare-chested and have a futuristic weapon for instance.

We were provided with a copy of an ink drawing of the character. I was unaware of who the illustrator was. I can say that the character depicted in the ink drawing I worked from was Clint Eastwood not Kurt. Bea Williams, our wardrobe stylist created the zippered-no-sleeve black shirt. The others in our crew were Steve Sayadian and Paulie Peterson. I'm sure Paulie cobbled together the prop gun and the tattoo. Kurt brought nothing special or any suggestions. We worked from the drawing plus any suggestions from the agency. My studio pretty much prepped and handled everything. My memory of Kurt was a cooperative bright-eyed young man eager to transition from Disney kid to full blown movie star.

Where were the photos taken, how long did it take to do the shoot, how many photos did you take and what kind of challenges did this project provide?

At our studio known as Francis Wolfe & Associates, 6646 Hollywood Boulevard, Hollywood, California. I can only say that the photography was done prior to the Cannes festival that year. If the movie was released in 1981 an educated guess would put the photo session in early 1980. The shoot went for three, four hours. I photographed using 2 1/4" square Ektachrome. Estimated frames expose, 144 plus countless polaroids. One brief challenge came when John Carpenter walked in mid-shoot instantly enamored of the way things were looking. He peered down the periscope finder on my Hasselblad. I think I remember a slight, "Wow." but ever the director John began to offer a lighting suggestion [something about pin lights in Kurt's eyes] then thought better of it realizing if it works don't risk collapsing the house of cards. [I used a custom-built Gordon Willis-inspired directional soft key light].

What's your favorite memory or memories of working on the movie? Also, what kind of comments from people have you got about the photos?

Like you, not that many are aware that I am the photographer so I can't think of too many comments. My own [immodest] comment. In a sense I feel the real Snake was born that day at our studio. Favorite memory, a big wet kiss [on the cheek] from Kurt when I presented him with a finished polaroid in the dressing room after the shoot.

What do you think of the movie personally?

I'm a fan of all of John's work and very much *Escape From New York*.

What are you currently doing and what do you enjoy doing in your spare time?

I am currently developing up to two dozen feature and television projects and have just finished the second draft of feature film script, *The Forger*. Our front burner series is entitled *Voodoo Guitar Man*. I read a lot in my spare time [Norman Mailer, Ernest Hemingway], listen to Bob Dylan and love to spend time with my kids, grandchildren, friends and goddaughter.

BARRY E. JACKSON
Poster Artist

How did you end up being an artist and a movie poster artist?

I began by walking the streets with my portfolio making cold calls from recommendations and going anywhere and everywhere. My first job was in the animation business doing backgrounds for Ralph Bakshi's animated film *The Lord of the Rings*. After a few years, I left there and began seeking work in the movie poster and album cover business. I just phoned people and asked if they would look at my work. That is very hard to do today.

How did you get the job to do an *Escape From New York* poster?

I had done a number of assignments for a design studio called Seiniger Productions in West L.A. An art director named David Renerick had the idea of the Statue of Liberty's head in the street. I composed a rough drawing that everyone liked so they asked me to paint the finished poster.

How was the poster conceived and can you elaborate a bit more about the decapitated head of the Statue of Liberty?

There was a lot of competition to get the poster for *Escape From New York*. John Carpenter was very hot at the time. When I heard David Renerick's idea, I knew it was a winner. I did one rough and one finished piece that took about two weeks. It came back for corrections that took another week. I had not seen the film. I don't think David had seen it either. David knew the decapitated head was not in the movie but felt it was a valid metaphor. I am sure some people felt cheated that they didn't get to see that scene, but the movie was not what you would call an effects extravaganza. It was more tongue in cheek. If people went to see the movie *Cloverfield*, they actually did the shot with the Statue of Liberty's head! I read that J.J. Abrams got the idea from my poster! It's weird how this industry works.

Did you have any other ideas or drawings prior to the final one?

I had done other ideas for the poster for other design studios. I can't remember all the roughs, but I did one finished B&W of a down shot of Manhattan in which the building tops spelled out *Escape From New York*. Not used. Prior to my poster an illustrator named Stan Watts had done an illustration of the Statue of Liberty's arm with a handcuff holding the torch. He was told he had the poster for the whole campaign. It was printed and used in film festivals I believe. I aced him out at the last second.

How long did it take to make the poster art and what reactions did you get?

As far as comments, they were all positive. I probably could have become a full-time poster artist if I wanted to, but I had plans to move to New York and try other things.

Did you ever get any comments from John Carpenter about the poster?

I never heard a word from John Carpenter.

Are there any other anecdotes you'd like to share with us about the poster?

The original art was stolen and still legally belongs to me. I never found out who stole it. Avco Embassy brought the job to Seiniger Productions. I made a deal to do the art but did not do it work for hire. I signed away rights to print the poster while maintaining the right to keep the original art. Seiniger Productions told me someone at Avco had the art. I went there and was stonewalled at the reception desk. I called and called but didn't have the power to shake things up. Avco went under the next year. That art is in somebody's closet somewhere.

What do you think of the movie personally?

The movie attempts to be nothing more than a classic lowbrow B-movie. It is funny and enjoyable if you watch it keeping that in mind.

What are you currently doing and what do you enjoy doing in your spare time?

I work as a designer at studio called Yu and Company. I am doing a lot of art for the opening titles for *The Great and Powerful Oz* as well as the new *300* movie. I play golf for physical activity. I work on my own animated film for pleasure.

STAN WATTS
Poster Artist

How did you end up being an artist and a movie poster artist?

Well, I wasn't really a poster artist. Freelance meant you did a lot of everything for anybody. From label art for toilet bowl cleaners to the coolest rock covers and big-name portraits. I was interested in making money to pay bills and took on any project I could and did so for thirty-five years. Not too many of my contemporaries made it that far. The onset of the computer wiped out most and then just killed me at a slower rate of time. Most posters were a nightmare, but they paid great and you just put up with the sometimes poor concepts. ENDLESS and MEANINGLESS changes. The deadlines were ALWAYS unrealistic and the quality ALWAYS suffered. They were never my favorite assignment [except for *The Howling*] but they were lucrative, and I always said yes to Hollywood.

As far as them being used, there are a couple of thoughts. Sometimes after doing a piece of art that HAD to be done over the weekend, you would then spend the next week and a half doing bullshit changes. By then you didn't care if it went to print or not. You just wanted to get paid. The joy and pleasure of a movie poster was stripped away early on in the process. I much more preferred to do comps [comprehensive layout]. They paid great. They were little mini posters and there was generally a little more freedom there. That's how *The Howling* was created. They looked for images for months and couldn't find one. I was asked to do a comp that I just experimented with and did. Turned out to be the one. Those were the fun ones.

How did you get the job to do an *Escape From New York* poster?

Artwork was commissioned through Craig Butler Design.

How was the poster conceived and did you have any other ideas or drawings prior to the final one?

Well, there isn't a lot to talk about when it comes to that particular image. The concept was comped out and I just did the finish. It wasn't one that I had much creative ownership to.

How long did it take to make the poster art and what reactions did you get from it?

As I alluded to, there was never enough time to do a project with care and attention and as I recall this was no exception. My average time on any project was five to seven days. That included gathering photo reference, props, models etcetera and approval times. Actual rendering time was usually three days.

How come another artist called Ben Bensen did the portraits on it?

Here's the deal. As far as the inset illustrations [portraits], I barely had enough time to do the poster. They always "subbed" things out that way. As far as them making sections to use it or not use, it was an industry standard. Happened all the time. Like I said, I usually didn't care what they did with it as long as they paid. Hey, and as an industry they sometimes tried NOT to.

Is it true that you were told that you had the poster for the whole campaign only at the very last moment being aced out to Barry E. Jackson's one?

The Barry Jackson piece was the kind of crap they would always land on. Not that it was a bad concept, but it was a dated piece the minute the paint dried. Somehow losing out to a piece like that made sense in a weird way. As standard procedure, they always chose a couple of comps to go to finish, so you never knew who was doing what for whom. They must have had mountains of money in those days. A comp could pay 2.5k to 5k. The finish 10k, 15k, 20k. So, you can see why my "dance with the movie industry" was a bittersweet arrangement.

Were you disappointed that your poster wasn't used except for film festivals?

As far as *Escape From New York*, I didn't have any input on the image. I like Kurt Russell and was somewhat hopeful about the image. The Kurt Russell image I was SICK about losing out at the last minute to a really CRAPPY image was *The Thing*. I did this sophisticated image of a steel door in a subarctic setting being smashed into from the outside with bright iridescent light coming in through a breach in the door. Loved the movie. Loved the image. It just wasn't meant to be.

Are there any other anecdotes you'd like to share with us about the poster?

I think I still retain the art.

What do you think of the movie personally?

As far as the movie goes, I wasn't a fan. It was a caricature of a film to me anyway. My favorite Kurt Russell films will always be *Big Trouble in Little China* and *The Thing*. Met him once at a dinner party. A nice man.

What are you currently doing and what do you enjoy doing in your spare time?

Well, as far as my career, the computer killed me slowly. I was convinced that I needed to convert which I did and began the slow spiral down. As more and more people piled on Photoshop, respect for the media plummeted. It was just a push button approach to illustration and very few of the younger art directors actually had a background or understood real illustration. Prices dropped, deadlines diminished, and the ability to show new work to new ADs [Art Directors] became impossible. My last portfolio showing was with a local Austin agency. It was a Monday morning. I showed my slides and when the house lights came on half of the twenty something's ADs were asleep. I didn't say a word, just loaded up and left. Humiliating. That was it for me.

I had seen older illustrators when I was a young illustrator at art shows in L.A. and I would always say to myself, "What the fuck are you doing here?" Well, I came full circle and it was now my time to gracefully take stage left. It was traumatic for a number of years. A few straggler jobs came in from New York which I would KILL myself doing. Shitty budgets, shitty art direction only to have a ho-hum reaction to the finish. Tough. So, I quit in midstream of a series of illustrations for a Japanese video game, character development thing. I knew then I had no business in illustration any longer. I don't sketch, cartoon [my first love] or have any appreciation for art, fine or otherwise any longer. It stole thirty plus years of my life. Spent hunched over a desk 7 AM to 2 AM every day. Even holidays. I will give it no more of myself. I retrained on a CAD [Computer-Aided Design] program and work for a traffic control company.

Designing highways/streets and doing traffic control for major utilities like PG&E and AT&T. I love doing it. It's mentally demanding, still involves building something from start to finish and I'm not dealing with anyone's egos including my own. Well, there it is. More than I talked art in a decade at least. Not sure if this is what you wanted to hear. You were probably looking for something flashy and upbeat. That's just not my reality.

BEN BENSEN III
Poster Artist

How did you end up being an artist and a movie poster artist?

I grew up in New Orleans, LA and lived between two airfields. One civil and one military. It was a big influence on me. I learned to paint trying to imitate the art on the boxtops of model airplane kits. Attending the Art Center College of Design after getting one degree in advertising in Louisiana, I met one of my heroes who was teaching illustration, Jack Leynnwood who made his living amongst other assignments creating artwork for plastic model kits at Revell and Aurora. I took every class I could get with Jack. Later, Jack would help me land a job at an aerospace company where I worked as an art director and product illustrator until I left four years later to pursue my freelance career. I got to be a movie poster artist through my agent at the time. I was hired as a storyboard and presentation artist. I created quite a few movie comps [comprehensive layout] for presentation to the client over a period of a year or so, but I seldom got to paint the finished artwork.

How did you get the job to do the portraits on Stan Watts' *Escape From New York* poster?

I was asked to present a concept for the *Escape* poster at the design firm Craig Butler Design, but it wasn't accepted. At the time, I heard some of L.A.'s finest illustrators were vying for the opportunity to paint the final concept. I didn't get accepted, so I blew it all off and moved on. Sometime later, Craig Butler called and asked if I was interested in painting the inset portraits of the stars. I knew Craig and Lexi Scott from the Graphic Artists Guild, so often I got asked to create tight comps that I later found being used as final art for print. I can point out quite a few of those jobs back in the day.

Opposite Page: Inset Portraits / Advance Poster
(Art Courtesy Ben Bensen III)

Kurt Russell as "Snake"  Lee Van Cleef as "Police Commissioner"

Isaac Hayes as the "Duke of NY"  Harry Dean Stanton as "Brain"

Donald Pleasence as "The President"  Ernest Borgnine as "Cabbie"

Adrienne Barbeau as "Girlfriend"

283

How was the art conceived?

As is usually the case, I am not afforded the time to create great art. There didn't seem to be too much time to explore any options other than to make the portraits fit in a particular size. I believe I was given black and white stills of the cast. One of each actor. I wasn't too happy with the 8" x 10" glosses of Harry Dean Stanton [Brain] or Donald Pleasence [President], but there didn't seem to be any alternatives.

How long did it take to make the portraits and what reactions did you get from it?

I probably spent about eight or ten hours per portrait. I'm pretty sure the 12" x 16" insets were completed in acrylics without approval of the roughs in a four-day weekend. My favorite portrait of the seven is the one of Isaac Hayes [The Duke]. Some came easier than others. I wasn't asked to do it, but I thought I'd create a misty otherworld mood by incorporating an airbrush. Sometimes one has the opportunity to view the film ahead of time, but this was not the case. I don't remember seeing Stan Watts' painting as a final, which is the one that my portraits were used for, but I did see Barry [E.] Jackson's version and it had that blue lit background, which is how I got the idea to use the blue misty feel. As for the reactions, I don't recall Craig or anyone else going apeshit over the finished portraits. "Thanks, the check's in the mail!" I did get the original artwork returned to me, which I still have in my possession.

Are there any other anecdotes you'd like to share with us about the art?

I didn't particularly like Barry's poster because I felt the people running away from the fallen head was a classic horror or science fiction cliché. It seemed to me as an add-on. Personally, I thought the Statue of Liberty's severed head was the perfect solution. It really didn't need much else. As for Stan's poster, I still hate the handcuffs. It doesn't seem to belong to the rest of the imagery and is a bit over the top. I wonder what Stan would have said. In a way the Statue of Liberty concept representing a dystopian situation was first used in the original *Planet of the Apes* I believe.

Is it true that you had no idea how your art was used prior to me telling you?

Yes. I really didn't know until you mentioned it to me that the portraits were actually used as final art. There was mentioned that the "comps" might be use for foreign promotion, but I never did follow up on that. At the time, to be honest, I really didn't think much about the film or that it would become a cult classic. I didn't see the film until years later.

What do you think of the movie personally?

When I first saw the movie, I wasn't all that impressed. It seemed to have a B-movie feel to it. Later, I rented the movie and felt it holds up well given the plethora of hell in a handbasket and end of the world movies.

What are you currently doing and what do you enjoy doing in your spare time?

Well, after twenty years, I've kinda retired from the U.S. Air Force Art Program as one of the chairpersons. The Pentagon has enough of my aviation paintings. I no longer design, paint, or create much that has a deadline as a requirement. My wife and I live on five acres in a small town sixty miles north of New Orleans. I paint aircraft, jazz musicians, and landscapes for local galleries.

RENATO CASARO
Italian Poster Artist

How did you end up being an artist and a movie poster artist?

See my biography at casaro-renato-art.com.

How did you get the job to do the Italian *Escape From New York* poster?

I did the poster in Italy on order of the world sales company of the film which was Medusa at that time.

How was the poster conceived and did you have any other ideas or drawings prior to the final one?

Yes, there were always some more ideas from which the client would decide which one would be the selection for the final artwork.

Why did you decide to have Snake Plissken wear an earring?

As to say the truth, I don't remember this, but there was definitely a reason to do so.

How long did it take to make the poster art and what reactions did you get from it?

Two weeks. After the artwork is done and the client likes it, the real reactions come from the public. The film was a success and so far.

Are there any other anecdotes you'd like to share with us about the poster?

Yes, in the movie Kurt Russell wears a patch over the left eye. By mistake, I did it on the right one. Only after the poster was printed did we realize this.

What do you think of the movie personally?

I generally like the work of Carpenter. It was one of the first movies of its kind and Carpenter did a very good job.

What are you currently doing and what do you enjoy doing in your spare time?

I'm working on a huge painting which will take part of my PAINTED MOVIES series. I love movies and have spent my lifetime to work with greatest pleasure for it. In my "leisure" time, I'm traveling in African countries and the Arabian deserts as to study the wildlife and landscapes, but it always ends up in paintings.

PAUL CHADWICK
Poster Artist

How did you end up being an artist, a movie poster artist, and a writer for comic books?

I was a comics fan as a teen but, at that time, the mid-70s, the conventional wisdom was that comics were dying, supplanted by TV and mortally wounded by the fading away of mom-and-pop candy stores. Of course, we couldn't have been more wrong. Hobbyists and comic book stores came to the rescue. Nevertheless, I figured I'd better use my love of drawing in another field. Illustration for magazines, advertising, and book covers. So, I went to Art Center College of Design in Pasadena, California and earned a BFA [Bachelor of Fine Arts] in illustration. I freelanced after that and also began storyboarding movies. Ironically, drawn and painted illustration has very nearly disappeared from magazines [which are themselves dying because of the internet] and books and advertising supplanted by Photoshop imagery. And comics have never had a higher cultural profile.

How did you get the job to do an *Escape From New York* poster?

When I graduated from Art Center in 1979, there were a number of small ad agencies in Los Angeles devoted to the movie industry known as "movie boutiques." B. D. Fox & Friends, Seiniger & Associates, and Rod Dyer are some that I remember working for. They'd commission numerous illustrators to execute perhaps twenty, thirty poster ideas. The studio people would pick one or combine elements of two to go to finish whereupon one of the top illustrators in town like Drew Struzan, Robert Tannenbaum, or John Solie would execute the finished art. I was one of the many comp [comprehensive layout] artists. I think *Escape From New York* might've been for B. D. Fox. I was a pretty good sketch artist, though my painting skills weren't top-drawer. Still, I eventually got three or four finish jobs for other movies.

How was the poster conceived and did you have any other ideas or drawings prior to the final one?

Agency people assigned us ideas that came out of their brainstorming sessions. We freelancers would paint the illustrations, then they'd overlay typography. It's strange to think of all the great ads and designs never seen by anybody but the clients then put in a closet or thrown away. Attached is the first finished drawing I turned in. As you see, they decided to have the crashed presidential plane in the background instead of Isaac Hayes [The Duke] and the gunner. Incidentally I originally turned in a sketch that didn't have the forced perspective on the gun, which seems out of place to me still.

How long did it take to make the poster and what reactions did you get from it?

I had four or five days as I recall. Never enough time. They liked it well enough. I think I got more work afterward, but of course it wasn't used. Sometime later I interviewed with director Joe Dante to do storyboards for the science fiction film *The Philadelphia Project*. He saw the piece in my portfolio and said that he'd lobbied John Carpenter to use mine. That gave me a glow for the rest of the day. Incidentally, directing chores passed to Stewart Raffill for that film, though I still did some illustration for the VFX department on it.

Were you disappointed that your poster art wasn't used?

Sigh. It would've been one of the highlights of my career, but I can't honestly say it would have been as good as Barry [E.] Jackson's beautiful, crazy poster that they used, despite its head-scratching logic. How the devil did the Statue of Liberty's head get on 6th Avenue!?

Are there any other anecdotes you'd like to share with us about the poster?

Just that I wish I had the original or at least a better record of it than the 35mm slide with parallax problems that form the basis of the scan attached. A lot of detail has dropped out. I also seem to have flopped it inadvertently! Entropy never rests. Hey internet, if anybody owns it contact me via my blog!

What do you think of the movie personally?

This may seem churlish, but I had been supplied the screenplay beforehand and thought it was the best thriller script I'd yet read. Fast, inventive, funny,

Poster Sketch
(Art Courtesy Paul Chadwick)

Revised Poster Sketch
(Art Courtesy Paul Chadwick)

Final Art [Unused]
(Art Courtesy Paul Chadwick)

and suspenseful, but they clearly didn't have the budget to achieve the kinetic drive present in the script and I was a little disappointed when I first saw it. It just wasn't as grand as the mental images the words inspired. Of course, I also knew all the surprises in the plot, so I was robbed of those little pleasurable discoveries. I still liked it enough to buy the spooky soundtrack though, which I played through many an hour at the drawing board. It's in my computer's music file to this day, in fact.

You know what still gives me a chuckle? There is a long lead time on Disney animated films and their soundtracks are recorded early in the process. So, a considerably younger Kurt Russell appeared as the adorable hound in *The Fox and the Hound* the same year he played battered, hard-bitten Snake Plissken in *Escape From New York*. Also, it's ironic that the script, probably written in the 70s when New York was going to hell, envisioned Manhattan walled off and abandoned to criminals when the 80s actually saw Manhattan gentrified into glossy unaffordability.

What are you currently doing and what do you enjoy doing in your spare time?

I'm finishing a graphic novel *Best Wishes* that will be out next year. Then more *Concrete*. I balance writing and art by caring for the family farm, hitting the gym most days, and wasting hours on the fascination machine - the internet. I simply cannot believe how different life is with every question quickly answerable, every subject easily investigated. Even thirty-four year old cult movies like *Escape From New York* have people documenting their every aspect!

KIM PASSEY
Poster Artist

How did you end up being an artist and a movie poster artist?

As a child, my mother would draw pictures to keep me from squirming around during church services. I was about four years old at the time and the proceedings were a little too long for my attention span. Sitting in the pew one Sunday, I received a revelation. While watching mom draw, it came to me like a bolt from above. I can do better than that! [Sorry, mom.] From that time on I was drawing constantly. I started out by copying cartoon characters from TV and books. Later I started drawing from memory [Popeye was the first character I remember drawing.] By the time I got to junior high, I graduated to comic books and started drawing superheroes. In the eighth or ninth grade, I discovered a massive book in the school library filled with Norman Rockwell paintings. That was it. My destiny was set. I was going to be an illustrator!

We were a military family and moved around the country during most of my school years. I'm not an extrovert by nature and making new friends wasn't easy. Each time we moved I had to establish a new social network. Drawing helped in a couple of ways. It allowed me to entertain myself when I was feeling isolated. It allowed me to retreat into my own fantasies/reality. On the other hand, my ability to draw attracted a lot of attention. It didn't really matter which class I was in I drew all of the time. Without intending it I received a lot of positive feedback from kids sitting nearby. This type of encouragement only reinforced my artistic ambitions. After my fourth year in college, I determined it was time to move to the "real world" and start my career as a freelance illustrator. In the Spring of 1979 with $1500 in my back pocket, I put two suitcases, my drawing board, and some art supplies into my 1973 VW Beetle and left school to seek my fortune in Los Angeles. I won't go much into the proverbial "starving artist" stereotype, but the first year or two was pretty rough. However, with a lot of luck, a few crucial connections, and an introduction to an inexperienced but eager agent [known as an artist's representative or "Rep" for short], I managed to get a foothold in the industry.

By my second year, I was actually starting to make a living as an illustrator. To build a career in Los Angeles, it was necessary to seek assignments in as many art markets as possible. Over a twenty year period, I worked for entertainment studios, advertising agencies, editorial clients, and toy manufacturers. For clarity, the "entertainment industry" includes movie studios, television, theme parks, and video games. By my second year I had the opportunity to do a number of movie posters and movie poster comps [comprehensive layout]. Comps were generally half the size of a full-sized movie poster [30" x 40"]. They were usually full color but not intended as finished art mainly to flesh out a concept. Most movie related work came to me through my hard-working agent.

How did you get the job to do an *Escape From New York* poster?

As mentioned, the chance to do a comp for *Escape From New York* came through my rep. Back in the day [1980s], movie studios didn't produce posters "in-house." Creating a print campaign was usually left to small advertising agencies known as "boutiques." Seiniger Advertising, B. D. Fox and New York West were three agencies I had a chance to work with. The *Escape* assignment came to me via New York West.

How was the poster conceived and did you have any other ideas or drawings prior to the final one?

The total creative process isn't in the hands of an individual illustrator. There's just too much money on the line and too little time for individual illustrators to be involved early in the process. Instead, a creative director or a small number of art directors at a boutique will come up with a number of ideas for several posters. These ideas can be crudely drawn on a napkin during lunch. In many cases ideas are given to a studio concept artist who makes a fast pencil sketch or loose marker rendering. Later, these rough layout sketches will be turned over to an illustrator. Between six to ten poster ideas are settled on. Illustrators are contacted at this point. Illustrators are chosen because of style but, more often than not, availability because illustrators are independent freelance talent and it's likely they are already committed to project and unable to accept a job when contacted. There's a certain random aspect to the whole thing. However, if the artist is available and interested, he'll jump at the chance. When an illustrator comes to an agency he is briefed on the movie's plot, who's starring in the film, given idea sketches and reference material [usually black and white movie stills and photos]. Rarely does an artist get to pre-screen a movie. Prior to release, studios want as little information to get out to the public as possible.

Final Art [Unused]
(Art Courtesy Kim Passey)

With limited background, a hand full of references, and a deadline the illustrator leaves to start work on the particular concept assigned to him. The *Escape From New York* assignment I received followed the procedure above. Each artist comes to the agency alone. We don't know what the competition is doing nor do we know what the other ideas are. There's not much leeway to interpret the concept assigned. The central figure, cityscape, laser blasting through the metal door, the keyhole, and metal rivets were all part of the assigned layout I received. Without a prior screening of the movie, I had no way of knowing whether or not the laser had anything to do with the storyline or not. All I had to go on was the briefing I received from the art director. Whatever originality or creativity I brought to the assignment was usually due to technique or execution. Once the comp was completed, it's delivered to the boutique on or before the deadline. All comps are gathered by the art director and delivered to the movie studio for review. A final comp is chosen through a process of elimination. Sometimes additional comps are done, but it's usually a refinement on one or more of the original pieces. At this point a specific artist is chosen to create the final movie poster. There's no guarantee the artist who did the original comp will do the finished poster. The finished poster may be handed over to a "big-name" artist to execute.

How long did it take to make the poster and what reactions did you get from it?

It's a little difficult recalling the exact circumstance surrounding a piece I did thirty years ago. Typically, New York West would give me a call on a Friday afternoon around 3 PM and need finished art by Monday morning at 9 or 10 AM. That meant I would leave my place immediately and drive thirty minutes to New York West's location in Hollywood. We'd spend around an hour going over specifics and gathering references. I'd leave their office around 5 or 5:30 PM just in time for rush hour traffic. Getting home would take twice as long as my drive into Hollywood. That meant another hour or so would get eaten up in transit. At this point, it would be around 6 PM before getting home. I'd eat an early dinner and start working by 7 PM. From that point on, it would be crunch-time until I delivered art on Monday morning. Overnighters were just accepted. Often the art director would drop by on Saturday or Sunday to check my progress. That might eat up another hour. Of course, if he/she had issues, my workload would be increased. That didn't matter. The deadline remained the same.

This was the typical turnaround time for New York West. Less frequently, they would call in the middle of the week and need a project done by the following

Monday. Instead of a two-and-a-half-day turnaround, I might have three or four days plus a weekend to complete a job. I want to say my *Escape From New York* assignment benefited from this schedule, but it's hard to recall. I'd always heard horror stories about deadlines in connection to the advertising industry, but ad agencies have nothing over entertainment clients. Anything connected to movies always put me under a lot of stress. On the positive side, budgets were usually better than other art markets. The entertainment industry's solution to a problem, just throw money at it. Problem solved! I wish I could recall the exact reactions to my *Escape From New York* comp when I turned it in. I felt fine about it considering the circumstances and turnaround time. Typically, most art directors are very non-committal until studio executives have a chance to review things. At that point they sometimes get back to you with feedback. Obviously, the comp chosen was the "winner." All other contenders are thanked with a paycheck. Whatever the outcome it's yesterday's news. On to the next movie!

Were you disappointed that your poster art wasn't used?

I never took things too personally. I always assumed that if they called me back for another project [which they did numerous times], they must be satisfied with my work. Without major creative input from the start, I really couldn't become overly invested in the end result. I did my best to do what was asked of me with the information I had in the time allotted in a professional manner. I'm not sure I could have done much more. I know this isn't how movie fans like to envision things. Movies are certainly entertainment but unfortunately much of the time it's just business.

Are there any other anecdotes you'd like to share with us about the poster?

No real anecdotes per say. Looking back thirty-four years, I see things I'd approach differently with my poster. Given the same parameters, I'd stress a much grungier look. The reflective door and rivets are too clean. I'd go with a rusted boilerplate look with plenty of corrosion. I'd enlarge the central figure more and make his pose more crouched and dramatic through the keyhole. The laser beam would still be there, but the blast would have more molten metal, smoke, and sparks shooting all over the place. Better yet, there's a scene in the movie where Kurt Russell shoots an automatic weapon through a wall and creates a perforated oval opening. Perhaps the laser should have been replaced all together with something along these lines. I think these changes would still be in keeping with the original assignment and better reflect the overall character of the movie. Keep in mind, the first time I viewed the movie was when it was released to the public. Had I seen a trailer prior to painting the poster, it would have been a big help.

What do you think of the movie personally?

I enjoyed it back in 1981 when it first came out. Plenty of action kept things moving. I have not seen it in years. I went to YouTube to view a trailer just to remind myself. These days it would get a bigger budget, even more dramatic camera angles, and more computer-generated special effects. For the most part, it holds up well.

What are you currently doing and what do you enjoy doing in your spare time?

I began my career as a freelance illustrator in 1979. The world of commercial art today bears little resemblance to art markets of the 1980s. Few artists could have predicted the impact of computers on commercial art back then. Most of us were working for clients in the entertainment, advertising, packaging and editorial markets. Nearly all artwork we produced was intended for print media. Print media was king. The work we created was reproduced in the form of posters, magazines, album covers, point-of-purchase advertising, greeting cards, and product packaging. In other words, our livelihoods depended on getting artwork distributed to the public through printed materials. This ended with the digital revolution. By the late 80s hand painted illustrations for movies posters was a thing of the past. You may have noticed there are no hand illustrated movie posters hanging at theater entrances or in lobbies these days. Instead, nearly all posters are photo compositions assembled in Adobe Photoshop today.

Through the 90s, the same trend moved through advertising agencies and product packaging. By the end of the decade "the writing was on the wall." Print media was dead for illustrators. The future was digital media. That meant computer monitors, TV sets, game consoles, laptops, tablets, and smart phones. Many of my contemporaries either left commercial art, transitioned to art galleries or found a niche in the developing digital world. Because there was a shortage of trained digital artists, many found work as concept artists in the computer game industry and from there received on-the-job training using digital media and software. This is the path I took. Starting in 2000, I found work in the computer game industry. I started as a concept artist, learned 3D modeling software [Maya], UVLayout and texture painting [Photoshop]. I gradually moved from concept artist to character modeler, then art director and finally to creative director. In 2008, the Great Recession hit and the company I worked for went out of business as a result of the collapse of Lehman Brothers bank. From 2009 to 2014, I bounced around between freelance work, contract work, odd jobs, unemployment, and a two-year stint as an art director working for a small company making games for social media and smart phones. While there, I gained experience using Adobe Illustrator and learned to created vector assets for online games. Finally in June of 2014, because of my Adobe Illustrator experience and thanks to a wonderful art director, I was hired as a concept artist at Wildworks Studios [Salt Lake City, Utah]. I really enjoy my work and the people I work with.

As of this writing, I have been part of the studio for just over a year and I love it. Outside of art [and employment] I enjoy traveling, dining out, movies, social dance, and outdoor activities like hiking, fishing and camping. I also enjoy studying philosophy, religion, mythology, sociology, and psychology.

HAROLD JOHNSON
Movie Tie-In Board Game Designer

How did you end up being a game designer/editor and author?

I started to war game in 1969. I was introduced to *Dungeons & Dragons* in summer of 1975 when I returned home for my brother's wedding. I got a gaming group together when I returned to Northwestern University and played for years. In the summer of 1976, I attended my first Gen Con Game Fair [first one run by TSR [Tactical Studies Rules] and first AD&D [Advanced Dungeons & Dragons] Open. I complained loudly how unfair and poorly designed the tournament was and was recruited to create and run an adventure that show. I've been working with Gen Con as volunteer and staff and manager ever since. I graduated summer of 1977 with a degree in biology and a minor in history [of ancient near eastern religions]. I did not like my job opportunities. In the summer of 1978, I discovered TSR was looking to hire an editor and applied [actually just as an exercise for interviewing, intended to turn it down if the job was offered to me]. I did not get offered the job. In the fall of 1978, I applied to be the lead designer for the *D&D* line and actually was offered the job. However, Gary [Gygax] [TSR Co-Founder] called and said they had lost an editor while they were working on the *Dungeon Masters Guide* and so he [and my gaming mates] convinced me to take the job of editor. David "Zeb" Cook was hired as designer.

In order to prove my design chops, I volunteered to write the AD&D Open on the side for Origins 79 [Origins International Game Expo, which became *C1: The Hidden Shrine of Tamoachan*]. Still an editor, I took to reinventing my job with each new assignment. I put a behind schedule product on hold to help our one-man staff for Gen Con. I took three months to create and draft three new *Player Character Record Sheets* and I finished several very late projects. Instead of making me the designer I had been promised, I was drafted as the new manager of editing and, in the summer of 1982, after some personnel changes I was offered the position of director of production and games [at that time called VP of publishing]. By the fall of that year, I had taken us from two years behind schedule to a year and a half ahead of schedule and feared TSR might not keep us on since they did not need us anymore. I secretly directed my staff on several Blue Sky projects and eventually selected Tracy Hickman and co-created *The Dragonlance Saga* over a weekend. I then spent a year getting it in shape to sell TSR on the concept of the first cross-merchandised lines for hobby games. I was never officially a game designer, but I did have my hands in every project for nearly a decade before I transferred to other duties. I often served as a rules developer, ghost writer, and editor. I guess it was because I was a fledgling author from fourth grade on and even wrote and published amateur writer magazines and later children's plays and read lots of comic books and other game products that helped me develop my skills as a storyteller. As an editor I parleyed my skills as a copywriter and copy editor and just told everyone I was an editor while I found and studied manuals on editing and writing. My writing as an author and designer were always done on the side in order to fill a gap in our schedule when I could not find anyone else to take on the task. So, I guess designer by accident and demand. I have only in this century got a chance to try my hand writing as a freelance author, but frankly am not really thrilled with the results because I never get to devote sufficient time to the task.

How did you and TSR [Tactical Studies Rules] get the assignment to do an *Escape From New York* movie tie-in board game?

During my time as director of games, we were approached by a number of movie companies to license their movies for games since Milton Bradley, Parker Brothers, Selchow and Righter, Coleco, Ideal, Mattel, and Hasbro were not interested. Movie properties offered to us included *Blade Runner* [I turned it down because it was a downer ending. Must have had everyone tell them that because they altered the script and movie in the end], *Dark Crystal* [Jim Henson Productions. Desperately wanted to do this one but could not convince TSR management to take the leap. Darn!], *Take This Job and Shove It* [actually designed a game for this one] and many more. It must be understood that mass market games were expensive for hobby game companies to make and produce and demanded a very low suggested retail price. It took creative design and a variety of short cuts to be able to make money on these games. A deck of cards cost over a dollar, so we had sheets of cards that players had to punch out to save cost. The hard game board cost over a dollar a piece so we went with a half-sized board and so on.

The Movie Tie-In Board Game

How did you, David Cook [Game Designer], and TSR prepare for this project and how did you come up with the game play and design? Is it true that you only had the advance press kit as the only reference material for instance?

When the *Escape From New York* script was offered to us, the design department howled that the story was silly and preposterous and that there was no way we could design a game for it. I disagreed. I said we can always design a great game on any topic. The trick was, could we design one on a topic that the public would want to buy? Zeb challenged me to tell him how we could design a game for *Escape From New York*. After a brief thought, I told him how I would do it based on some game mechanics we had already been play-testing. The next day, Zeb walked in and said, "You were right, Harold. I designed that game last night based on your ideas," and because we then had a fun game already designed, I agreed we should take a chance with the license to use as an example of what we could do for other movies. Over the years that followed we developed games or adventures for a variety of films including *2001: A Space Odyssey, 2010: The Year We Make Contact, Dynasty, All My Children, Indiana Jones,* and *Conan*.

As already answered, that game design occurred as the result of my describing the game mechanics I would use based on recent playtests and discussion of game mechanics we had already been toying with at the shop. After that, Zeb brainstormed and created the board and cards straight out of his head and brought it in for us to playtest and tweak as a result. Over the years Zeb often surprised me with quick designs taking inspiration from a variety of places. I was concerned with the components and pricing and printing once we had our final design. In addition, the release of a movie tie-in required a quick completion of the product [we normally took two years plus to create and market a game] and lots of lead time for advertising. That required a cover NOW! [we had never done this before] and so the only art available at that time [since the film was still in production] was the concept art in the press kit. Placement in vital catalogs such as Sears and JC Penney required a lot of lead time and would make the difference between a successful mass market release and a failure. So there was no time to waste. In those decades [who are we kidding. They still do it today] many film companies kept their productions secret so they could not be scooped [George Lucas, Steven Spielberg, James Cameron, Paramount and Universal all required non-disclosure agreements]. Therefore, it was more a matter of the deadlines for marketing that drove us to use pre-production art so we could get it out in time for a coordinated release of the film seven months later. Once it was published in catalogs, we could not change it. We did have a first or second draft of the script as a reference and barring them making major changes to the story. That proved good enough.

What kind of challenges did this project provide, where was it made, how long did it take to make the game and how well did it sell?

What kind of challenges did this project provide? Since I do not possess the company's actual sales records anymore [Wizards of the Coast has them], the best I can recall is based on dim memories from over three decades ago. As mentioned in a prior response, a lot of the issues centered around producing and marketing a mass market game for the first time. Under our pricing structure and overhead costs, we had to spend no more than ten percent of the final desired price and we wanted to keep the suggested retail at $10-$15. A deck of cards would have cost $1, a double board $1, pawns and dice are pennies but a traditional box with four color was another $1. So, I had to be creative and develop cost savings to keep the product within the project cost of goods budget.

Where was it made? The game was written at 772 Main Street, Lake Geneva, Wisconsin on the third floor above Kilwin's Chocolate. TSR used to own that building and production offices were on the third floor. Printed? In those days our go-to printer was Patch Press who is located in South Beloit, Illinois. Every time we wanted to do a product in a new format we had to work with them to determine what their limits were. They were the ones that helped us change over from label wrapped chipboard game boxes [also used for jigsaw puzzles] to set up boxes which were printed on thin poster board and die-cut then folded into shape and did not require us to glue a label on chipboard and saved us a lot of money. Patch Press was an invaluable partner and taught me a lot about the printing industry.

How long did it take to make the game? Once play-testing was finished and the rules edited [about three weeks], it took all of two weeks to complete the typesetting and art and ready for paste up and the printers. As noted, this was an incredibly short production time in comparison to other games we had published over the years. During this time, I had to convince marketing and then the executives that this was a good thing to do as a dip our toe into the world of licensing other properties as well as selling mass market games and not just hobby market games. Because of catalog deadlines with Sears and Toys "R"

Us, our biggest accounts we had to make do with using conceptual art instead of final promotional art which had yet to be finished for the movie.

How well did it sell? I no longer possess the sales records that I did from those early days. It was no Milton Bradley volume of one million copies, but we did print about 100,000 copies and place them in all our mass market outlets including Sears. We did not do a second print run and let the license run its length and not renew it. I was surprised that the movie *Escape From New York* gained a cult following but the game never really did.

What's your favorite memory or memories of working on this project?

Well, my favorite memory of this game was conceptualizing the game in minutes and then Zeb Cook designing it in an evening and telling me I was right. I don't get a lot of "attaboys." Mostly it is a constant struggle of conceptualization, engineering and pricing, salesmanship and constant negotiation and renegotiations to keep a game on track and on schedule. It is kind of like movies. You have to be championing your creations all the time or someone new comes in and says, "I didn't have anything to do with that product. Cancel it!"

Is it true that Avco Embassy, the studio was pleased with the game and even invited you to a special screening in a private Milwaukee theater?

Yes, there was a special screening of the *Escape From New York* movie for our company. I believe that was the brainchild of our marketing guru Gordon Giles [but I may be misremembering that].

Do you agree or disagree with John Carpenter who says that the tie-in board game is pretty hard?

I never heard that John Carpenter thought the game was hard. I will admit that it followed the formula set by games like *Source of the Nile* and *Knights of Camelot* which has since been adopted by many zombie games that the chance for survival is low without a good amount of luck and some backstabbing treachery to help you survive just a little longer than your opponents. Though we got the components and pricing to work for the mass market, we had yet to be schooled by Mike Gray of Milton Bradley and for a time TSR in the proper method of designing a family friendly board game with better odds. For that matter, if we had been Milton Bradley we would never have had as quick a turnaround because we would have engaged in several months of focus group testing and then redesign and retesting.

Is there anything you would've done differently in retrospect to the game?

The game was a war game with grim consequences dictated by the story. However, I love the countdown game mechanic with its unexpected arrival and would definitely keep it. Today, knowing better how to make a mass market game, I would re-analyze the odds and try to make them a better match for family satisfaction. When we wrote *Knights of Camelot*, the original odds of elimination was one in six with each die roll and there might be several rolls in one turn. I changed it to one in thirty-six using two dice to make elimination less frequent. Perhaps even put in some catch up/short cut features [but probably not. I like the dire nature of the game]. If I was doing this game today, I would include a real deck of four-color cards and a bigger map of Manhattan with perhaps a subway/sewers or rooftop route to escape since producing board games is more economical today. But generally, I would put my focus in the printed rules and maybe even include illustrated character profiles and maybe some fiction to set the tone of the world for players and the rules would also be in four-color.

What do you think of the movie personally?

The movie is a hoot, goofy, melodramatic, overly allegorical [though not as much as *Escape From L.A.*]. I prefer *Big Trouble in Little China* for the obvious humor and wise cracking, but that's just me. I like superhero stories [that's why I brought *Marvel Super Heroes* to TSR] but more the Marvel story style than the DC style. I guess it's the existence of pathos and drama mixed with humor and flippancy that I like.

What are you currently doing and what do you enjoy doing in your spare time?

Spare time. What's that? Let's see. I work for UPS [United Parcel Service] as a preload supervisor and deal with the chaos of getting trucks loaded every weekday from 2-10 AM. I own a bookstore [Breadloaf Bookstore] that is open every day from noon till 5 PM-ish [sometimes 6 or 7] and am 50 percent of the staffing and help manage the mall property as time permits. I work at conventions and do events and help with some of the management duties. I am a grandfather of three little girls whom I never see but think about all the time and a father to three great kids who are all grown but still value a relationship with me. I have a mother who is in her 90s and very with it and whom I want to spend as much time enjoying her company while she is still here. I am an elder in my church [Dutch Reformed which is sort of Dutch Presbyterian which is sort of what I was raised in]. I do theater every month and charitable events to benefit community charities and host a book festival, public speaking and radio. I read a lot and watch movies, television shows and theater as I can. I game whenever I can squeeze it in and do models for miniature games to run events at all the game conventions. And I write and write. Stories, articles, plays [two so far this year], speeches and gaming adventures morning, noon and night. And every so often, say three or four times a year I design game rules for whatever inspires me. A *Dark Sun* chariot race/gladiatorial game, Mega Bloks Dragons, interesting abstract games inspired by certain floor tiles, plastic easter eggs with dinosaur heads on them etcetera. Oh yes, and I give interviews on blogs, radio and answer questions like yours as I can.

BILL WILLINGHAM
Movie Tie-In Board Game Artist

How did you end up being an artist and writer for comic books?

They were two tracks that eventually converged into a single related profession. In my early days trying to break into comics, I was under the understandable impression that one had to either choose to be a writer of comics or an artist. While I was interested in both, thinking I had to choose, I chose to pursue drawing comics, which after more than a year of trying [after I left TSR [Tactial Studies Rules] I finally got to do. Drawing a page of comics day in and day out is tough. I began to become frustrated at putting so much work in for less than thrilling stories. After a few years of getting less than sterling scripts from many comics writers, I decided to start writing what I drew. After that, it was only a matter of time before I began writing what other artists drew.

How did you get the job to be an illustrator for the *Escape From New York* movie tie-in board game?

It was my turn. Seriously, we had a rotating system where whoever finished a job was the first guy to begin the next job in line. I was the first available artist in the rotation when the *Escape* project came down to us, so I was assigned by virtue of availability. That occurred in the summer of 1980 to the summer of 1981 when I was a staff artist for TSR, the publishers of *Dungeons & Dragons*.

How did you and Erol Otus [Illustrator] prepare for this project and how did you collaborate? Is it true that you only had the advance press kit as the only reference material for instance?

I'm not entirely sure how Erol prepared for the undertaking. Most of the preparation on my part as the first artist in the rotation available to take on the new project involved begging. This was long before the internet. I couldn't just look up references to the stars of *Escape* or images of the film-in-progress the way one can now. My only source of reference for the film was an advance publicity/

Movie Tie-In Board Game Art

press package that contained many photos of the film being shot and the stars in it. Unfortunately, that press package when it arrived at TSR's main offices was scooped up by Gary Gygax [TSR Co-Founder] who was determined to keep it all to himself [one can only guess at his reasons]. In any case, with the deadline clock ticking away to produce the cover painting and other illustrations I kept calling over to the main offices begging Gary to let me use the photo references just long enough to do the work. Finally, he reluctantly sent a messenger over with some of the photos from the press package, but none containing shots of Adrienne Barbeau [Maggie] whom he specially adored. At first his messenger was going to stand over me while I perused the photos, but our art director Dave Sutherland was able to coax the fellow away long enough for me to get some work done. I eventually had a fraction of the photos in the press package to look at plus I had a copy of the screenplay.

As the first artist on this particular job, it fell to me to read up on any written material that came along. This included a copy of the screenplay, which was carefully monitored. Since the story was a closely guarded secret, strict records were kept on who had what watermarked copies. I don't recall who at TSR had to sign with John Carpenter's people to receive a copy of the screenplay. I think it might have been [David] "Zeb" Cook [Game Designer] but don't hold me to that, but it certainly wasn't me. When Zeb dropped off the screenplay for me to read, he quickly forgot all about it. I read it, gleaned what I could from the story, and put the thing away in a drawer. Eventually, the Carpenter people came looking for their screenplay back but by then no one at TSR could remember who had it [except for me but I wasn't telling]. My half-assed plan at the time was to clandestinely sell the screenplay to *Starlog*, a pop culture magazine at the time because they'd been mentioning how desperate they were to find out anything about the new production. Of course, I never tried to follow through on that scheme. Truth is, I never follow through on my best schemes. It seems my criminal impishness is limited to planning and wondering what if. That screenplay was still in my desk drawer when I left TSR. I wonder what became of it.

How long did it take to make all the illustrations and were any art/ideas discarded?
Two work days because that's all the time left to us to do the art once the contracting people were done messing around and second-guessing everything. Like the *Indiana Jones* game, the *Escape* game was a constantly on-again, off-again project. TSR had a reputation [well deserved I think] for being a tough group to negotiate with and would often raise ridiculous demands. In any case, one day the project was suddenly on-again, but by then most of the advance time had been burned up, leaving us almost no time to actually create the game. By then, the development boys [one floor above] had cobbled some rules together with the very little time they had to work. The art department only ever got whatever time to work on a given project that the other stations of creation and development left us once they took their sweet time finishing their parts of the job. We had to rush the job out and it looks it. Too bad. It could've been much better. Nothing on the *Escape* game was discarded because we didn't have time to make mistakes. Anything we finished got used no matter how good or bad it was. I have no idea what became of the originals for *Escape From New York* the board game. TSR kept all original art produced for any of their publications. There's an equal chance they were thrown out or pilfered away by one of the TSR suits.

What's your favorite illustration or illustrations for the game and which were the most challenging and fun to work on?
I'm sorry to say, I have no favorite illustrations for this game for the reasons mentioned above. I was given so little time to do it that every part of it was rushed in a ridiculous fury of last-minute effort and it looks rushed and perfunctory. One

of my motivations for leaving TSR for greener pastures was that the time available to do the art for any given project was always whatever amount of time was left over once the other departments had finished their parts. There was always a rush on every project by the time it made its way to the artists. I began to despair at how rushed and slipshod my art was becoming so I began to plot my exit.

What's your favorite memory or memories of working on this project?

As the first of the art team to become available for this game when it came up in the work rotation, it was incumbent upon me to read the source material so that I could suggest things to be illustrated and generally begin to form the idea of what the game would look like. In this case, the first bit of source material available was the *Escape From New York* screenplay. I was quite taken with the story. It was a good screenplay. Possibly a great one. I was a little disappointed when the movie came out that it didn't include the opening scene where we got to see Snake Plissken get captured. I heard much later that it was filmed but edited out of the final cut for time.

What do you think of the movie personally?

I liked it. Though using some of the more depressed [meaning inexpensive] areas of St. Louis as a stand-in for New York City made for some clunky bits here and there. I like most of John Carpenter's film work and I'm quite the fan of Kurt Russell as an actor.

Did you attend the special screening for TSR [Tactial Studies Rules]?

Nope. By the time the movie came out, I had already moved on from TSR and probably wasn't considered a good ally of the company. They never informed me there would be a special screening.

What are you currently doing and what do you enjoy doing in your spare time?

Currently I'm doing what I've been doing for the past forty-plus years. Using a combination of art and words to tell [what I hope are] interesting stories. I read. I swim. I cook. I host/call bingo games for one of the local activity clubs. I take naps. I occasionally sit down in a poker game. A few years ago, I was approached by BOOM! Studios to write an *Escape From New York* comic series for which they'd obtained the rights. I went so far as to plot out the three big arcs of the series. John Carpenter's original plan was to do a trilogy. *Escape From New York*, *Escape From L.A.* and finally *Escape From Earth*. Of course, he never got to do that last one, so I plotted out a similar trilogy. In my trilogy the first arc was *Escape From New York*. If you'll recall, the *L.A.* movie ended with Snake plunging all of Earth into a new dark age. My story would've taken up where that left off. Earth is a post-apocalyptic hell hole. But where did Snake disappear to? Well, knowing what was coming, he decided to return to the one place where they'd had many years worth of time adjusting to exactly such a standard of living. New York City. That's where a young and frisky group of rebels track him down and talk him into joining them in their plans to leave Earth entirely. There's a space station up there where all of the elite live. It's called Heaven. Their cushy lives continues while Earth suffers. They're going to steal a supply shuttle and get off of this world but first they have to escape from New York. The second arc was going to be called *Escape From Earth* which details how they steal the shuttle and lift off to the space station which they do only to find out Heaven has also fallen into savagery and now it's called Hell. The final arc was going to be called *Escape From Hell* which I imagine they would've found a way to do, but where do they go from there? Who knows because I never got to write it. Talks stalled over pay and time to do the work. I wasn't going to be able to get to it right away. Too bad too as it would've involved meeting John Carpenter and [perhaps] Kurt Russell. I did hear second hand that Carpenter liked the outline. Oh well.

EROL OTUS
Movie Tie-In Board Game Artist

How did you end up being an artist and game designer?

I've always been interested in art. I drew a lot as a little kid. Eventually, it became a dream to somehow make a living doing artwork. This seemed a bit of a trick when I started at university. I was trying to make a possible go at architecture, starting off with environmental design classes. This, however, was not looking good as I was certain I would be miserable doing such things. From junior high up to this point, I had been keeping up playing *D&D* [*Dungeons & Dragons*] and doing a lot of artwork for the games I would run as DM [Dungeon Master]. I would also do various fantasy and science fiction illustrations. Some of these I started sending unsolicited to *The Dragon Magazine*. They did end up publishing some and when TSR [Tactical Studies Rules] needed a staff artist they contacted me.

How did you get the job to illustrate the *Escape From New York* tie-in game?

As a staff artist at TSR, we would usually work on almost every product that was published in-house.

How did you and Bill Willingham [Illustrator] prepare for this project and how did you collaborate? Is it true that you only had the advance press kit as the only reference material for instance?

Bill and I were both staff artists at TSR. We received our assignments through our art director Jim Roslof or directly from the design staff. We had a pretty good amount of artistic freedom. The amount of contribution per artist on any given project varied a lot. I only really remember the illustration of the things coming out of the sewer [The Crazies]. The cover is plainly Willingham. I think we had some photos.

How come the Crazies look so ghoulish?

I think that just comes from my unconscious.

Movie Tie-In Board Game Art

How long did it take to make all the illustrations and were any art/ideas discarded?

I think it probably took me about a day to do.

What's your favorite illustration or illustrations for the game and which were the most challenging and fun to work on?

I only remember doing the one illustration, so that would have to be my favorite.

What do you think of the movie personally?

I liked the film, though it's been a very long time since I've seen it.

Did you attend the special screening for TSR [Tactical Studies Rules]?

I did not attend a TSR special screening.

What are you currently doing and what do you enjoy doing in your spare time?

I'm keeping up a slow but steady stream of freelance artwork. Playing *D&D* and tennis.

E.T. STEADMAN
Movie Tie-In Novel Artist

How did you end up being an artist and cover artist?

I have always been involved in art since fourth grade. Later in life I wanted to illustrate children's books. Maurice Sendak was one of my teachers at Parsons School of Design. When I first got out of school, I had a B&W cross hatching style. I illustrated many stories for *Analog* and *Isaac Asimov's Science Fiction Magazine*. About a million and half hatching lines later, I realized I could do things faster with an airbrush. I started getting work in color and soon three years after I started an agent approached me and asked if wanted to become a serious illustrator. I did advertising art for the next eight years. I worked for Coke, Sprite, IBM, Subaru, Crest, Seagrams, lots of airlines and many, many more. Something changed in the world market and I moved into painting book covers. I did lots of fantasy for Bantam Books. I can't remember, but I think this was for them. From Bantam I went to them all. I had new agents. Scholastic, Simon and Schuster, Troll, Zebra, Putnam and others too. I became momentarily famous with all twelve-year olds when *Goosebumps* was out. I did not do them but I did five other creepy for kids thrillers. I did three hundred covers in five years. From there I worked for *Playboy*, did postage stamps, and began to teach.

How did you get the job to do the cover art for the 1985 re-release of the U.S. *Escape From New York* movie tie-in novel?

My style fit what the art directors were looking for.

How was the cover art conceived and did you have any other ideas or drawings prior to the final one?

It was so long ago. I really can't remember. At that time, I usually presented four sketches. One was chosen and I would do a photo shoot, a tight sketch, then a final. There was always a deadline. I did all my work from photos, so the model who posed as Snake Plissken for this was my brother-in-law, Phillip Schlegel.

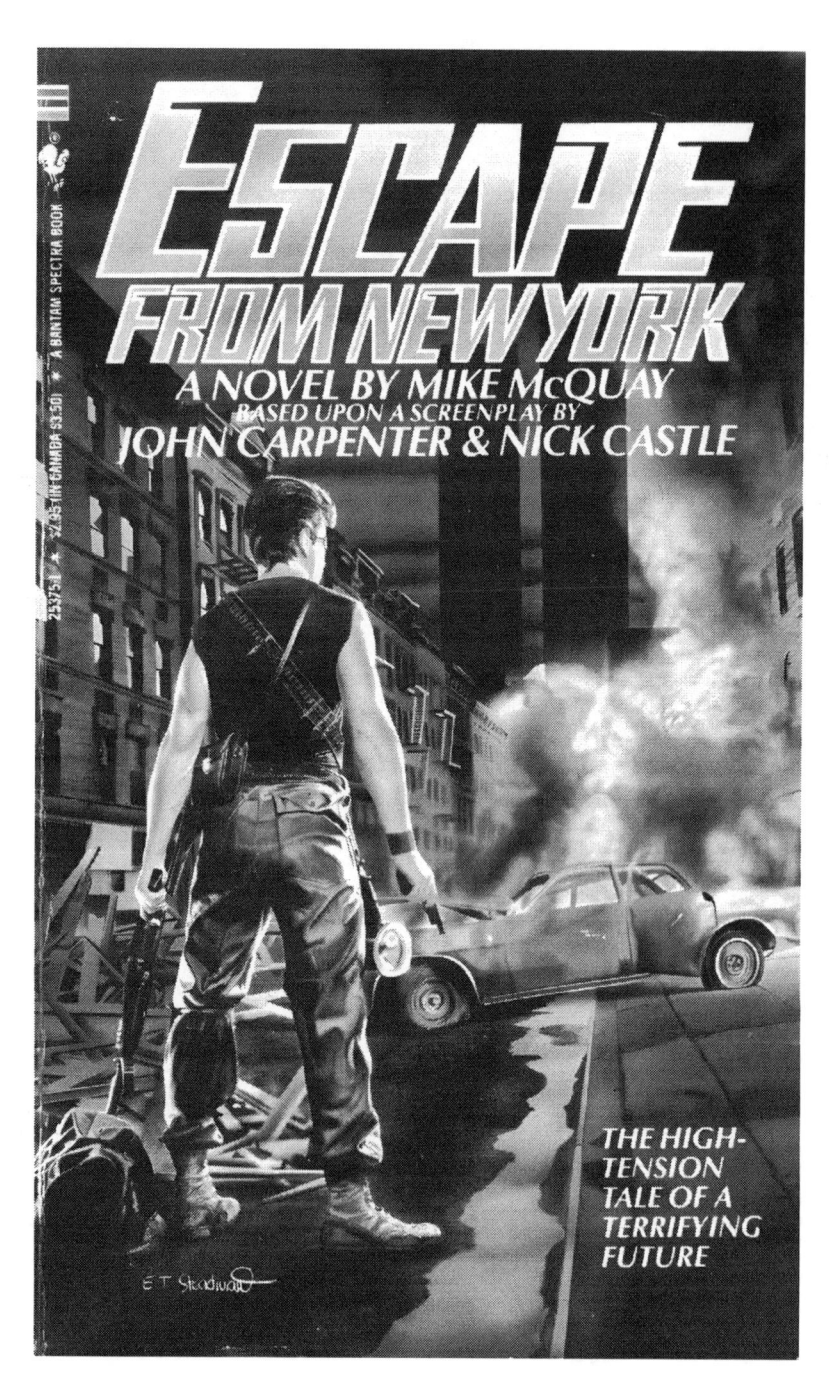

Movie Tie-In Novel [Third Cover] [December, 1985]

Kurt Russell was unavailable. The street scene was a photo I took down 97th Street [New York] looking west. I lived on 96th Street at the time.

How come Snake Plissken looks nothing like him in your art?

I did not have the rights to paint Kurt Russell. It must have been the art director who lead me in that direction.

How long did it take to make the cover art and what reactions did you get from it?

The normal time frame was two weeks for sketches and two weeks for the finished artwork.

Are there any other anecdotes you'd like to share with us about the cover art?

I gave the original artwork to my brother-in-law who was the model.

Did you ever read the movie tie-in novel and if so, what did you think of it?

I did not. At this point in my career there were editors who read and met with art directors who would usually give me a paragraph or two of the description of the book and characters.

What do you think of the movie personally?

I loved the movie. I like Kurt Russell in anything.

What are you currently doing and what do you enjoy doing in your spare time?

I'm painting murals now and teaching. Our local school system was looking for someone to paint a mural in their cafeteria that blossomed into what I do these days. Murals in people's homes, businesses, etcetera. I'm a gardener, a beekeeper, a bread maker, a good cook. My kids are twenty-six and twenty-nine now and I'm so proud of both of them. They grew up watching me cook, would pitch in and help and now they both surpass me.

On Living with Snake
By Mike McQuay

As a property, *Escape From New York* has had an interesting endurance rate over the last six years or so. Its continuing popularity has always been a source of interest to me [both economically and artistically] and something that I've always wanted to examine close up. So when Judi [Raish] and Linda [Ojard] flattered me by asking me to write a piece for *Snakebit*, it struck me that it might be the perfect time to take a look at the phenomenon through my own involvement in it, through my skewered view, as it were.

If the dynamics of the film and book business working in concert [disconcert] is of no interest to you, I suggest you tear out this page and use it taped to your window to keep out that little aggravating ray of sunshine that always comes in and hits you in the eye. Thanks. The rest of us will proceed. I may even have a couple of things to tell you about your favorite eye-patched hero that you didn't know.

My first association with the project that would eventually become *Escape* came during the summer of 1980. My editor at Bantam at the time was a lady named Karen Haas, who had just purchased one of the novels that turned out to be a series about a future private eye named Matt Swain. Karen asked me if I'd be interested in a novelization job of an unnamed film [the first thing you learn in the book business is that nobody tells you anything unless they have to] that was being done by "the guy who made *Halloween*." Being basically easy and agreeable little shit, I said sure. At which time she told me that fifteen other people were also up for it and thank you very much.

I never heard anything else until about four months later. I got a call from a man in L.A., who asked me if I was still interested in the novelization. I said, again, sure and he gave me the job on the spot and told the title was *Escape From New York*. He also gave me the second rule of the book business - they need it right away. No matter that they sat on the property for five extra months while bumping percentage points from a quarter to a half and back again. They have to have the book rights away - six weeks tops, not even enough time for the contract to get written and a check made, which is rule #3 - the writer is always the last one paid.

Movie Tie-In Novel

Fine. I enjoy pressure [and money]. I said, "Sure. Send me a script." They were happy to oblige, and, in the delivery, cut another week and half off my already brief schedule.

Three things struck me upon receipt of the red-bound manuscript: one, it had a 1974 completion script that had probably been written totally ten more times since this edition; two, the script bore a strong resemblance to a film Carpenter had already made [more on this later]; and, three, the story had an antihero as its protagonist - usually no, no in the book business.

I rejected the script, knowing it wouldn't resemble the film that was still being shot [this was October, 1980]. They promised me another from the middleman in L.A. [I never spoke with Carpenter or any of his people], and while waiting for the new script, I set about trying to figure out how to expand a 120 page script into a 300 page novel. I did it by killing two birds with one stone.

I'd learned enough in script #1 to know that they'd really done nothing to expand the motivations or backgrounds of the characters [in the first script the film opens with Snake's robbing the Federal Reserve in Colorado, then being caught after a long, drawn out chase sequence where he tries to escape on his specially equipped motorcycle that expanded the Snake imagery - bet you didn't know that!], so I decided to give him good, solid motivations and set them out in the book, which served the purpose of building sympathy for him with the book reader. I finished out the process by taking Carpenter's McGuffin, the tape, and making it a harmful instead of helpful thing. In so doing, the government is not only stuck with responsibility for the ways things are [instead of out-of-control crime], but it also makes Snake a humane hero instead of a cad. And in the book, I think that's the way he should be. [Why you ask - because in a book you identify with the protagonist in ways that you don't in a film, and nobody wants to identify for any amount of time with an asshole; plus, you spend more time with a book hour-wise than you do with a film and consequently have to like the characters better]. All the extra characterization and motivation would more compensate for the extra pages.

I'd found out from Karen that I was hired because they'd read my first Swain book, so that took care of my next problem - style. I used a modified Swain style, changing from first to third person on *Escape*, and I think it was a good decision. I'd also found out the story behind the film. Apparently, *Escape* was the first script Carpenter wrote after his film school experience. He'd been unable to sell it [probably because of natural anti-s/f bias and the cost of the production], so it simply languished. Later, he had the opportunity to revive the script as an urban drama that was eventually called, *Assault on Precinct 13*.

If you've never seen this film, take a look. In many ways it's superior to *Escape*, predating it by several years. The same situations and characters are duplicated in both films with minor changes. Carpenter does similar music in both films. The Snake Plissken character has several of the same lines in both films. Two of the actors, Frank Doubleday and Charles Cyphers from *Escape* play nearly identical roles in *Assault*.

In another week and a half another script arrived. This one was, as I suspected, very dissimilar from the first. By now, I already had a pretty good feel for Snake and his world [once I had adequately explained it to myself] and I dove in.

I spent four or five weeks in the actual writing, finishing in November of 1980. It was a relatively simple write because the story was simplistic. In fact, I found myself complicating it just for fun with subliminal subplots and by starting scenes well ahead of the action in the film. The only real problem I had was with the aforementioned McGuffin. In the film, the tape is music-only "Bandstand Boogie", and believe it or not, music-only does not translate very well to the printed page. Ta ta ta ta-da, Ta ta ta ta da-da da... you get the message. So, it became necessary to change the McGuffin music. Simple enough to me - I just used the words for "Satisfaction" by the Stones. It fit perfectly. My new editor [I'd been kicked up to the movie tie-in department], Fred Klein, did not agree.

Fred called and told me that Bantam Books nor any combined thirty publishers could afford the royalties it would cost to get permission to use that song. He suggested that I write one. Better still, he suggested that <u>he</u> write one because he always wrote skits for the reps down at the sales conferences in Florida every summer [rough work if you can get it].

That got me to the typewriter [we still used typewriters back in those days], and I turned out a wonderful little ditty called, "Night Music", and sent it to Fred who then informed me that he had written a song called "Gettin' Even", that was sung to the tune of "Satisfaction" [of course]. I argued. Fred disagreed. He turned it over to a higher authority [his secretary] to ask for her unbiased opinion as to which song was better. If there's any doubt as to which song Fred's secretary chose, get a copy of my novelization and try to remember the tune to "Satisfaction".

When I finished the thing, my real problems began. Everybody wanted the right to edit, from the filmmaker on down. I went through Carpenter corrections, the L.A. middleman corrections, then corrections in New York by Fred [he did not edit anything out of his song, though], leaving very little of my initial manuscript. They did things like, cut out all the humor [there's nothing funny about this!] and all the philosophy [what's this shit?!], then, remembering rule #2, they proceeded to send it back to me in late April to tell me I had to hurry and get my galley corrections back in five days or they'd miss pub date in June. They were so rushed this time they told me if I couldn't get them mailed back in time, that I could call them in to somebody in production.

The beauty of every system is that it has been created by humans and has loopholes. I held my manuscript; I held it for too long and then called it in to a sweet young lady in production who was just soooo happy to meet a real writer and would you please be kind enough to put all those nasty deletions right back in that manuscript and oh yes, I'd be glad to do whatever you say and - Voila! The butchery was done in by my heads-up trench fighting. Every unkind cut was readded to the manuscript, the thing going out exactly as written, humor and all. It was a move worthy of Snake Plissken. Production was rushed to get it out at film release, so rushed that the first cover was taken from a still of Kurt Russell instead of the cover art, though the cover art was stuck on the second edition.

The opening was fun. We happened to be in New York when the movie premiered there in June of '81. They had a real media blitz and even had stenciled the name of the film all over the streets around Broadway. I stood in the B. Dalton's at 666 Fifth Avenue and watched people buy my book [I also watched one woman pick it up, read the last page, and put it back down - I learned my lesson about hanging around the racks]. It was fun. It also did things for me.

Escape was only my second published novel. I'd written others, but this was rushed out ahead of them because of the timing of the film release. It had an initial printing of 150,000 copies, which is great for science fiction. Within two weeks we were back to press for an additional 50,000. There were a number of overseas editions. In the book's healthy run, it's been through three American covers and four printings, the latest just last year.

As a writer, the impact was tremendous for me. The book sold well and I became more recognizable in a very short time. We had some fun *Escape* parties for awhile [for a time I feared my eleven year old son would become Snake; he did a great impersonation]. Then, of course, it faded.

One of the very sad things about writing is that if you do it, you usually aren't able to enjoy it once you've done it. I've never reread anything I've ever written. I daresay very few writers have. So, I've never gone back and peeked through the book again to see if it's any good. It was a fun write, but not so spectacularly innovative write since I was basically doing someone else's ideas, ideas that I would have taken in entirely different directions. It went quick; I probably had the money spent even before I got it - but then that's usually a safe bet with me.

I don't think the movie had a very successful run first time around. It did well in the big cities, then died in the heartland. It may have done well oversees, though. But for some reason, for a pretty solid cult, the story still lives and breathes. This publication is proof enough of that. Why? Maybe you guys can answer that better than me. But I'd like to take a shot at it anyway.

Snake's a loner in the Ollie North/Clint Eastwood/John Wayne mold, a singular type of <u>individual</u> who cuts through the bullshit to get something done. In *Escape*, the tangle of the city could be a metaphor for the endless red tape that seems to entangle our lives anymore, over which we are powerless to act or change anything. But the tangle isn't an obstacle to Snake. He goes in, alone, and faces up to all the pitfalls that society can dig for him. Snake is our revenge against our modern world and the new problems that it brings.

Now, add to this the idea that Snake isn't just a loner, but an <u>outsider</u> as well, someone who'll never fit in, and you begin to see the appeal to s/f fans who think of themselves as outside the general order of the world anyway. Snake is not a representative of society on any level. He is, above all, an individual operating under his own set of rules and ethics totally removed from the conflicting ethics of society. Ollie North may be a sociopath, but he at least knows what he wants out of life and how to get it. Snake isn't crazy like North; his ethics work on a more personal level, one on one. He is the man we'd all like to be, and he don't take shit from nooooobody.

It's a simplistic definition, but, I feel, one that's on the mark. We, both unfortunately and otherwise, live with a great deal of control [for it also means protection], it sure is fun to live out Snake's life for just awhile.

I hear that Carpenter's making a sequel. Hmmm. To tell you the truth, I'd love to be connected to it. Only nobody's asked me. After living with Snake all these years, I really think I'd be able to contribute something to the man and his world. Take matches, for instance. Don't you think Snake should be able to light matches on his face? Just a thought. Maybe Carpenter knows what he's doing after all.

[*This article first appeared in* Snakebit 2 *(Nov, 1988). It appears here courtesy Chris McQuay.*]

The Story Behind the Soundtrack for Escape From New York

By Alex Denney

Thirty-four years ago, *Escape From New York* burst onto the screen. Written in response to the Watergate scandal, John Carpenter's film follows the attempts of its hard-bitten antihero, Snake Plissken, to rescue the U.S. President from Manhattan, which in the dystopian future of 1988 has been turned into a giant maximum security prison. Quirky, thrilling, and tough, it's as vivid a nightmare vision of the city-as-hellscape as anything this side of *Taxi Driver*.

Crucial to its impact was its pulsating score, composed by Carpenter and sound designer Alan Howarth, who went on to work with the director on other films including *They Live, Big Trouble in Little China*, and *Prince of Darkness*. The soundtrack made terrific use of synthesizers at a time when Hollywood scores were chiefly an orchestral beast, albeit with a few noteworthy exceptions [see Goblin's indelibly creepy work on *Suspiria* or Tangerine Dream's pulse-jacking score for *Sorcerer*] and set the template for a decade's worth of hard-boiled crime thrillers churned out by Hollywood. It's also been influential for a new wave of filmmakers looking to bring retro charm to their work - think *Drive*, or the throbbing synth menace of *It Follows* - so it's strangely fitting that Howarth has decided to revisit the score by taking it out on the road for the first time. We spoke to him to find out how it all came together.

ALAN'S WORK ON *STAR TREK* GOT HIM THE JOB ON *ESCAPE*

"I moved to L.A. in the 70s to work with Weather Report, a jazz band I'd been touring with. An old biker buddy of mine was working in the sound department of a film studio making copies of tapes and he overheard two sound editors talking about how they needed someone who knew about synthesizers for this movie they were making. So my buddy says, "Hey man, you have to talk to my buddy Alan, man he works for Weather Report" - like that's going to mean something to them - and they look at him and go, 'Weather Report? Is that the one at 7 o'clock or 11 o'clock?' Anyway, they took my number and gave me a call, so I went down and

L-R: John Carpenter [Director/Co-Writer/Co-Composer], Alan Howarth [Co-Composer/Special Synthesizer Sound]
(Photo by/Courtesy Philip D'angelo)

it turned out they were making *Star Trek: The Motion Picture*. It was my work on that [as a sound FX specialist] which brought me into John's world [*a picture editor working on the movie passed his tapes on to Carpenter*]."

JOHN CARPENTER CAME ROUND TO HIS HOUSE AND HIRED HIM

"He just came over to my house in Glendale, California. I had my own rig at home, and it worked out well because Carpenter didn't want to know anything about the equipment, he just said, "That's your job." We hung out and I played him some music and he was like, "Let's do it!" All very casual, no formal stuff, no attorneys or big-money exchange - just a bunch of guys, you know?"

THEY MADE IT AT THE SAME TIME AS WATCHING THE MOVIE

"One thing I brought to the party that John liked was the idea of using videotape. Normally when you score a film, you would literally do it to a stopwatch. You say, "I need some music that goes for a minute and thirty-four seconds," then you decide on a tempo, put a click track down and play blindly along, sort of imagining what the scene was. But I put up a video so that you could watch the video and play to it, which he loved because you could really sculpt a picture that way. He referred to that as a kind of coloring book."

MOST OF IT WAS MADE UP ON THE SPOT

"Pretty much everything was improvised. Occasionally, John would come in with something he wanted to do that he'd figured out at home. But a lot of the time he'd just kind of look at me and say, "Alan, give me something." One of the very first cues I did was one we called the "69th Street Bridge," where the car chase takes place and they go across the bridge and the taxi cab blows up. John let me run with that one to see what I would do, just to kind of figure out who I was. The last thing we did was actually the opening title sequence, because originally there was this whole bank robbery scene at the beginning of the movie that was taken out, so we had scored the movie starting with that."

IT BLAZED A TRAIL FOR SYNTH-LED HOLLYWOOD SCORES

"What we were doing was all relatively new at the time, I guess. Certainly the drum machine thing was new - that Linn drum I had literally been over to Roger Linn's garage and got one of the first ones. I remember when we first sat down to do the music for *Escape*, John brought two LPs with him, one was The Police and the other one was Tangerine Dream [German prog-rockers who composed early synth scores for William Friedkin and Michael Mann]. So, there were some clues as to where he was going with this."

IT'S TOTALLY INFLUENTIAL

"I think we made some musical statements that appeal to younger filmmakers and musicians. It's simple. Rather than trying to be the next John Williams, being the next Carpenter and Howarth is a lot easier! You never know when you're doing it, you just do it, but here we are thirty some years later still talking about it, so there must have been something there that had some timeless quality, some vision that still holds up. It's funny, after we did *Escape*, John's next movie was *The Thing*, which he got Ennio Morricone to score Morricone-style.

But it was a challenge for John because some of it wasn't really working for him, so he turned around and played Morricone our score from *Escape From New York* and said, 'Can you do something like this?' So Morricone went back and did a second pass, and that's where that opening title that sounds very much like John Carpenter came from. It was Morricone watching *Escape From New York* and going back and doing John Carpenter as Ennio Morricone!"

JOHN CARPENTER DGAF

"I remember telling Carpenter I wanted to make an LP out of the soundtrack, and he was like, 'Really? Someone will want to listen to that?' I said, 'Yeah, it's cool, man!' His view was that it was just a utility item that we created in order to make the movie... If you ask him, he'll tell you I was the cheapest guy he could get."

[*This article first appeared in* Dazed Digital *(Oct 30, 2015). It appears here courtesy Alex Denney.*]

A NOTE ON SOURCES

The following original interviews were conducted by author Andreas Johansson between 2012 and 2023. The authors of any archival interviews in this book have been noted in the byline where the articles themselves appear.

Season Hubley [Girl in Chock full o'Nuts] [2017/Email]
Adrienne Barbeau [Maggie] [2013/Email]
Larry Franco [Producer/First Assistant Director] [2018/Email]
Todd C. Ramsay [Editor] [2018/Email]
Joe Alves [Production Designer] [2013/Phone]
Dean Cundey [Director of Photography] [2020/Phone]
Frank Doubleday [Romero] [2017/Email]
John Strobel [Cronenberg] [2016/Email]
John Cothran Jr. [Gypsy #1] [2016/Phone]
Garrett Bergfeld [Gypsy #2] [2015/Email]
Joel Bennett [Gypsy #4] [2016/Email]
Tobar Mayo [Third Indian] [2017/Phone]
Steven M. Gagnon [Secret Service #1] [2020/Phone]
Dale E. House [Helicopter Pilot #1] [2017/Email]
Tony Papenfuss [Theater Assistant] [2016/Email]
Alan Shearman [Dancer] [2015/Email]
John Contini [Extra] [2015/Email]
Jeff Sillifant [Extra] [2015/Email]
Ken Tipton [Extra] [2016/Phone]
David Udell [Extra] [2019/Email]
Dick Warlock [Stunt Coordinator/Stunts] [2015/Email]
Jeffrey Chernov [Second Assistant Director] [2018/Phone]
Louise Jaffe [Script Supervisor] [2023/Email]
Raymond Stella [Camera Operator] [2020/Email]
Clyde E. Bryan [First Assistant Camera] [2020/Phone]
Christopher Horner [Assistant Art Director] [2021/Phone]

Cloudia Rebar [Set Decorator] [2015/Email]
Arthur Gelb [Graphic Designer] [2022/Email]
Steve Mathis [Flicker Box Technician] [2023/Email]
Ken Chase [Makeup Artist Supervisor] [2015/Email]
Kim Gottlieb-Walker [Stills] [2023/Email]
Eddie Surkin [Special Effects] [2017/Phone]
Tom Thomas [Transportation Captain] [2023/Phone]
Geoffrey Ryan [Production Assistant] [2015/Email]
Donald P. Borchers [Avco Nominee] [2020/Email]
Mario Simon [Driver] [2022/Email]
Sharon Tucci [TalentPlus: Extra Casting] [St. Louis] [2023/Email]
R.J. Kizer [Project Supervisor: Special Visual Effects] [2016/Email]
Brian Chin [Miniature Construction] [2023/Email]
Tom Campbell [Engineer: Special Visual Effects] [2021/Email]
Steve Caldwell [Camera Assistant: Special Visual Effects] [2021/Phone]
Eugene P. Rizzardi [Miniature Construction] [2016/Email]
Bruce MacRae [Miniature Construction] [2021/Email]
John C. Wash [Graphic Displays] [2015/Email]
Mark Stetson [Miniature Construction] [2015/Email]
John L. Hammontree [Special Thanks] [2021/Email]
Gino LaMartina [Special Thanks] [2020/Phone]
Richard Hescox [Pre-Production Ad Artist] [2015/Email]
Francis Delia [Pre-Production Portrait Photographer] [2018/Email]
Barry E. Jackson [Poster Artist] [2012/Email]
Stan Watts [Poster Artist] [2015/Email]
Ben Bensen III [Poster Artist] [2021/Email]
Renato Casaro [Italian Poster Artist] [2015/Email]
Paul Chadwick [Poster Artist] [2015/Email]
Kim Passey [Poster Artist] [2015/Email]
Harold Johnson [Movie Tie-In Board Game Designer] [2018/Email]
Bill Willingham [Movie Tie-In Board Game Artist] [2023/Email]
Erol Otus [Movie Tie-In Board Game Artist] [2020/Email]
E.T. Steadman [Movie Tie-In Novel Artist] [2017/Email]

THE ADVENTURE CONTINUES...

ESCAPE ARTISTS VOL. 2 IS AVAILABLE NOW!

More interviews, more rare photos, more vintage articles. Available in Paperback, Hardcover, and eBook.

Learn more at HarkerPress.com

Learn more at
HarkerPress.com

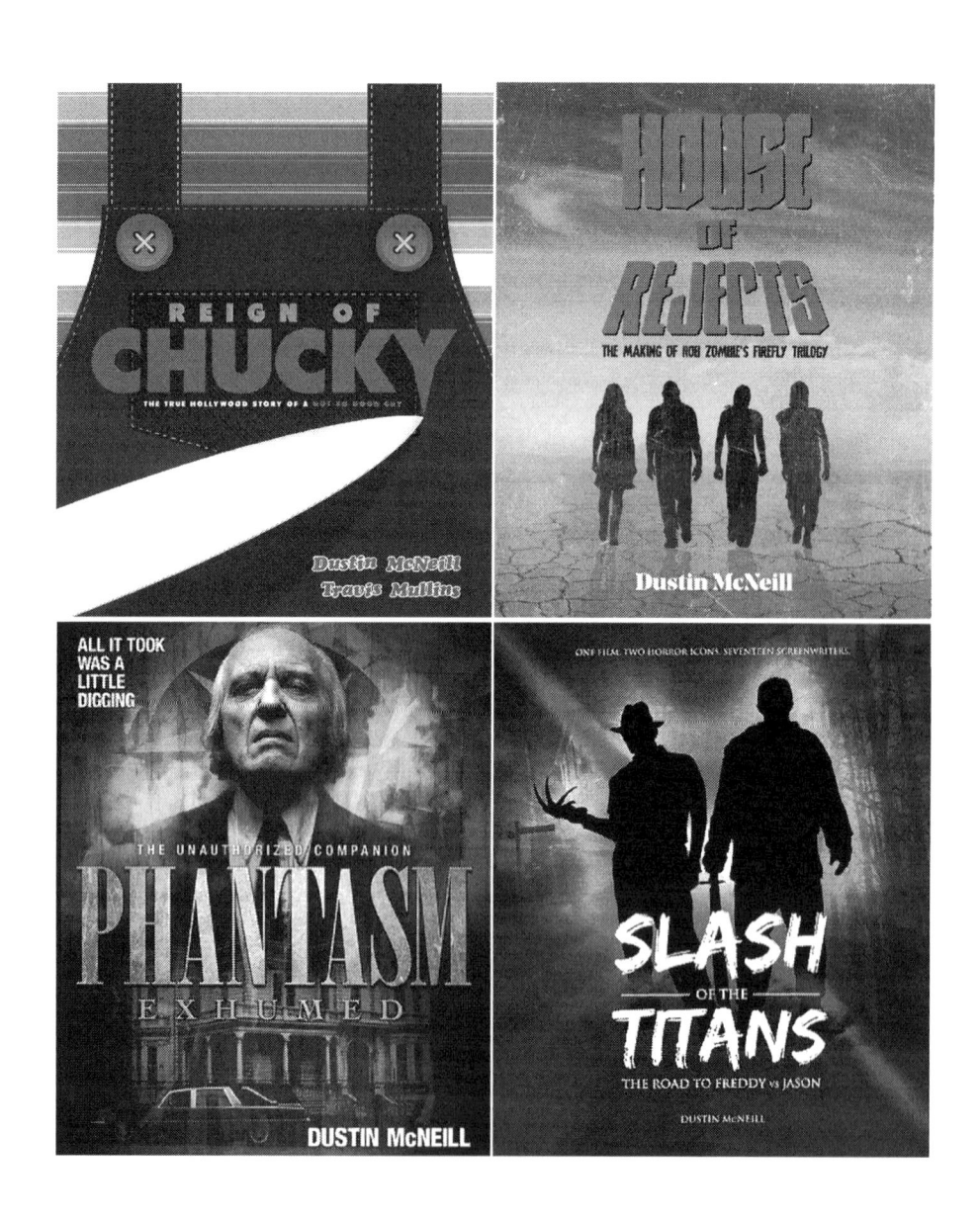

If you enjoyed this book, consider other titles from

HARKER PRESS
PUBLISHER OF SCARY GOOD BOOKS

ESCAPE ARTISTS VOL 2

ESCAPE FROM L.A. INTERVIEWS

ANDREAS JOHANSSON